Railway Clearing House.

DISTANCES

BETWEEN THE

STATIONS AND JUNCTIONS

OF THE

RAILWAYS

ON WHICH THE

CLEARING SYSTEM

IS IN OPERATION.

SEPTEMBER, 1853.

LONDON:

M'CORQUODALE & CO., PRINTERS, CARDINGTON STREET.
WORKS, NEWTON.

MDCCCLIII.

INDEX TO COMPANIES.

NOTE.—In printing the following Distance Tables the certified lists of Distances furnished by the Companies have been strictly adhered to. There is, however, some reason to believe, that, notwithstanding the delay which has taken place, the distances given are not in every case correct; for when correcting the proofs, the following discrepancies were detected :—

Between Leeds and Dewsbury Junction, the distance is given by the London and North Western Company as 10½ Miles; the Lancashire and Yorkshire Company give the distance between the same points as 10¼ Miles.

Between Heaton Lodge and Dewsbury Junction, the distance is given by the London and North Western Company as 2½ Miles; and by the Lancashire and Yorkshire Company as 2¾ Miles.

Between Broughty Ferry and Dundee, the distance is given by the Dundee and Arbroath as 3¾ Miles; and by the Edinburgh, Perth, and Dundee, as 4¼ Miles.

Between Wichnor Junction and Burton, the distance is given by the Midland as 5¾ Miles, and by the South Stafford Company as 6 Miles.

Between Askern Junction and Knottingley, the distance is given by the Lancashire and Yorkshire as 10¼ Miles, and by the Great Northern as 10½ Miles.

Between Wakefield and Knottingley, the distance is given by the Lancashire and Yorkshire as 10¾ Miles, and by the Great Northern as 10¼ Miles.

ERRATA.

Caledonian.—Page 6.—Edinburgh to Carlisle, for 100¾, read 100.

Midland.—Page 121.—Keighley to Wichnor Junction, for 118¾, read 108¾.

Lancashire and Yorkshire.—Page 59.—Moses Gate to Kirkdale Junction, for 28, read 28½.

In the Note appended to the Midland Table, for "between Woodhouse Mill and Beighton Junction," read between "Eckington and Beighton Junction."

INDEX TO COMPANIES.

(ENGLISH AND SCOTCH.)

(IRISH.)

INDEX TO STATIONS.

b

c

INDEX TO IRISH RAILWAYS.

ENGLISH RAILWAYS.

ABERDEEN RAILWAY.

STATIONS.	Aberdeen.	Arbroath.	Forfar.	
Aberdeen	...	55½	57	
Arbroath	55½	...	15	
Auldbar Road	51¾	9¾	5¼	
Border Offset	49¾	5¾	9¼	
Brechin.... A	45¼	18¼	19¾	
Bridge of Dun	41¼	14¼	15¾	
Clocksbriggs	54½	12½	2½	
Colliston	52	3½	11½	
Cove	4¼	51¼	52¾	
Craigo	35½	20	21½	
Drumlithie	22¾	32¾	34¼	
Dubton	38¾	16¾	18¼	
Farnell Road	44½	11	12½	
Fordoun	26¾	28¾	30¼	
Forfar	57	15	...	
Friockheim	49¼	6¼	8¾	
Glasterlaw	47¾	7¾	9¼	
Guthrie	49¾	7¾	7¼	
Laurencekirk	30¼	25¼	26¾	
Letham Mill Offset	53¾	1¾	13¼	
Leysmill	50¾	4¾	10¼	
Marykirk	33½	22	23½	
Montrose	41¾	19¾	21¼	
Muchalls	11¼	44¼	45¾	
Newmills Offset	21¼	34¼	35¾	
Newton Hill	10	45½	47	

STATIONS.	Aberdeen.	Arbroath.	Forfar.	
Portlethen	7½	48	49½	
Stonehaven	15¾	39¾	41¼	
Waulkmill Offset	53¼	2¼	12¾	

M'Corquodale & Co., Printers.

AMBERGATE, NOTTINGHAM, AND BOSTON RAILWAY.

STATIONS.	Grantham.	Nottingham.								
Aslockton	11½	11¼								
Bingham.......................	13¾	9								
Bottesford.....................	7	15¾								
Elton	9¾	13								
Grantham......................	...	22¾								
Nottingham	22¾	...								
Ratcliffe......................	17½	5¼								
Sedgebrooke	4¼	18½								

ARDROSSAN RAILWAY.

STATIONS.	Dubbs.	Kilwinning.	Perceton.								
rdrossan	4¼	6	10¼								
orsehillhead....................	1½	2½	4½								
irraus	1	2	5								
ubbs	...	1	6								
glinton...................... ..	1	2	5								
ergushill	2½	3½	3½								
ilwinning	1	...	7								
erceton	6	7	...								
altcoats	2¾	4	8¾								
tevenson	1½	2	7½								

BIRKENHEAD, LANCASHIRE, & CHESHIRE JUNC. RAILWAY.

STATIONS.	Birkenhead Goods.	Birkenhead Passengers.	Chester.	Victoria, Manchester.*	Walton Junction.
Bebington	3¾	2¾	12¼	51¾	29¼
Birkenhead Goods	...	1	16	55½	33
Birkenhead Passengers	1	...	15	54½	32
Bromboro'	6¼	5¼	9¾	49¼	26¾
Chester	16	15	...	39½	17
Dunham	21¼	20¼	5¼	34¼	11¾
Frodsham	25¾	24¾	9¾	29¾	7¼
Helsby	23¼	22¼	7¼	32¼	9¾
Hoole Siding	17	16½	1½	38	15½
Hooton	8	7	8	47½	25
Kenyon Junction*	42¾	41¾	26¾	12¾	9¾
Limekiln Lane	2	1	14	53½	31
Mollington	13	12	3	42½	20
Moore	31¼	30¼	15¼	24¼	1¾
Newton Bridge*	39¾	38¾	23¾	15¾	6¾
Norton	29¼	28¼	13¼	26¼	3¾
Ordsall Lane*	64½	53½	38½	1	21½
Patricroft*	50½	49½	34½	5	17½
Rock Lane	2¾	1¾	13¼	52¾	30¼
Runcorn	27½	26½	11½	28	5½
Spital	5	4	11	50½	28
Sutton	9¼	8¼	6¾	46¼	23¾
Victoria, (Manchester)*	55½	54½	39½	...	22½
Walton Junction	33	32	17	22½	...
Warrington*	34	33	18	21½	1

* These are Stations on the London and North Western to which the Birkenhead, Lancashire, and Cheshire, have power to run.

CALEDONIAN RAILWAY.

STATIONS.	Carlisle.	Gartsherrie.	Gretna Junction.	Greenhill.	Morningside.	Paisley Junction.	Shields Bridge Junction.				
Abington	58		49¼	48¾		50	44½				
Auchengray	79½		70¾	39		40¼	34¾				
Barrhead Railway	102¼		93½	30¾		6½	1				
Beattock	39¾		31	67		68	62½				
Bishopton	112¾		104¼	41½		5	10½				
Blantyre	98		89¼	26½		14½	9				
Braidwood	80¾		72	26		27	21½				
Calder Iron Works	93½		84¾	18		23	17½				
Cambuslang	97¼		88½	25¾		10½	5				
Cambuslang Colliery	97		88¼	25½		10¾	5¼				
Carfin	93		84¼	16¾		22½	17				
Carlisle	...		8¾	106¾		107¾	102¼				
Carluke	82		73¼	24¾		25¾	20¼				
Carnbroe Colliery	92¼		83½	14½		21¾	16¼				
Carnbroe Iron Works	93¼		84½	18½		22¾	17¼				
Carnwath	75		66¼	34½		35½	30				
Carstairs	73½		64¾	33		34¼	28¾				
Castlehill Siding	82¾		74	24		25	19½				
Chapel Siding	86		77½	23¼		24½	19				
Clyde Iron Works	97¾		89	26		10	4½				
Coatbridge	94¾		86	12		24¼	18¾				
Coltness Siding	86		77¼	23		24¼	18¾				
Core Quarry Siding	14		5¼	92¾		93½	88				
Craigenhill Siding	78¾		69¾	28		29¼	23¾				
Cumbernauld	101¼		92½	5½		30¾	25¼				
Currie	95½		86¾	55		56¼	50¾				

CALEDONIAN RAILWAY—*Continued.*

STATIONS.	Carlisle.	Gartsherrie.	Gretna Junction.	Greenhill.	Morningside.	Paisley Junction.	Shields Bridge Junction.				
Paisley	107¾		99	36¼		...	5½				
Paisley Canal	101½		92¾	30		...	...				
Port Glasgow	121		112¼	49½		13	18½				
Provan Mill	102		93½	17		31½	26				
Rockliffe	4		4¾	102¾		103¾	98¼				
Rutherglen	99		90¼	27½		8¾	3¼				
Shiel Muir Siding	87½		78¾	19		20¼	14¾				
Shields Bridge Junction	102¼		93½	30¾		5½	...				
Slateford	98¾		89¾	58¼		59½	54				
Steps Road	100		91¼	15		29½	24				
Stevenston	92¾		83¾	16¼		22¼	16¾				
Stirling Road	86		77¼	23¼		24¼	18¾				
Stonelaw	98¾		90¼	27		9	3½				
Summerlee	95¼		86½	11½		24¾	19¼				
Symington	66¾		57¾	40		41¼	35¾				
Thankerton	68½		59¾	38		39¼	33¾				
Uddingstone	93¾		85	22		14	8½				
Upper Thankerton	91½		82¾	15		21	15½				
Wamphray	34½		25¾	72		73¼	67¾				
Waterlands Siding	83½		74¾	23		24¼	18¾				
West-Calder, or Torphine	85½		76¾	45		46¼	40¾				
West of Scotland Iron Works	90		81¼	16¾		19½	14				
Whifflet	93¾		85	13		23¼	17¾				
Windmill Hill Siding	88¾		79¾	18		19¼	13¾				
Wishaw	86½		77¾	20¼		21¼	15¾				
Wishaw Pits (6) Siding	87		78¼	19¾		20¾	15¼				

CALEDONIAN RAILWAY—*Continued.*

STATIONS.	Carlisle.	Gartsherrie.	Gretna Junction.	Greenhill.	Morningside.	Paisley Junction.	Shields Bridge Junction.				
Wrangham	92½		83¾	16		22	16½				

CALEDONIAN RAILWAY—*Continued.*

STATIONS.	Carlisle.	Gartsherrie.	Gretna Junction.	Greenhill.	Morningside.	Paisley Junction.	Shields Bridge Junction.				
Paisley	107¾		99	36¼		...	5½				
Paisley Canal	101½		92¾	30		...	...				
Port Glasgow	121		112¼	49½		13	18½				
Provan Mill	102		93½	17		31½	26				
Rockliffe	4		4¾	102¾		103¾	98¼				
Rutherglen	99		90¼	27½		8¾	3¼				
Shiel Muir Siding	87½		78¾	19		20¼	14¾				
Shields Bridge Junction	102¼		93½	30¾		5½	...				
Slateford	98¾		89¾	58¼		59½	54				
Steps Road	100		91¼	15		29½	24				
Stevenston	92¾		83¾	16¼		22¼	16¾				
Stirling Road	86		77¼	23¼		24¼	18¾				
Stonelaw	98¾		90¼	27		9	3½				
Summerlee	95¼		86½	11½		24¾	19¼				
Symington	66¾		57¾	40		41¼	35¾				
Thankerton	68½		59¾	38		39¼	33¾				
Uddingstone	93¾		85	22		14	8½				
Upper Thankerton	91½		82¾	15		21	15½				
Wamphray	34½		25¾	72		73¼	67¾				
Waterlands Siding	83½		74¾	23		24¼	18¾				
West-Calder, or Torphine	85½		76¾	45		46¼	40¾				
West of Scotland Iron Works	90		81¼	16¾		19½	14				
Whifflet	93¾		85	13		23¼	17¾				
Windmill Hill Siding	88¾		79¾	18		19¼	13¾				
Wishaw	86½		77¾	20¼		21¼	15¾				
Wishaw Pits (6) Siding	87		78¼	19¾		20¾	15¼				

CALEDONIAN RAILWAY—*Continued.*

STATIONS.	Carlisle.	Gartsherrie.	Gretna Junction.	Greenhill.	Morningside.	Paisley Junction.	Shields Bridge Junction.				
Wrangham	92½		83¾	16		22	16½				

CHESTER AND HOLYHEAD RAILWAY.

STATIONS.	Chester.	Ffrith Junction.	Mold Junction.	Saltney Junction with S. & C.
Aber	54¼	58½	51¼	52¼
Abergele	34¼	38½	31¼	32¼
Admiral Dundas's Siding	6¼	10½	3¼	4¼
Bagilt	14½	18¾	11½	12½
Bangor	59½	63¾	56½	57½
Bodorgan	72½	76¾	69½	70½
Britannia Bridge	61¾	66	58¾	59¾
Broughton	4¾	5½	1¾	2¾
Brundrilt and Whitewag's Siding	50½	54¾	47½	48½
Caernarvon	68¼	72	64¾	66½
Chester	...	10¼	3	2
Coed Talon	11¾	1½	8¾	9¾
Colwyn	40¼	44½	37¼	38¼
Conway	45½	49¾	42½	43½
Dee Bank Siding	15¼	19½	12¼	13¼
Eytons Siding	19¼	23½	16¼	17¼
Ffrith Junc., or Padeswood.	10¼	...	7¼	8¼
Flint	12½	16¾	9½	10½
Foryd	31½	35¾	28½	29½
Gaerwen	66½	70¾	63½	64½
Garreglwyd	10¼	...	7¼	8¼
Gronant Siding	24¾	29	21¾	22¾
Holyhead	84½	88¾	81½	82½
Holywell	16¾	21	13¾	14¾
Hope	9	1¼	6	7
Llanfair	63½	67¾	60½	61½

CHESTER AND HOLYHEAD RAILWAY—*Continued.*

STATIONS.	Chester.	Ffrith Junction.	Mold Junction.	Saltney Junction with S. & C.
Llong	11½	1¼	8½	9½
Lysfaen	37¼	41½	34¼	35¼
Mold	13¼	3	10¼	11¼
Mold Junction	3	7¼	...	1
Mostyn	20	24¼	17	18
Penmaenmaur	50	54¼	47	48
Pennant Col[l]. Siding	58½	62¾	55½	56½
Penlan Siding	58	62¼	55	56
Pentregwyddel	37½	41½	34¼	35¼
Port Dinonvic	64	67¾	60½	62¼
Prestatyn	26¼	30½	23¼	24¼
Queen's Ferry	7	11¼	4	5
Rhyl	30	34¼	27	28
Saltney Junction	2	8¼	1	...
Saltney Wharf	2½	7¾	½	½
Steele's Siding	26	30¼	23	24
Ty Croes	75½	79¾	72½	73½
Valley	81	85¼	78	79

COCKERMOUTH AND WORKINGTON RAILWAY.

STATIONS.	Cockermouth.	Workington.								
Brigham	2½	6½								
Broughton Cross..............	3	6								
Camerton	5½	3½								
Cockermouth..................	...	9								
Marron	4	5								
Ribton Bridge.................	5½	3½								
Workington	9	...								
Workington Bridge	7¼	1¾								

DUNDEE AND ARBROATH RAILWAY.

STATIONS.	Arbroath	Dundee.	Broughty Pier.								
Arbroath	...	16¾	13								
Barry..........................	8	8¾	5								
Broughty Ferry..............	13	3¾	2¼								
Broughty Pier.................	13	6	...								
Carnoustie....................	6¼	10½	6¾								
Dundee.........................	16¾	...	6								
Easthaven....................	4½	12¼	8½								
Kelly Field											
Milton	11½	5¼	1½								
Monifieth......................	10¾	6	2¼								
Panbride.......................	5½	11¼	7½								

DUNDEE AND NEWTYLE RAILWAY.

STATIONS.	Dundee Wards.	Newtyle.
Auchterhouse	7¼	3
Balbeuchley (Foot of)	4¾	5½
Balbeuchley (Top of)	5¾	4½
Baldovan	2¼	8
Baldragon	3¼	7
Cross Roads	1	9¼
Hatton	9½	¾
Newtyle	10¼	...

DUNDEE AND PERTH RAILWAY.

STATIONS.	Dundee.	Perth.									
Dundee	...	24½									
Errol	10½	14									
Glencarse	14½	10									
Inchture.........................	8¼	16¼									
Invergowrie	3¾	20¾									
Kinfauns	17¼	7¼									
Longforgan	5¾	18¾									
Perth.........................	24½	...									

EAST ANGLIAN RAILWAY.

STATIONS.	Dereham.	Ely.	Ely Junction.	Huntingdon.	St. Ives.	Wisbeach.					
Bilney	19¾	33¾	32¼			22½					
Denver	39¼	14¼	12¾			16					
Dereham	...	53½	52			42¼					
Downham	37¾	15¾	14¼			14½					
East Winch	21¾	31¾	30¼			20½					
Ely	53½	...	1½			30¼					
Ely Junction	52	1½	...			28¾					
Emneth	40	28	26½			2¼					
Fransham	7	46½	45			35¼					
Harbour Junction	28½	25	23½			13¾					
Hilgay	42¼	11¼	9¾			19					
Holme	34	19½	18			10¾					
Huntingdon	...	...	...		5¼	...					
Little Dunham	8¼	45¼	43¾			34					
Littleport	47¾	5¾	4¼			24½					
Lynn	26¾	26¾	25¼			15½					
Magdalen Gate	34	22	20½			8¼					
Middle Drove	37	25	23½			5¼					
Middleton	23¾	29¾	28¼			18½					
Narborough	18¼	35¼	33¾			24					
Ouse Bridge	40¾	12¾	11¼			17½					
St. Ives	...	...	...	5¼		...					
St. Germains	31	22½	21			11¼					
Scarning	2½	51	49½			39¾					
Smeeth Road	38½	26½	25			3¾					
South Lynn	29½	26	24½			14¾					

EAST ANGLIAN RAILWAY—*Continued.*

STATIONS.	Dereham.	Ely.	Ely Junction.	Huntingdon.	St. Ives.	Wisbeach.				
Sporle	9¾	43¾	42¼			32½				
Stow	35¼	18¼	16¾			12				
Swaffham......................	12¼	41¼	39¾			30				
Walsoken......................	41¾	29¾	28¼			½				
Watlington.............	32¾	20¾	19¼			9½				
Wendling.......................	4	49½	48			38¼				
Wisbeach......................	42¼	30¼	28¾			...				

EASTERN COUNTIES RAILWAY.

STATIONS.	Bow.	Brandon.	Cambridge.	Colchester.	Ely.	Ely Junction.	Marks Tey.	Peterborough.	Shepreth.	St. Ives.	Wisbeach.
Audley End	41¼	44¾	14	87¾	28¾		82¾	58½	16¾	28¾	52
Barking Road	3	86½	55¾	49½	70½		44½	100¼	58½	70½	93¾
Bishop Stortford	30	56	25¼	76½	40		71½	69¾	28	40	63¼
Black Bank	75	21	19¾	121½	5		116½	24¾	28	29¼	18¼
Blackwall	4	87½	56¾	50½	71½		45½	101¼	59½	71½	94¾
Bow	...	86	55¼	49	70		44	99¾	58	70	93¼
Braintree	42¼	125¾	95	19¼	109¾		14¼	139½	97¾	109¾	133
Brandon	86	...	30¾	132½	16		127½	45¾	39	45½	39¼
Brentwood	15½	99	68¼	33½	83		28½	112¾	71	83	106¼
Broxbourne	16¾	69¼	38½	63¼	53¼		58¼	83	41¼	53¼	76½
Bulford	40¼	123¾	93	17¼	107¾		12¼	137½	95¾	107¾	131
Burnt Mill	22¼	63¾	33	68¾	47¾		63¾	77½	35¾	47¾	71
Cambridge	55¼	30¾	...	101¾	14¾		96¾	44½	8¼	14¾	38
Chatteris	80¾	39½	25½	127¼	23½		122¼	22¼	33¾	10¾	15¾
Chelmsford	27	110½	79¾	22	94½		17	124¼	82½	94½	117¾
Cheshunt	14	72	41¼	60½	56		55½	85¾	44	56	79¼
Chesterford	45¼	40¾	10	91¾	24¾		86¾	54½	12¾	24¾	48
Chittisham	73¼	19¼	18	119¾	3¼		114¾	26½	26¼	31	20
Colchester	49	132½	101¾	...	116½		5	146¼	104½	116½	139¾
Eastrea	93	39	37¾	139½	23		134½	6¾	46	26¼	15¼
Edmonton	8¼	79¾	49	54¾	63¾		49¾	93½	51¾	63¾	87
Elsenham	35¼	50¾	20	81¾	34¾		76¾	64½	22¾	34¾	58
Ely	70	16	14¾	116½	...		111½	29¾	23	29½	23¼
Ely Junction											
Enfield	10¼	81¾	51	56¾	65¾		51¾	95½	53¾	65¾	89
Forest Gate	2½	86	55¼	46½	70		41½	99¾	58	70	93¼

EASTERN COUNTIES RAILWAY—*Continued.*

STATIONS.	Bow.	Brandon.	Cambridge.	Colchester.	Ely.	Ely Junction.	Marks Tey.	Peterborough.	Shepreth.	St. Ives.	Wisbeach.
Foxton	57	38	7¼	103½	22		98½	51¾	1	22	45¼
Harlow	24	62	31¼	70½	46		65½	75¾	34	46	69¼
Harston	55¼	36¼	5½	101¾	20¼		96¾	50	2¾	20½	43½
Hartford	23¾	76¼	45½	70¼	60¼		65¼	90	48¼	60¼	83½
Histon	60	35½	4¾	106½	19½		101½	43	13	10	36½
Ilford	4¾	88¼	57½	44¼	72¼		39¼	102	60¼	72¼	95½
Ingatestone	21	104½	73¾	28	88½		23	118¼	76½	88½	111¾
Kelvedon	39½	123	92¼	9½	107		4½	136¾	95	107	130¼
Lakenheath	82¼	3¾	27	128¾	12¼		123¾	42	35¼	41¾	35½
Langford	40½	124	93¼	17½	108		12½	137¾	96	108	131¼
Lea Bridge	3½	82½	51¾	50	66½		45	96¼	54½	66½	89¾
London	2¼	88¼	57½	51¼	72¼		46¼	102	60¼	72¼	95½
Long Stanton	64½	40	9¼	111	24		106	38½	17½	5½	32
Maldon	41¾	125¼	94½	18¾	109¼		13¾	139	97¼	109¼	132½
Manea	79¾	25¾	24½	126¼	9¾		121¼	20	32¾	24½	13½
March	85½	31½	30¼	132	15½		127	14¼	38¼	18¾	7¾
Marks Tey	44	127½	96¾	5	111½		...	141¼	99½	111½	134¾
Mildenhall Road	77	9	21¾	123½	7		118½	36¾	30	36½	30¼
Mile End	1¼	87¼	56½	50¼	71¼		45¼	101	59¼	71¼	94½
Newport	39½	46½	15¾	86	30½		81	60¼	18½	30½	53¾
Oakington	62	37½	6¾	108½	21½		103½	41	15	8	34½
Park	6½	79½	48¾	53	63½		48	93¼	51½	63½	86¾
Pear Tree Hill	87¾	33¾	82½	134¼	17¾		129¼	16½	40½	21	5½
Peterborough	99¾	45¾	44½	146¼	29¾		141¼	...	52¾	33	22
Ponder's End	9½	76½	45¾	56	60½		51	90¼	48½	60½	83¾
Romford	9¾	93¼	62½	39¼	77¼		34¼	107	65¼	77¼	100½

EASTERN COUNTIES RAILWAY—*Continued.*

STATIONS.	Bow.	Brandon.	Cambridge.	Colchester.	Ely.	Ely Junction.	Marks Tey.	Peterborough.	Shepreth.	St. Ives.	Wisbeach.
Roydon	19¾	66¼	35½	66¼	50¼		61¼	80	38¼	50¼	73½
Rye House....................	18½	71	40¼	65	55		60	84¾	43	55	78¼
Sawbridgeworth	26¼	59¾	29	72¾	43¾		67¾	73½	31¾	43¾	67
Shelford..........................	52	34	3¼	98½	18		93½	47¾	5	18	41¼
Shelford Junction	52½	33½	2¾	99	17½		94	47¼	5½	17½	40¾
Shepreth	58	39	8¼	104½	23		99½	52¾	...	23	46¼
Stanstead	32¾	53¼	22½	79¼	37¼		74¼	67	25¼	37¼	60½
Stonea	81¾	27¾	26½	128¼	11¾		123¼	18	34¾	22½	11½
Stratford	1¼	84¾	54	47¾	68¾		42¾	98½	56¾	68¾	92
Stratford Bridge	1½	85	54¼	48	69		43	98¾	57	69	92¼
St. Ives	70	45½	14¾	116½	29½		111½	83	23	...	26½
St. Margaret's	19¾	72¼	41½	66¼	56¼		61¼	86	44¼	56¼	79½
Somersham	75½	44¾	20¼	122	28¾		117	27½	28½	5½	21
Swavesey	66¾	42¼	11½	113¼	26¼		108¼	36¼	19¾	3¼	29¾
Tottenham	5½	80½	49¾	52	64½		47	94¼	52½	64½	87¾
Waltham	12½	73½	42¾	59	57½		54	87¼	45½	57½	80¾
Ware.............................	21¾	74¼	43½	68¼	58¼		63¼	88	46¼	58¼	81½
Waterbeach	60¾	25¼	5½	107¼	9¼		102¼	39	13¾	20¼	32½
Water Lane	7¼	78¾	48	53¾	62¾		48¾	92½	50¾	62¾	86
Whittlesford	48¾	37¼	6½	95¼	21¼		90¼	51	9¼	21¼	44½
Whittlesea......................	94½	40½	39¼	141	24½		136	5¼	47½	27¾	16¾
Wickham	38½	122	91¼	15½	106		10½	135¾	94	106	129¼
Wimblington	84½	35¾	29¼	131	19¾		126	18½	37½	14½	12
Wisbeach	93¼	39¼	38	139¾	23¼		134¾	22	46¼	26½	...
Witham	36	119½	88¾	13	103½		8	133¼	91½	103½	126¾
Woolwich	6	89½	58¾	52½	73½		47½	103¼	61½	73½	96¾

EASTERN UNION RAILWAY.

STATIONS.	Colchester.	Marks Tey.	Norwich.	Trowse.							
Ardleigh	4¼	9¼	58	59							
Bentley	11¼	16¼	51	52							
Bramford	19½	24½	42¾	43¾							
Bures	12	7	74¼	75¼							
Burston	45¾	50¾	16½	17½							
Bury	43¼	48¼	43	44							
Capel	13½	18½	53¼	54¼							
Chapple	8½	3½	70¾	71¾							
Claydon	21¾	26¾	40½	41½							
Colchester	...	5	62¼	63¼							
Diss	43¼	48¼	19	20							
Elmswell	34¾	39¾	34½	35½							
Finningham	34¾	39¾	27½	28½							
Florden	54¾	59¾	7½	8½							
Forncett	52¼	57¼	10	11							
Hadleigh	18½	23½	58¼	59¼							
Haughley, Junction with Bury Line	31¼	36¼	31	32							
Hythe	1¾	6¾	64	65							
Ipswich	16¾	21¾	45½	46½							
Manningtree	7¾	12¾	54½	55½							
Marks Tey	5	...	67¼	68¼							
Mellis	39¾	44¾	22½	23½							
Needham	25½	30½	36¾	37¾							
Norwich	62¼	67¼	...	1							
Rayden	16¼	21¼	56	57							
Swainsthorpe	58	63	4½	5¼							

NOTE.—The distances calculated in the above Table include the 5 miles from Marks Tey to Colchester, which is the property of the Eastern Counties Company.

EASTERN UNION RAILWAY—*Continued.*

STATIONS.	Colchester.	Marks Tey.	Norwich.	Trowse.							
Stowmarket	29	34	33¼	34¼							
Sudbury	16¾	11¾	79	80							
Tivetshall	48¾	53¾	13½	14½							
Thurston	39¼	44¼	39	40							
Trowse	63¼	68¼	1	...							

NOTE.—The distances calculated in the above Table include the 5 miles from Marks Tey to Colchester, which is the property of the Eastern Counties Company.

EAST LANCASHIRE RAILWAY.

STATIONS.	Blackburn.	Burnley Junction.	Bury.	Clifton Junction.	Colne.	Farrington Junction.	Kirkdale Junction.	Patricroft.	Preston, via Extension.	Salford.	Walton Junction.
Accrington	5¼	6	12¼	18¼	11½	15½	39	21¾	16¼	22¼	37½
Aintree	30¾	42	48¼	54¼	47½	22	3	57¾	23¾	58¼	1½
Bacup	20½	21	12	18¼	26¾	30¾	54¼	21¾	31½	22	52½
Bamber Bridge	8	19¼	25¾	31¾	25	2¼	25¾	35¼	3	35¾	24
Bamber Bridge Junction	8¼	19½	26	32	25¼	2	25½	35½	2¾	36	23¾
Baxenden	7½	8¼	10	16	13¾	17¾	41¼	19½	18½	20	39¾
Blackburn	...	11¼	17½	23½	16¾	10¼	33¾	27	11	27½	32
Bolton Junc. (Darwen Line)	¼	11½	17¾	23¾	17	10	33½	27¼	11	27¾	32
Bootle Lane	33¼	44½	51	57	50	24½	½	60½	26¼	60¾	1¼
Burnley	11½	1¾	18½	24½	5¼	21¾	45¼	28	22½	28½	43½
Burnley Barracks	11	1¼	17¾	24	6	21	44½	27½	22	27¾	43
Burnley Junction	11¼	...	18¼	24¼	7¼	21½	45	27¾	22¼	28¼	43½
Burscough	20¾	32	38½	44½	37¾	12¼	18	48	14	48½	11¼
Bury	17½	18¼	...	6	28¾	27¾	51¼	9½	28¾	10	49¾
Cherry Tree	2	13¼	19½	25½	18¾	8¼	31¾	29	9	29½	30¼
Church	4¼	7	13¼	19¼	12½	14½	38	22¾	15¼	23¼	36½
Clifton Junction	23½	24¼	6	...	29¾	33¾	57¼	3½	34¾	4	55¾
Cocker Bar	13½	24¾	31¼	37¼	30¼	4¾	20¼	40¾	6½	41	18½
Colne	16¾	7¼	23¾	29¾	...	27	50½	33¼	27¾	33¾	49
Croston	15½	26¾	33	39	32¼	6¾	18¼	42½	8½	43	16¾
DaisyField Junc. (Clitheroe Line)	½	10¾	17	23	16¼	10¾	34¼	26½	11½	27	32¾
Ewood Bridge	15	15½	6½	12½	21	25	48¾	16	26	16½	47
Farrington Junction (N.U.)	10¼	21½	27¾	33¾	27	...	25	37¼	3¼	37¾	23½
Gannow Junction	10½	¾	17½	23½	6¼	20¾	44¼	27	21½	27½	42½
Hapton	8½	2¾	16½	21½	8½	18¾	42¼	25	19½	25½	40½
Haslingden	9	9½	8¾	14¾	15	19	42¾	18¼	20	18¾	41

EAST LANCASHIRE RAILWAY—*Continued.*

STATIONS.	Blackburn.	Burnley Junction.	Bury.	Clifton Junction.	Colne.	Farrington Junction.	Kirkdale Junction.	Patricroft.	Preston, via Extension.	Salford.	Walton Junction.
Haslingden Grane	9¾	10½	7¾	13¾	16	20	43½	17¼	20¾	17¾	42
Helmshore	10¾	11½	6¾	12¾	17	21	44½	16¼	21¾	16¾	43
Hoghton	5¼	16½	22¾	28¾	22	5	28½	32¼	5¾	32¾	27
Hoghton Tower	4¼	15½	21¾	27¾	21	6	29½	31¼	7	31¾	28
Huncoat	7½	3¾	14½	20½	9½	17¾	41¼	24	18½	24¼	39½
Kirkdale Junction, (Southport Railway	33¾	45	51¼	57¼	50½	25	...	60¾	26¾	61¼	1¾
Liverpool Exchange	35¾	47	53¼	59¼	52½	27	2	62¾	28¾	63¼	3½
Liverpool Goods	35¼	46½	52¾	58¾	52	26½	1½	62¼	28¼	62¾	3¼
Lostock Hall	9¾	21	27¼	33¼	26½	1	24	36¾	2¾	37¼	22½
Lostock Junction	9½	20¾	27	33	26¼	¾	24¼	36½	2½	37	22¾
Maghull	28¼	39½	45¾	51¾	45	19½	5½	55¼	21¼	55¾	4
Marsden	13½	4	20½	26½	3¼	23¾	47¼	30	24¾	30½	45¾
Mill Hill	1¼	12½	18¾	24¾	18	9	32½	28¼	10	28¾	31
Molyneux	22¾	23½	5¼	¾	29	33	56½	4¼	34	4¾	55
Molyneux Junction	23¼	23¾	5¾	½	29½	33½	57	4	34¼	4¼	55¼
Nelson	14¾	5¼	21¾	27¾	2	25	48½	31¼	25¾	31¾	47
Newchurch Goods	18¼	18¾	10	16	24½	28½	52	19½	29¼	19¾	50¼
Newchurch Passengers	18	18½	9¾	15¾	24¼	28¼	51¾	19¼	29	19½	50
Ormskirk	23½	34¾	41	47	40¼	14¾	10¼	50½	16½	51	8¾
Patricroft Junction	27	27¾	9½	3½	33¼	37¼	60¾	...	38¼	7½	59¼
Pleasington	3	14¼	20½	26½	19¾	7¼	30¾	30	8	30½	29¼
Preston, *via* Extension	11	22¼	28¾	34¾	27¾	3¼	26¾	38¼	...	38½	25¼
Radcliffe Bridge	20¼	21	2¾	3¼	26½	30½	54	6¾	31¼	7¼	52¼
Ramsbottom	18¾	14¼	4	10	19¾	23¾	47¼	13½	24¾	14	45¾
Rawtenstall	16¼	17	8	14	22½	26½	50	17½	27¼	18	48¼
Ringley Road	21¼	21¾	3½	2½	27½	31½	55	6	32¼	6½	53¼

EAST LANCASHIRE RAILWAY—*Continued.*

STATIONS.	Blackburn.	Burnley Junction.	Bury.	Clifton Junction.	Colne.	Farrington Junction.	Kirkdale Junction.	Patricroft.	Preston (*via*) Extension.	Salford.	Walton Junction.
Rishton	2¾	8½	14¾	20¾	14	13	36½	24¼	13¾	24¾	35
Rose Grove	10	1¼	17	23	7	20¼	43¾	26½	21	26¾	42
Rufford	18	29¼	35½	41½	34¾	9¼	15¾	45	11	45½	14¼
Salford	27½	28¼	10	4	33¾	37¾	61¼	7½	38½	...	59¾
Skelmersdale Branch (End of)	26½	37¾	44	50	43¼	17¾	13¼	53½	19½	54	11¾
Stacksteads	19¼	20	11	17	25½	29½	53	20½	30¼	21	51¼
Stubbins........................	13	13½	4¾	10¾	19¼	23¼	46¾	14¼	24	14½	45
Summerseat ....:............	15	15¾	2½	8½	21¼	25¼	48¾	12	26	12½	47¼
Todd Lane Junction	9	20¼	26½	32½	25¾	1¼	24¾	36	2	36½	23¼
Town Green	25½	36¾	43	49	42¼	16¾	8¼	52½	18½	53	6¾
Walton	32	43¼	49¾	55¾	48¾	23¼	1¾	59¼	25	59½	...
Walton Junction	32	43¼	49¾	55¾	49	23½	1¾	59¼	25¼	59¾	...
Withins Lane	19¼	20	1¾	4¼	25½	29½	53	7¾	30½	8¼	51½

M'Corquodale & Co., Printers.

EAST & WEST INDIA DOCK & BIRMINGHAM JUNC. RAILWAY.

STATIONS.	Hampstead Road, L. & N. W. Junc., Camden.	Stepney.
Blackwall	10	2
Bow	6½	1½
Camden Road	¾	7½
Hackney	4¼	3¾
Hampstead Road (L. & N. W. Junction, Camden)	...	8
Islington	2	6
Kingsland	3½	4¾
Limehouse	8½	½
London, (Fenchurch Street)	9¾	1¾
Poplar	9½	1½
Shadwell	8½	½
Stepney	8	...
West India Docks	9	½

EDINBURGH AND GLASGOW RAILWAY.

STATIONS.	Campsie Junction	Causewayend Junction.	Edinburgh.	Garngabber.	Greenhill Junction.	Larbert Junction.	Morningside.	Ratho Junction.	Slamannan Junction.
Alum Works Siding	5	26¾	45¾	5¼	15¾	29	62¼	37¾	25¾
Barracks Siding...............	42¾	22¾	18	42¼	31¾	29½	15	10	21¾
Bathgate	43½	23¾	19	43¼	32½	30¼	14½	10¾	22¾
Bents Siding	48	28¼	23¼	47¾	37	34¾	9½	15¼	27¼
Bishop Briggs	3¼	25	44	3½	14	27¼	60½	36	24
Bishop Briggs Siding	3½	25½	44½	3¾	14½	27½	61	36¼	24½
Boghead	44¼	24½	19½	44	33¼	31	13¼	11½	23¼
Bonnymuir Siding............	12¼	9¾	28¾	12	1¼	12	45¼	20¾	8¾
Broomhouse Siding	30¼	10½	10¾	30	19½	17	27¼	2½	9½
Broxburn	36	16	11¼	35¾	25	22¾	21½	3¼	15
Campsie Junction	...	22	41	½	11	24¼	57½	33	21
Castlecarry	9¼	12¾	31¾	9	1¾	15	48¼	23¾	11¾
Causewayend Junction......	22	...	21¼	21¾	11	8¾	37¾	13	1¼
Coal Branch Junction	57¼	37½	32¾	57	46½	44	¼	24½	36½
Coalrees	49¾	30	25¼	49½	39	36½	7¾	17	29
Coltness Branch Junction...	50	30¼	25½	49¾	39	36¾	7½	17¼	29¼
Corstorphine	37½	17¾	3½	37¼	26½	24¼	29½	4¾	16¾
Cowlairs........................	5	26¾	46	5¼	16	29	62½	37¾	25¾
Crofthead	50¼	30½	25½	50	39¼	37	7¼	17½	29¼
Croy	5¼	16¾	35¾	5	5¾	19	52¼	27¾	15¾
Darngavel Siding	55	35	30¼	54¾	44	41¾	2¾	22¼	34
Davy Dykes Siding	56	36	31¼	55¾	45	42¾	1¾	23¼	35
Dechmont	39¼	19¼	14½	39	28¼	26	18½	6½	18¼
Edinburgh.......................	41	21¼	...	40¾	30	27¾	32¾	8¼	20¼
Falkirk	15½	6½	25½	15¼	4¾	8¾	42	17½	5½
Garngabber Junction	½	21¾	40¾	...	10¾	23¾	57¼	32½	20¾

EDINBURGH AND GLASGOW RAILWAY—*Continued.*

STATIONS.	Campsie Junction.	Causewayend Junction.	Edinburgh.	Garngabber.	Greenhill Junction.	Larbert Junction.	Morningside.	Ratho Junction.	Slamannan Junction.		
Glasgow	6½	28¼	47¼	6¾	17¼	30½	63¾	39¼	27¼		
Gogar	35½	15¾	5½	35½	24¾	22¼	27½	2¾	14¾		
Grahamston	22	6½	25½	21¾	11	2¼	42	17½	5½		
Greenhill Junction	11	11	30	10¾	...	13¼	46½	22	10		
Haymarket	40	20	1¼	39½	29	26½	30¾	6	19		
Headless Cross	52¾	33	28¼	52½	41¾	39½	4¾	20	32		
Houston	37½	17¾	13	37¼	26¾	24¼	20	4¾	16¾		
Inch Cross Siding	45	25	20¼	44½	34	31¾	12¾	12¼	24		
Kirkintilloch	1¾	23¾	42¾	2¼	12¾	26	59¼	34½	22¾		
Larbert Junction	24¼	8¾	27¾	23¾	13¼	...	44¼	19¾	7¾		
Lennoxtown	5½	27¼	46¼	5¾	16½	29½	62¾	38¼	26¼		
Linlithgow	23½	3½	17¾	23¼	12½	10¼	34¼	9½	2½		
Livingstone	40¼	20½	15¾	40	29½	27	17¼	7½	19½		
Longridge	48¾	29	24¼	48½	38	35½	8¾	16	28		
Longridge Siding	49¼	29½	24½	49	38¼	36	8¼	16½	28¼		
Manuel Siding	21½	1½	19¾	21	10½	8¼	36¼	11½	½		
Middlemuir Branch Junction	1	23	42	1½	12	25¼	58½	34	22		
Milton	3½	25½	44½	3¾	14½	27½	61	36¼	24½		
Morningside	57½	37¾	32¾	57¼	46½	44¼	...	24¾	36¾		
Netherwood Siding	8¾	13¼	32¼	8½	2¼	15½	48¾	24	12¼		
New Bridge Siding	34	14¼	9½	33¾	23	20¾	23½	1¼	13¼		
Pardovan Siding	25¾	6	15¼	25½	15	12½	31¾	7¼	5		
Polmont Junction	18¾	3¼	22¼	18½	7¾	5½	38¾	14¼	2¼		
Ratho Junction	33	13	8¼	32½	22	19¾	24¾	...	12		
Redding Siding	17½	4½	23½	17¼	6¾	6¾	40	15½	3½		
Shieldhill Junction	21¾	¼	21	21½	10¾	8½	37½	12¾	¾		

EDINBURGH AND GLASGOW RAILWAY—*Continued.*

STATIONS.	Campsie Junction.	Causewayend Junction.	Edinburgh.	Garngabber.	Greenhill Junction.	Larbert Junction.	Morningside.	Ratho Junction.	Slamannan Junction.		
Shotts Junction	53¾	34	29¼	53½	43	40½	3¾	21	33		
Slamannan Junction	21	1¼	20¼	20¾	10	7¾	36¾	12	...		
Stane Siding..................	54¾	35	30¼	54½	44	41½	4¾	22	34		
Uphall Junction	37¼	17½	12¾	37	26½	24	20¼	4½	16½		
Whitburn	45¾	26	21	45½	34¾	32½	11¾	13	35		
Wilsontown, Morningside, and Coltness Junction...	43¼	23½	18¾	43	32½	30	14¼	10½	22½		
Winchburgh....................	29	9¼	12	28¾	18	15¾	28½	4	8¼		

EDINBURGH, PERTH, AND DUNDEE RAILWAY.

STATIONS.	Broughty Ferry.	Dundee.	Dunfermline.	Edinburgh.	Hilton Junc., for S. Central.	Perth.	St. Andrews Junction.				
Abernethy	28¼	32¾	33¾	37¼	5¾	7¾	21¾				
Balburnie Coal Siding, see Markinch											
Balgonie Coal Siding, see Thornton Junction											
Beath Colliery, see Cowdenbeath Station											
Bow of Fife Lime Siding	16½	21	25	28½	17½	19½	10				
Bridge of Earn	32	36½	37½	41	2	4	25½				
Broughty	...	4½	41½	45	34	36	6½				
Burnt Island	37	41½	26	8	35	37	30½				
Cappledrae Colliery, see Cardenden Station											
Cardenden	32	36½	9½	24½	30	32	25½				
Cluny Coal Siding	30½	35	11	23	28½	30½	24				
Cluny Lime Siding	30¼	34¾	11¼	22¾	28¼	30¼	23¾				
Collessie	20½	25	26	29½	13½	15½	14				
Cowdenbeath	36¼	40¾	5¼	28¾	34¼	36¼	29¾				
Crossgates	38	42½	3½	30½	36	38	31½				
Cupar	12¾	17¼	28¾	32¼	21¼	23¼	6¼				
Cuttlehill Coal Siding	38½	43	3	31	36½	38½	32				
Dairsie	9¾	14¼	31¾	35¼	24¼	26¼	3¼				
Dundee	4½	...	46	49½	38½	40½	11				
Dundonald Colliery, see Cardenden Station											
Dunfermline	41½	46	...	34	39½	41½	35				
Dunnikier Coal Siding	30½	35	19½	14½	28½	30½	24				
Dysart	29¼	33¾	18¼	15¾	27¼	29¼	22¾				
Dysart Coal Siding, North Boreland	27½	32	16½	17½	25½	27½	21¼				
Dysart Coal Siding, South Boreland	28½	33	17½	16½	26½	28½	22½				

NOTE.—In the above Table only Single Mileage is allowed for the Forth and Tay Ferries. The Mileage to be added for these Ferries is as follows:—Forth Ferry, between Burnt Island and Granton, five miles additional; Tay Ferry, between Broughty and Tayport, two miles.

EDINBURGH, PERTH, AND DUNDEE RAILWAY—*Continued*.

STATIONS.	Broughty Ferry.	Dundee.	Dunfermline.	Edinburgh.	Hilton Junc., for S. Central.	Perth.	St. Andrews Junction.				
Edinburgh	45	49½	34	...	43	45	38¼				
Falkland Road	21	25½	20½	24	19	21	14½				
Fod Siding, see Halbeath } Station					●						
Fordel Coal Siding	37½	42	4	30	35½	37½	31				
Forthew Lime Siding	20¼	24¾	21¼	24¾	18¼	20¼					
Foulford Pit Siding	35¾	40¼	5¾	28¼	33¾	35¾					
Granton	42¼	46¾	31¼	2¾	40¼	42¼	35¾				
Halbeath	39¼	43¾	2¼	31¾	37¼	39¼	32¾				
Hilton Junction	34	38½	39½	43	...	2	27½				
Kinghorn	34¼	38¾	23¼	10¾	32¼	34¼	27¾				
King's Kettle	19	23½	22½	26	17	19	12½				
Kirkaldy	31¼	35¾	20¼	13¾	29¼	31¼	24¾				
Kirkaldy Harbour Branch	31¼	35¾	20¼	15	29¼	31¼	24¾				
Kirkness Colliery, see } Cardenden Station											
Ladybank	18	22½	23½	27	16	18	11½				
Leith	45	49½	34	2½	43	45	38¼				
Leuchars	5¾	10¼	35¾	39¼	28¼	30¼	¾				
Lochgeily	34	38½	7½	26½	32	34	27½				
Lochgelly East Siding	33¾	38¼	7¾	26¼	31¾	33¾	29¾				
Lochgelly Nott'm Pit Siding	35	39½	6½	27½	33	35	28¼				
Lochgelly Saw Mill Pit Siding	34½	39	7	27	32½	34½	27¾				
Lumphinans Coal Siding	35¼	39¾	6¼	27¾	33¼	35¼	38¾				
Markinch	24	28½	17½	21	22	24	17½				
Newburgh	25¼	29¾	30¾	34¼	8¾	10¾	18¾				
Perth	36	40½	41½	45	2	...	29½				
St. Andrew's Junction	6½	11	35	38¼	27½	29½	...				
Scotland Street	45	49½	34	...	43	45	38¼				

NOTE.—In the above Table only Single Mileage is allowed for the Forth and Tay Ferries. The Mileage to be added for these Ferries is as follows:—Forth Ferry, between Burnt Island and Granton, five miles additional; Tay Ferry, between Broughty and Tayport, two miles.

EDINBURGH, PERTH, AND DUNDEE RAILWAY—*Continued.*

STATIONS.	Broughty Ferry.	Dundee.	Dunfermline.	Edinburgh.	Hilton Junc., for S. Central.	Perth.	St. Andrews Junction.				
Sinclairtown	30	34½	19	15	27¾	29¾	23½				
Springfield......................	15	19½	26½	30	19	21	8½				
Strathore Siding..............	28¾	33¼	12¾	21¼	26¾	28¾					
Tayport	¾	5¼	40¾	44¼	33¼	35¼	5¾				
Thornton........................	26¼	30¾	15¼	18¾	24¼	26¼	19¾				
Thornton Siding..............	27	31½	14½	19½	25	27	20½				
Townhill and Wellwood Coal Siding..............	39¾	44¼	1¾	32¼	37¾	39¾	33¼				
Trinity	45	49½	34	...	43	45	38¼				

NOTE.—In the above Table only Single Mileage is allowed for the Forth and Tay Ferries. The Mileage to be added for these Ferries is as follows;—Forth Ferry, between Burnt Island and Granton, five miles additional; Tay Ferry, between Broughty and Tayport, two miles.

FLEETWOOD, PRESTON, & WEST RIDING RAILWAY.

STATIONS.	Maudland.	Preston.									
Grimsargh	$4\frac{3}{4}$	$3\frac{3}{4}$									
Longridge	7	6									
Maudland	...	$1\frac{3}{4}$									
Preston	$1\frac{3}{4}$	...									

M Corquodale and Co., Printers.

FURNESS RAILWAY.

STATIONS.	Broughton	Piel										
Barrow	13½	4½										
Broughton	...	15½										
Dalton	10¾	6¾										
Furness Abbey	10¼	5¼										
Kirkby	3½	12										
Lindal	12¼	8¼										
Piel	15½	...										
Ulverstone Road	13½	9½										

GLASGOW & SOUTH WESTERN RAILWAY.

STATIONS.	Ayr.	Carlisle.	Glasgow.	Gretna Junction.	Kilwinning, Ardrossan Junction.	Paisley, Greenock Junction.	Shields Bridge Junction.
Annandale Branch Junction	12¾	93¼	35¾	84¾	13	28¾	34¾
Annandale Lye, No. 1	13½	94	36½	85½	13¾	29½	35½
Annandale Lye, No. 2	13¾	94¼	36¾	85¾	14	29¾	35¾
Annan	88½	17½	107½	9	84½	100½	106½
Annick Branch Junction ...	19½	95¾	29	87¼	9	22	28
Annicklodge Lye	19¾	96	29¼	87½	9¼	22¼	28¼
Ardrossan Railway Junction	14	102	26	93½	...	19	25
Auchenskeith Lye............	18	100¾	24¼	92¼	4	17¼	23¼
Auchinleck	28¾	77¼	47½	68¾	24¾	40½	46½
Auldgirth	65½	40½	84¼	32	61½	77¼	83¼
Ayrshire Iron Works Lye	17½	102	22¾	93½	3½	15¾	21¾
Ayr	...	105¾	40	97¼	14	33	39
Baird's Ironstone Lye, No. 1	18½	103	21¾	94½	4½	14¾	20¾
Baird's Kerseland Lye, No. 2	18¼	103¼	22	94¾	4¼	15	21
Balgray Lye	19½	96	28¾	87½	8¾	21¾	27¾
Barassie Junction	7	98¾	33¼	90¼	7¼	26¼	32¼
Barleith Lye	17¼	88¾	36¼	80¼	13¼	29¼	35¼
Bartonholme Lye	12¾	100½	27½	92	1½	20½	26½
Beith	22¼	107	17¾	98½	8¼	10¾	16¾
Birnieknowe Lye	30	78¼	48¾	69¾	26	41¾	47¾
Blair Iron Co.'s Lye, No. 5	19	103½	22¼	95	5	15¼	21¼
Bogside Branch Junction...	12½	93½	36	85	12¾	29	35
Bogside Lye	11¾	99½	28½	91	2½	21½	27½
Bonnytod Siding	15¾	91¾	33	83¼	10¼	26	32
Bonnytod Lyes, Nos. 1 & 2	15½	91¼	33½	82¾	10¾	26½	32½
Bonnytod Lye, No. 3	15	91	33¾	82½	11	26¾	32¾

GLASGOW & SOUTH WESTERN RAILWAY—*Continued.*

STATIONS.	Ayr.	Carlisle.	Glasgow.	Gretna Junction.	Kilwinning, Ardrossan Junction.	Paisley, Greenock Junction.	Shields Bridge Junction.				
Borestone Loading Bank ...	19¼	103¾	22½	95¼	5¼	15½	21½				
Braehead Pit Lye	32	80¼	51	71¾	28¼	44	50				
Braehead Tile Works Lye...	32	80¼	51	71¾	28¼	44	50				
Broomlands Lye	12	97	31	88½	5	24	30				
Brownhill Lye	19	103½	21¼	95	5	14¼	20¼				
Burnbrae Lye	20½	97	27¾	88½	7¾	20¾	26¾				
Busby	16¼	92¾	32	84¼	9¼	25	31				
Capringstone Lye, No. 1 ...	13½	95½	32½	87	6½	25½	31½				
Capringstone Lye, No. 2....	14	96	32¾	87½	6¾	25¾	31¾				
Caprington Branch Junction	13½	93¼	37	84¾	13¾	30	36				
Caprington Lye................	14¾	94½	38¼	86	15	31¼	37¼				
Carbella Lye	32¾	81	51¾	72½	29	44¾	50¾				
Carronbridge	55½	50½	74½	42	51¾	67½	73½				
Closeburn	61½	44½	80½	36	57¾	73½	79½				
Cochranemill	28¾	113¼	11½	104¾	14¾	4½	10½				
Colinnan Quarry	7¾	98¼	34	89¾	8	27	33				
Cummertrees..................	85	20¾	104	12¼	81¼	97	103				
Dalry	17½	102¼	22½	93¾	3½	15½	21½				
Dornock	92	14	111	5½	88	104	110				
Dowra Lye	20	96½	28¼	88	8¼	21¼	27¼				
Dreghorn	13	96¼	31¾	87¾	5¾	24¾	30¾				
Drybridge	10	96	36¼	87½	10¼	29¼	35¼				
Dumfries	73¼	32¾	92	24¼	69¼	85	91				
Dykehead Lye	17½	90	36¼	81½	13½	29¼	35¼				
Earlstone Lye	14¾	94½	38¼	86	15	31¼	37¼				
Eglinton Colliery Lye	20¾	98	26¾	89½	6¾	19¾	25¾				

GLASGOW & SOUTH WESTERN RAILWAY—*Continued.*

STATIONS.	Ayr.	Carlisle.	Glasgow.	Gretna Junction.	Kilwinning, Ardrossan Junction.	Paisley, Greenock Junction.	Shields Bridge Junction.			
Eglinton Iron Works Lye...	13¼	101	26¾	92½	¾	19¾	25¾			
Fairlie Branch Junction ...	12½	93½	36	85	12¾	29	35			
Fairlie Lye, No. 3............	13¾	94¾	37¼	86¼	14	30¼	36¼			
Fairlie Lye, No. 4............	13¾	94¾	37¼	86¼	14	30¼	36¼			
Fergushill Lye	21	97½	27¼	89	7¼	20¼	26¼			
Galston Branch Junction.,..	16¾	89¼	35½	80¾	12¾	28½	34½			
Galston	20¼	93	39¼	84½	16¼	32¼	38¼			
Gargiestone Branch Junction	13¾	92¼	34¾	83¾	12	27¾	33¾			
Gargiestone Lye	13¾	92¼	34¾	83¾	12	27¾	33¾			
Garfel Lye	38¼	86½	57¼	78	34¼	50¼	56¼			
Gaswater Branch Junction..	32¾	81	51¾	72½	29	44¾	50¾			
Gaswater Lime Wharf.......	34¼	82½	53¼	74	30½	46¼	52¼			
Gaswater Pit Lye, No. 1 ...	34	82¼	53	73¾	30¼	46	52			
Gaswater Pit Lye, No. 2 ...	34¼	82½	53¼	74	30¼	46¼	52¼			
Gatehead	12¼	93¾	36¼	85¼	12½	29¼	35¼			
Gatehead Colliery Lye	12	94	36½	85½	12¼	29½	35½			
Gateside Lye, K. & T. Branch	7¾	98¼	34	89¾	8	27	33			
Gateside Lye, Main Line ...	45½	60½	64¼	52	41½	57¼	63¼			
Gauchland Lye	19¾	92¼	38½	83¾	15¾	31½	37½			
Glasgow	40	124¾	...	116¼	26	7	1			
Glengarnock Coal Lye	20½	105	19¾	96½	6½	12¾	18¾			
Glengarnock Iron Lye	20¾	105¼	19½	96¾	6¾	12½	18½			
Greenhill Lye	16	92¼	32¼	83¾	9½	25¼	31¼			
Gretna Junction	97¼	8½	116¼	...	93½	109¼	115¼			
Gretna	96½	9½	115½	1	92½	108½	114½			
Hillhead Lye	15¼	91¼	33½	82¾	10¾	26½	32½			

GLASGOW & SOUTH WESTERN RAILWAY—*Continued.*

STATIONS.	Ayr.	Carlisle.	Glasgow.	Gretna Junction.	Kilwinning. Ardrossan Junction.	Paisley. Greenock Junction.	Shields Bridge Junction.				
Holmes Lye	18½	91	37¼	82½	14½	30¼	36¼				
Holywood	69¾	36¼	88½	27¾	65¾	81½	87½				
Horsecleugh Junction	32¾	78	51¾	64½	29	44¾	50¾				
Howood Coal Lye............	27¼	112	13	103½	13½	6	12				
Howood Lime Lye	27¾	112½	12½	104	13¾	5½	11½				
Hurlford	16¾	89¼	35¾	80¾	12¾	28¾	34¾				
Irvine and Busby Branch Junction, Ayr Branch.	10¾	98½	29½	90	3½	22½	28½				
Irvine and Busby Branch Junction, Main Line...	16¼	92¾	32	84¼	9¼	25	31				
Irvine Harbour	11½	99¼	30¼	90¾	4½	23¼	29¼				
Irvine..............................	10¾	98½	29½	90	3½	22½	28½				
Johnstone	30	114¾	10¼	106¼	16	3¼	9¼				
Kerseland Lye	19	103½	21¼	95	5	14¼	20¼				
Kilbirnie	20¼	105	19¾	96½	6¼	12¾	18¾				
Kilcush Junction	17	101¾	23¼	93¼	3	16¼	22¼				
Kilmarnock and Troon Branch Junction	14¾	91¼	33¾	82¾	10¾	26¾	32¾				
Kilmarnock	15	91	33¾	82½	11	26¾	32¾				
Kilwinning	14	102	26	93½	...	19	25				
Kirkconnell	43½	62½	62½	54	39¾	55½	61½				
Knockintibber Lye	16¼	92¾	32	84¼	19¼	25	31				
Langhouse Lye	30¾	75	49¾	66½	27	42¾	48¾				
Lochwinnoch..................	24¼	109	15¾	100½	10¼	8¾	14¾				
Longbar Lye	20¼	105	19¾	96½	6¼	12¾	18¾				
Lovemill Lye...................	10¼	94¾	37¼	86¼	11¼	30¼	36¼				
Lugar Branch Junction ...	31½	79½	50¼	71	27½	43¼	49¼				
Lugar Iron Works' Lye ...	32	80¼	51	71¾	28	44	50				
Lugar..............................	31½	79½	50¼	71	27½	43¼	49¼				

GLASGOW & SOUTH WESTERN RAILWAY—*Continued.*

STATIONS.	Ayr.	Carlisle.	Glasgow	Gretna Junction.	Kilwinning, Ardrossan Junction.	Paisley, Greenock Junction.	Shields Bridge Junction.				
Mansfield Lye	37½	68½	56¼	60	33½	49¼	55¼				
Mauchline	24¼	81½	43¼	73	20½	36¼	42¼				
Merry & Co.'s No. 18, Pit Lye	19½	104	23	95½	5½	16	22				
Milton Branch Junction	11¾	94¼	36¾	85¾	11¾	29¾	35¾				
Milton Lye, No. 14	12½	94¾	37¼	86¼	12¼	30¼	36¼				
Minnock Lye	48½	57½	67¼	49	44½	60¼	66¼				
Monkton	4	103¾	36	93¼	10	29	35				
Moorfield Lye	13	93¼	36	84¾	13¼	29	35				
Mossroad Lye	36½	121¼	3½	112¾	22½	3½	2½				
Muirkirk Branch Junction	28¾	77	47¾	68½	25	40¾	46¾				
Muirkirk Iron Works Lye	39	87¼	57¾	78¾	35	50¾	56¾				
Muirkirk	39	87¼	58	78¾	35	51	57				
Muirs Lye	21½	106¼	18½	97¾	7½	11½	17½				
New Cumnock	36	69¾	55	61¼	32¼	48	54				
Newmilns	22¼	94¾	41	86¼	18¼	34	40				
Old Cumnock	30¾	75	49¾	66½	27	42¾	48¾				
Paisley	33	117¾	7	109¼	19	...	6				
Parkthorn Lye	8¼	97¾	34½	89¼	8½	27½	33½				
Pierceton Branch Junction	13½	95½	32½	87	6½	25½	31½				
Pierceton Lye, No. 3	14	96¼	33	87¾	7	26	32				
Pitcon Lye, No. 3	19	103½	22¼	95	5	15¼	21¼				
Pitcon Lye, No. 4	19¼	104	22¾	95½	5¼	15¾	21¾				
Portland Iron Co.'s Coal Lye	16¼	89½	35¼	81	12¼	28¼	34¼				
Portland Iron Lye	16½	89¼	35½	80¾	12¾	28½	34½				
Portland Ironstone Lye	26	78	46¾	69½	24	39¾	45¾				
Prestwick	2½	103¼	37½	94¾	11½	30½	36½				

GLASGOW & SOUTH WESTERN RAILWAY—*Continued.*

STATIONS.	Ayr.	Carlisle.	Glasgow.	Gretna Junction.	Kilwinning, Ardrossan Junction.	Paisley, Greenock Junction.	Shields Bridge Junction.
Racks	77	29	95¾	20½	73	88¾	94¾
Reidstone Lye	20	98¾	26	90¼	6	19	25
Ruthwell	81½	24½	100½	16	77½	93½	99½
Sandhills Lye	34¾	83	53½	74½	30¾	46½	52½
Sanquhar	47	59	65¾	50½	43	58¾	64¾
Sheddows, Western Coal Lye	32½	117	7¾	108½	18½	¾	6¾
Shields Bridge Junction	39	124	1	115½	25	6	...
Smithstone Lye	14½	102¼	25½	93¾	½	18½	24½
Southoak Lye	14¾	94¼	33½	85¾	7¾	26½	32½
Sovereign, High, No. 15, Lye	12¾	95¼	37¾	86¾	12¾	30¾	36¾
Sovereign, New, No. 10, Lye	12¾	95¼	37¾	86¾	12¾	30¾	36¾
Sovereign, New, No. 17, Lye	12½	95	37½	86½	12½	30½	36½
Springside Lye	14¼	95	33	86½	7	26	32
Stewarton	18¾	95	29¾	86½	9¾	22¾	28¾
Swinlees Branch Junction	18½	103	21¾	94½	4½	14¾	20¾
Swinlees Loading Bank	19¾	104¼	23	95¾	5¾	16	22
Thirdpart Lime Kilns Lye	12¾	93¼	35¾	84¾	12¾	28¾	34¾
Thornhill	58¾	47	77¾	38½	55	70¾	76¾
Thornton Lye	12	94½	37	86	12	30	36
Todhill Lye	18	102¾	22	94¼	4	15	21
Troon Harbour	9¼	101	35¼	92½	9¼	28¼	34¼
Troon	6¼	99¾	34	91¼	8	27	33
Wellhill Lye	33¾	72¼	52½	63¾	29¾	45½	51½
Weltrees Lye	36	84¼	54¾	75¾	32	47¾	53¾
Wellwood Lye	36¼	84½	55¼	76	32½	48¼	54¼
West Thornton Lye	14½	94½	33¼	86	7¼	26¼	32¼

M'Corquodale & Co., Printers.

GREAT NORTHERN RAILWAY.

STATIONS.	Askern Junction.	Doncaster.	Gainsboro', *via* Sykes Junction.	Grantham.	Great Grimsby.	Hitchin.	Huntingdon.	Knottingley.	Leeds Midland.	Lincoln.	Methley.
Alford	96¼	92	71¼	77	24½	98½	71½	106¾	122¼	54¼	113¼
Algarkirk	79½	75¼	54½	47¼	54¼	68½	41¾	90	105½	37¾	96½
Arlsey	123½	119¼	118	68	117¾	5	21¾	134	149½	101¼	140½
Askern Junction	...	4¼	43½	55¼	120¾	128½	101¾	10½	26	42	17
Authorpe	100¾	96½	75¾	81½	20	103	76	111¼	126¾	58¾	117¾
Bardney	51¼	47	26¼	62¼	69½	97	70	61¾	77¼	9¼	68¼
Barnet	151¼	147	146	96	145½	22¾	49½	161¾	177¼	129	168¼
Bawtry	12½	8¼	31	42¾	108	116	89	23	38½	29¼	29½
Biggleswade	119½	115¼	114	64¼	113¾	9	17¾	130	145½	97¼	136½
Boston	73	68¾	48	54	47¾	75¼	48¼	83½	99	31	90
Burgh	90¼	86	65¼	71	30½	92½	65½	100¾	116¼	48¼	107¼
Carlton	34¼	30	33¾	21	110¾	94¼	67½	44¾	60¼	32	51¼
Claypole	45¼	41	44¾	10	121¾	83¼	56½	55¾	71¼	43	62¼
Claythorpe	99¼	95	74¼	80	21½	101½	74½	109¾	125¼	57¼	116¼
Corby	63½	59¼	63	8¼	93¼	65	38	74	89½	61¼	80½
Crowland, or St. James Deeping	85¼	81	71¾	30	71½	51½	24½	95¾	111¼	55	102¼
Dogdyke	62	57½	37	65	58¾	86¼	59½	72½	88	20	79
Doncaster	4¼	...	39¼	51	116½	124¼	97½	14¾	30¼	37½	21¼
Eastville	82¾	78½	57¾	63½	38	85	58	93¼	108¾	40¾	99¾
Essendine	72	67¾	71½	16¾	84¾	56½	29½	82½	98	68¼	89
Firsby	88¼	84	63¼	69	32½	90½	63½	98¾	114¼	46¼	105¼
Gainsboro', *via* Sykes Junc.	43½	39¼	...	54¾	95¾	123¼	96¼	54	69½	17	60½
Grantham	55¼	51	54¾	...	101½	73¼	46½	65¾	81¼	52¾	72¼
Great Grimsby	120¾	116½	95¾	101½	...	123	96	131¼	146¾	78¾	137¾
Great Ponton	58½	54¼	58	3¼	104¼	70	43	69	84½	56¼	75½
Hatfield	142¾	138½	137½	87½	137	14¼	41	153¼	168¾	120½	159¾

GREAT NORTHERN RAILWAY—*Continued.*

STATIONS.	Milford Junction.	Newark.	Peterboro'.	Retford.	Sykes Junction.	Wakefield.	Warrington Jun.	York.
Alford	111¾	91¾	54	74	62	117¼	51	126¾
Algarkirk	95	62	24¼	57½	45¼	100¾	21¼	110
Arlsey	139	83	39¼	101½	108¾	144½	42¼	154
Askern Junction	15½	40½	84¼	22	34¼	21	81¼	30½
Authorpe	116¼	96¼	58½	78½	66½	121¾	55½	131¼
Bardney	66¾	47½	52¾	29	17	72¼	49¾	81¾
Barnet	166¾	110¾	67	129¼	136½	172¼	70	181¾
Bawtry	28	28	71¾	9½	21¾	33¾	68¾	43
Biggleswade	135	79	35¼	97½	104¾	140½	38¼	150
Boston	88½	68¾	31	51	38¾	94	28	103½
Burgh	105¾	85¾	48	68	56	111¼	45	120¾
Carlton	49¾	6¼	50	12¼	24½	55½	47	64¾
Claypole	60¾	4¾	39	23¼	35½	66½	36	75¾
Claythorpe	114¾	94¾	57	77	65	120¼	54	129¾
Corby	79	23	20¾	41½	53¾	84¾	17¾	94
Crowland, or St. James Deeping	100¾	44¾	7	63¼	62½	106½	4	115¾
Dogdyke	77½	58¼	42	39¾	27½	83	39	92½
Doncaster	19¾	36¼	80	17¾	30	25½	77	34¾
Eastville	98¼	78¼	40½	60½	48½	103¾	37½	113¼
Essendine	87½	31½	12¼	50	62¼	93¼	9¼	102½
Firsby	103¾	83¾	46	66	54	109¼	43	118¾
Gainsboro', *via* Sykes Junc.	59	40	79	21½	9¼	64¾	76	74
Grantham	70¾	14¾	29	33¼	45½	76½	26	85¾
Great Grimsby	136¼	116¼	78½	98½	86½	141¾	75½	151¼
Great Ponton	74	18	25¾	36½	48¾	79¾	22¾	89
Hatfield	158¼	102¼	58½	120¾	128	164	61½	173¼

GREAT NORTHERN RAILWAY—*Continued.*

STATIONS.	Askern Junction.	Doncaster.	Gainsboro', *via* Sykes Junction.	Grantham.	Great Grimsby.	Hitchin.	Huntingdon.	Knottingley.	Leeds Midland.	Lincoln.	Methley.
Hitchin	128½	124¼	123¼	73¼	123	...	27	139	154½	106¼	145½
Holme	91¼	87	86	36	85½	37¼	10½	101¾	117¼	69	108¼
Holton-le-Clay	115½	111¼	90½	96½	5¼	117¾	90¾	126	141½	73½	132½
Hornsey	156½	152¼	151¼	101¼	151	28	55	167	182½	134¼	173½
Hougham	49¼	45	48½	6	107½	79½	52½	59¾	75¼	46¾	66¼
Huntingdon	101¾	97½	96¼	46½	96	27	...	112¼	127¾	79½	118¾
Kirkstead	57½	53	32½	68½	63¼	90¾	64	68	83½	15½	74½
Kirton	76¾	72½	51¾	50	51½	71½	44½	87¼	102¾	35	93¾
Knottingley Junction	10½	14¾	54	65¾	131¼	139	112¼	...	15½	52½	6½
Langrick	68	63¾	43	59	52¾	80¼	53¼	78½	94	26	85
Lea, *Via* Sykes Junction ...	40	35¾	3½	50¼	92¼	119¾	92¾	50½	66	13½	57
Leake..........................	79½	75¼	54½	60½	41¼	81¾	54¾	90	105½	37½	96½
Leeds Midland	26	30¼	69½	81¼	146¾	154½	127¾	15½	...	68	9
Legbourne	104	99¾	79	85	16½	106¼	79½	114½	130	62¼	121
Lincoln	42	37½	17	53	78¾	106¼	79½	52½	68	...	59
Little Bytham	68½	64¼	68	13¼	94½	60	33¼	79	94½	66¼	85½
Little Steeping	86	81¾	61	67	34¾	88¼	61¼	96½	112	44	103
Littleworth	89¾	85½	67½	34½	67¼	55¾	28¾	100¼	115¾	50½	106¾
London Goods Station	160¼	156	155	105	154½	31¾	58¾	170¾	186¼	138	177¼
„ Kings Cross	160½	156¼	155¼	105¼	155	32	59	171	186½	138¼	177½
Louth	106¾	102½	81¾	87½	14	109	82	117¼	132¾	64¾	123¾
Ludborough	112	107¾	87	93	8¾	114¼	87¼	122½	138	70	129
Marton, *Via* Sykes Junction	37¼	33	6¼	48½	89½	117	90	47¾	63¼	10½	54¼
Methley	17	21¼	60½	72¼	137¾	145½	118¾	6½	9	59	...
Milford Junction	15½	19¾	59	70¾	136¼	144	117¼	5	20½	57½	11½
Newark	40½	36¼	40	14¾	116¼	88	61	51	66½	38¼	57¾

GREAT NORTHERN RAILWAY—*Continued.*

STATIONS.	Milford Junction.	Newark.	Peterboro'.	Retford.	Sykes Junction.	Wakefield.	Werrington Jun.	York.
tchin	144	88	44¼	106½	114	149¾	47¼	159
olme	106¾	50¾	7	69¼	76½	112½	10	121¾
lton-le-Clay	131	111¼	73½	93½	81¼	136½	70½	146
rnsey	172	116	72¼	134½	142	177¾	75¼	187
ugham	64¾	8½	35	27	39¼	70¼	32	79¾
ntingdon	117¼	61	17½	79½	87	122¾	20½	132¼
rkstead	73	53¾	46½	35¼	23	78½	43½	88
rton	92¼	64¾	27	54¾	42½	98	24	107¼
ottingley Junction	5	51	94¾	32½	44¾	10½	91¾	20
ngrick	83½	64½	36	46	33¾	89	33	98½
, *Via* Sykes Junction	55½	36½	75½	18	5¾	61¼	72½	70½
ke	95	75¼	37½	57½	45¼	100½	34½	110
ds Midland	20½	66½	110¼	48	60¼	22	107¼	35½
bourne	119½	99¾	62	82	69¾	125¼	59	134½
ooln	57½	38¼	62	19¾	7½	63	59	72½
tle Bytham	84	28	15¾	46½	58½	89½	12¾	99
tle Steeping	101½	81¾	44	64	51¾	107	41	116½
leworth	105¼	49¼	11½	67¾	58¼	111	8½	120¼
don Goods Station	175¾	119¾	76	138¼	145½	181½	79	190¾
, Kings Cross	176	120	76¼	138½	146	181¾	79¼	191
th	122¼	102¼	64½	84½	72½	127¾	61½	137¼
borough	127½	107¾	70	90	77¾	133	67	142½
ton, *Via* Sykes Junction	52¾	33¾	72½	15¼	3	58½	69½	67¾
hley	11½	57½	101¼	39	51¼	13	98¼	26½
ford Junction	...	56	99¾	37½	49¾	15½	96¾	15
vark	56	...	43¾	18½	30¾	61¾	40¾	71

GREAT NORTHERN RAILWAY—*Continued.*

STATIONS.	Askern Junction.	Doncaster.	Gainsboro', *via* Sykes Junction.	Grantham.	Great Grimsby.	Hitchin.	Huntingdon.	Knottingley.	Leeds Midland.	Lincoln.	Methley.
North Thoresby	113¾	109½	88¾	94½	7	116	89	124¼	139¾	71¾	130¾
Offord	104¾	100½	99¼	49½	99	24	3	115¼	130¾	82½	121¾
Peakirk	83¾	79½	73½	28½	73¼	49¾	22¾	94¼	109¾	56½	100¾
Peterboro'	84¼	80	79	29	78½	44¼	17½	94¾	110¼	62	101¼
Potters Bar	147¾	143½	142½	92½	142	19¼	46	158¼	173¾	125½	164¾
Ranskill	16½	12	27¼	39	104¼	112¼	85¼	27	42½	25½	33½
Retford	22	17¾	21½	33¼	98½	106½	79½	32½	48	19¾	39
Rossington	9	4¾	34½	46¼	111¾	119½	92¾	19½	35	33	26
Sandy	116½	112¼	111	61¼	110¾	12	14¾	127	142½	94½	133½
Saxilby	35¾	31½	10¾	47	85	112½	85½	46¼	61¾	6	52¾
Scrooby	14½	10¼	29	40¾	106¼	114	87¼	25	40½	27½	31½
Sibsey	77¾	73½	52¾	58¾	43	80	53	88¼	103¾	36	94¾
Southgate, or Colney Hatch	154¼	150	148¾	99	148½	25½	52½	164¾	180¼	132	171¼
Southrey	53¾	49½	28¾	64¾	67	94½	67½	64¼	79¾	11¾	70¾
Spalding	87¼	83	62¼	39¾	62	61	34	97¾	113¼	45¼	104¼
Stevenage	132	127¾	126½	76¾	126¼	3½	30¼	142½	158	109¾	149
Stixwould	55¼	51	30¼	66½	65½	93	66	65¾	81¼	13½	72¼
Stockbridge	2¼	2	41¼	53	118½	126¼	99½	12¾	28¼	39½	19¼
St. Neots	109	104½	103½	53½	103¼	19¾	7¼	119½	135	86½	126
Surfleet	83¼	79	58¼	43½	58	65	38	93¾	109¼	41½	100¼
Sutton	18½	14¼	25	36¾	102	110	83	29	44½	23¼	35½
Sykes Junction	34¼	30	9¼	45½	80½	114	87	44¾	60¼	7½	51¼
Tallington	76	71½	75¼	20½	81	52¾	25¾	86½	102	64½	93
Tattershall	61	56¾	36	66	59¾	87¼	60¼	71½	87	19	78
Tuxford	28¾	24½	28¼	26½	105¼	99¾	73	39½	54¾	26½	45¾
Wakefield	21	25½	64¾	76½	141¾	149¾	123¾	10½	22	63	13

GREAT NORTHERN RAILWAY—*Continued.*

STATIONS.	Milford Junction.	Newark.	Peterboro'.	Retford.	Sykes Junction.	Wakefield.	Warrington Jun.	York.
North Thoresby	129¼	109¼	71½	91½	79½	134¾	68½	144¼
Offord	120¼	64	20½	82½	90	125¾	23½	135¼
Peakirk	99½	43¼	5½	61½	64¼	105	2½	114¼
Peterboro'	99¾	43¾	...	62¼	69½	105½	3	114¾
Potters Bar	163¼	107½	63½	125¾	133	169	66½	178¼
Ranskill	32	24¼	68	5¾	18	37½	65	47
Retford	37½	18½	62¼	...	12¼	43¼	59¼	52½
Rossington	24½	31½	75¼	13	25¼	30	72¼	39½
Sandy	132	76	32¼	94½	101¾	137½	35¼	147
Saxilby	51¼	32¼	68	13¾	1½	57	65	66¼
Scrooby	30	26	69¾	7½	19¾	35½	66¾	45
Sibsey..........................	93¼	73½	35¾	55¾	43½	99	32¾	108¼
Southgate, or Colney Hatch.	169¾	113½	70	132	139½	175¼	73	184¾
Southrey	69¼	50	50¼	31½	19½	74¾	47¼	84¼
Spalding........................	102¾	54½	16¾	65	53	108¼	13¾	117¾
Stevenage	147½	91½	47¾	110	117¼	153	50¾	162½
Stixwould	70¾	51¾	48½	33¼	21	76½	45½	85¾
Stockbridge	17¾	38¼	82	19¾	32	23½	79	32¾
St. Neots	124½	68¼	24½	86¾	94¼	130	27½	139½
Surfleet	98¾	58¼	20½	61¼	49	104½	17½	113¾
Sutton	34	22	65¾	3½	15¾	39¾	62¾	49
Sykes Junction	49¾	30¾	69½	12¼	...	55½	66½	64¾
Tallington	91½	35¼	8½	53¾	66	97	5½	106½
Tattershall.....................	76½	37½	43	39	26¾	82	40	91½
Tuxford	44¼	11¾	55½	6¾	19	50	52½	59¼
Wakefield	15½	61¾	105½	43¼	55½	...	102½	30½

GREAT NORTHERN RAILWAY—*Continued.*

STATIONS.	Askern Junction.	Doncaster.	Gainsboro', *via* Sykes Junction.	Grantham.	Great Grimsby.	Hitchin.	Huntingdon.	Knottingley.	Leeds Midland.	Lincoln.	Methley.
Waltham	117½	113¼	92½	98½	3	119¾	93	128	143½	75¾	134½
Washingborough	44½	40¼	19½	55½	76¼	103¾	76¾	55	70½	2½	61½
Welwyn	138½	134¼	133¼	83½	133	10	37	149	164½	116¼	155½
Willoughby	93¾	89½	68¾	74½	27	96	69	104¼	119¾	51¾	110¾
York	30½	34¾	74	85¾	151¼	159	132¼	20	35½	72½	26½

GREAT NORTHERN RAILWAY.—*Continued.*

STATIONS.	Milford Junction.	Newark.	Peterboro'.	Retford.	Sykes Junction.	Wakefield.	Werrington Jun.	York.			
Waltham	133	113¼	75½	95½	83¼	138¾	72½	148			
Washingborough	60	41	59½	22½	10¼	65½	56½	75			
Welwyn	154	98	54¼	116½	124	159¾	57¼	169			
Willoughby	109¼	89¼	51½	71½	59½	114¾	48½	124¼			
York	15	71	114¾	52½	64¾	30½	111¾				

M'Corquodale & Co., Printer

KENDAL & WINDERMERE RAILWAY.

STATIONS.	Oxenholme.									
Burneside	4									
Kendal, Goods	2½									
Kendal, Passengers	2									
Oxenholme	...									
Staveley	6½									
Windermere	10¼									

LANCASHIRE & YORKSHIRE RAILWAY.

STATIONS.	Ardwick.	Askern Junction.	Barnsley.	Blackburn.	Bolton.	Bradford.	Burnley.	Burton Salmon Junction.	Bury.	Clifton Junction.	Dewsbury Junc.	Euxton Junction.	Farrington Junc.	Heaton Lodge.	Huddersfield.
Adlington	22¾	79½	65	22	8½	51¼	38¾	69	14½	14½	50¾	6¼	9¼	48	50½
Ainsdale	54	110¾	96¼	53¼	39¾	82½	70	100¼	45¾	45¾	82	48¾	52	79¼	81¾
Aintree	38	94¾	80¼	37¼	23¾	66½	54	84¼	29¾	29¾	66	32¾	35¾	63	65¾
Ardwick	...	69¼	55	27¾	14¼	41¼	28¾	59¼	14	8¾	41	29	32	38	40½
Ashton	6½	72½	58	30½	17	44	31½	61¾	16½	11	43¾	31¾	34¾	40¾	43¼
Askern	67	2½	29½	82	68½	38¼	55½	8	62½	70¾	26¼	83¼	86¼	29	32¾
Askern Junction ...	69½	...	32	84½	71	40¾	58	10½	65	73¼	28¾	85¾	88¾	31	35¼
Barnsley	55	32	...	70	56½	26¼	43½	21½	50½	58¾	14¼	71¼	74¼	17½	20¾
Berrybrow............	42½	37½	23	57½	44	17¾	31	27	38	46½	8¾	58¾	61¾	6	2¼
Birkdale...............	55¾	112½	98	55	41½	84¼	71¾	102	47¼	47½	83¾	50½	53¾	81	83½
Blackburn	27¾	84½	70	...	13½	56¼	43¾	74	19½	19½	55¾	28	31¼	53	55½
Blackpool	52½	109¼	94¾	51½	38	80¾	68½	98½	44¼	44¼	80¼	23½	20½	77½	80
Black Lane	17¾	67¼	52¾	17¼	3¾	39	26½	56¾	2¼	9½	38¼	18½	21½	35½	38¼
Blue Pits	9½	60	45½	24½	11	31¾	19¼	49½	5	13¼	31	25¾	28¾	28¼	31
Bolton	14¼	71	56½	13½	...	42¾	30¼	60½	6	6	42¼	14¾	17¾	39½	42
Bootle Lane	40¾	97¼	83	39¾	26¼	69	56½	86¾	32½	32½	68½	35½	38½	65¾	68¼
Bradford	41¼	40¾	26¼	56¼	42¾	...	29¾	30¼	36¾	45	12	57½	60½	12	15¾
Bradley Fold....	16½	68½	54	16	2½	40¼	27¾	58	3½	8¼	39½	17¼	20½	36¾	39¼
Brighouse	35¼	34¼	19¾	50¼	36¾	13½	23¾	23¾	30¾	39	5½	51½	54½	2¾	5¼
Brockholes............	44¾	39½	25	59¾	46¼	20	33¼	29	40¼	48½	10¾	61	64	8	4¼
Bromley Cross	17¼	74	59½	10½	3	45¾	33¼	63½	9	9	45	17½	20¾	42¼	44¾
Burnley	28¾	58	43½	43¾	30¼	29¾	...	47½	24¼	32½	29	45	48	26¼	28¾
Bury	14¼	65¼	50¾	19¼	5¾	37	24½	54¾	...	11½	36¼	20½	23½	33½	36
Chapeltown	18½	75¼	60¾	9¼	4¼	47	34½	64¾	10¼	10¼	46½	19	22	43¾	46¼
Chatburn	40¾	97½	83	13	26½	69¼	56¾	87	32½	32½	68½	41	44¼	65¾	68¼
Chew Moor	18¼	75	60½	17¼	4	46¾	34¼	64½	10	10	46	13	16	43¼	45¾

NOTE.—The Lancashire and Yorkshire Co. are allowed by Act of Parliament double toll between Miles Platting and Victoria; it is not included in this Table.

LANCASHIRE AND YORKSHIRE RAILWAY—*Continued.*

STATIONS.	Kirkdale Junc.	Knottingley	Leeds, Central.	Liverpool.	Maudlands.	Methley Junc.	Normanton.	Penistone Junc.	Preston.	Preston Road Junction.	Salford.	Staleybridge Junction.	Wakefield.	Wigan Junc.	Victoria.
dlington	29¾	69¼	61	31½	12½	72	61¾	64	11¾	28	18½	26¾	58½	12¼	19¼
insdale...............	13	100½	92¼	14¾	55	103¼	93	95¼	54¼	14½	49¾	58	89¾	30½	50½
intree	3¼	84½	76¼	5	39	87	76¾	79¼	38¼	1½	33¾	42	73¾	14½	34¼
rdwick...............	41¼	59¼	51	43	35¼	61¾	51¾	54	34½	39¼	4½	7¾	48¾	23¾	3¾
shton	44	62	53¾	45¾	38	64¾	54½	56¾	37¼	42¼	7¼	1¼	51½	26½	6½
skern	95¼	7¾	36½	97¼	89½	14½	21½	46¼	88¾	93¾	67¼	71	18½	77¾	66¼
skern Junction ...	97¾	10¼	39	99¾	92	16¾	24	48¾	91¼	96¼	69¾	73½	21	80¼	68¾
arnsley	83½	21¾	24¾	85¼	77½	24½	14¼	34½	76¾	81¾	55¼	59	11	65¾	54¼
errybrow............	71	27¼	19	72¾	65	29¾	19½	11½	64¼	69¼	42¾	46¾	16½	53½	41¾
irkdale...............	14¾	102¼	94	16¾	57	105	94¾	97	56¼	16¼	51½	59¾	91¾	32¼	52¼
ackburn	40¼	74¼	66	42¼	34½	76¾	66¾	69	33¾	38¾	23½	31¼	63½	22¾	24
ackpool	59¼	98¾	90½	61¼	17½	101½	91¼	93½	18	57¾	48¼	56½	88¼	41¾	48¾
ack Lane	30¾	56¾	48¾	32½	24¾	59½	49¼	51¾	24	29	13½	21¾	46¼	13¼	14
ue Pits	37¾	49¾	41½	39¾	32	52¼	42	44½	31¼	36¼	9¾	13½	39	20¼	8¾
lton	26¾	60¾	52½	28¾	21	68½	53¼	55½	20¼	25¼	10	18¼	50	9¼	10¾
otle Lane	½	87	78¾	2¼	41¾	89¾	79½	81¾	41	1	36¼	44½	76½	17	37
adford	69½	30½	22¼	71½	63¾	33	22¾	29¼	63	68	41¼	45¼	19¾	52	40½
ndley Fold.........	29½	58	49¾	31¼	23½	60¾	50½	52¾	22¾	27¾	12¼	20½	47½	12	12¾
ighouse	63½	24	15¾	65½	57¾	26¾	16½	18¾	57	62	35¼	39¼	13¼	46	34½
ockholes............	73	29¼	21	75	67¼	32	21¾	9¼	66½	71½	44¾	48¾	18¾	55½	44
omley Cross	29¾	63½	55½	31½	23¾	66¼	56	58½	23	28	13	21¼	53	12¼	13½
rnley	57	47½	39½	59	51¼	50¼	40	42½	50½	55½	28¾	32¾	37	39½	28
ry	32¾	54¾	46¾	34½	26¾	57½	47¼	49¾	26	31	14¼	18¼	44¼	15¼	13¼
apeltown	31	65	56¾	33	25¼	67¾	57½	59¾	24½	29½	14¼	22½	54¼	13½	15
atburn	53¼	87	79	55	47¼	89¾	79½	81¾	46½	51½	36½	44¾	76½	35¾	37
ew Moor	23	64½	56½	24¾	19¼	67¼	57	59½	18½	21¼	14	22¼	54	5½	14½

NOTE.—The Lancashire and Yorkshire Co. are allowed by Act of Parliament double toll between Miles Platting and Victoria; it is not included in this Table.

LANCASHIRE AND YORKSHIRE RAILWAY—*Continued.*

STATIONS.	Ardwick.	Askern Junction.	Barnsley.	Blackburn.	Bolton.	Bradford.	Burnley.	Burton Salmon Junction.	Bury.	Clifton Junction.	Dewsbury Junc.	Euxton Junction.	Farrington Junc.	Heaton Lodge.	Huddersfield.
Chorley	25¾	82½	68	25	11½	54¼	41¾	72	17½	17½	53¾	8¼	6¼	50¼	58¼
Clayton Bridge	3¼	69¼	54¾	27½	14	41	28½	58¾	14¼	8	40¼	28¼	31¾	37¾	40¼
Cleckheaton	40¾	35¼	20¼	55¾	42¼	5¼	29¼	24¾	36¼	44½	6¼	57	60	6¼	10¼
Clifton	8½	73½	59	19½	6	45	32½	62¾	11¾	...	45½	20¾	23¾	41¼	44¼
Clifton Junction	8¼	73¼	59	19½	6	45	32½	62¾	11¾	...	44½	20¾	23¾	41¾	44¼
Clitheroe	38¾	95½	81	11	24½	67¼	54¾	85	30¼	30¼	66¼	39	42¼	63¾	66½
Cooper Bridge	37¼	32¼	17¾	52¼	38¾	12½	25¾	21¾	32¼	41	3¼	53½	56¼	½	4¾
Crigglestone	48¼	25	7	63	49¾	19¼	36¼	14½	43½	52	7½	64¼	67½	10¼	14
Crosby	45½	102¼	87¾	44½	31¼	74	61½	91¼	37¼	37¼	78¼	40¼	43¼	70½	73
Daisy Field	28¾	85½	71	1	14½	57¼	44¾	75	20½	20½	56¾	29¼	32¼	54	56½
Darcy Lever	14¾	70	55¾	14½	1	41¾	29¼	59½	5¼	6½	41¼	15¼	18¾	38¼	41
Darton	51½	28¼	3½	66½	53	22¾	40	18	47	55½	11	67¾	70¼	13¼	17¾
Denby Dale	49¾	44½	30¼	64¾	51¼	25	38¼	34	45¼	53½	15¾	66	69	13	9¾
Dewsbury Junction.	41	28¼	14¼	55¾	42¼	12	29	18¼	36¼	44½	...	56¾	60	2¾	6¾
Dixon Fold	9¾	74¾	60¼	18	4¼	46¼	34	64¼	10¼	1½	46	19¼	22¼	43¼	45¾
Droylsden	4½	70½	56¼	28¾	15¼	42¼	30	60¼	15¼	1¼	41¾	30	33	39	41¾
Eastwood	22¼	47¼	32¾	37¼	23¾	19	10½	36¾	17½	9¼	18¼	38¼	41¼	15¾	18¾
Elland	32½	87	22¼	47¼	34	10¾	20¾	26½	28	26	8¼	48½	51¾	5½	8
Entwistle	20¼	77	62½	7½	6	48¾	36¼	66½	12	12	48¼	20¾	23¾	45¼	47¾
Euxton	28¾	85½	71	28	14½	57¼	44¾	75	20½	20½	56¾	½	3¼	54	56¾
Euxton Junction.....	29	85¾	71¼	28¼	14¾	57½	45	75¼	20¾	20¾	56¾	...	3	54	56¾
Farrington Junction.	32	88¾	74¼	31¼	17¾	60¼	48	78¼	23¾	23¾	60	8	...	57¼	59¾
Featherstone	54¾	15	17	69½	56¼	25¾	43	4½	50	58¼	14	70¾	78¾	16¾	20¾
Fleetwood	54½	111½	96¾	53¾	40¼	83	70½	100¾	46¼	46¼	82¼	25¼	22¼	79¾	82
Formby	50¼	107	92½	49½	36	78¾	66¼	96½	42¼	42¼	78¼	45	48¼	75½	78
Goole	75½	26¼	38¼	90¾	77¼	46¾	64	16¾	71	79½	33¼	91¾	95	37¾	41¾

NOTE.—The Lancashire and Yorkshire Co. are allowed by Act of Parliament double toll between Miles Platting and Victoria; it is not included in this Table.

LANCASHIRE AND YORKSHIRE RAILWAY—*Continued.*

STATIONS.	Kirkdale Junc.	Knottingley.	Leeds, Central.	Liverpool.	Maudlands.	Methley Junc.	Normanton.	Penistone Junc.	Preston.	Preston Road Junction.	Salford.	Staleybridge Junction.	Wakefield.	Wigan Junc.	Victoria.
Chorley	32¾	72¼	64	34½	9½	74¾	64½	67	8¾	31	21½	29¾	61½	15¼	22
Clayton Bridge	40¾	59	50¾	42¾	35	61¾	51½	53¾	34¼	39¼	4¼	4¼	48¼	28¼	3¼
Cleckheaton	69	24¾	16¾	71	63¼	27½	17¼	23¾	62½	67½	40¾	44¾	14¼	51½	40
Clifton	32¾	63	54¾	34¾	27	65¾	55½	58	26¼	31¼	4	12¼	52½	15¼	4½
Clifton Junction	32¾	63	54¾	34¾	27	65¾	55½	57¾	26¼	31¼	4	12¼	52½	15¼	4½
Clitheroe	51¼	85¼	77	53	45¼	87¾	77½	80	44½	49½	34½	42¾	74½	33¾	35
Cooper Bridge	63¾	21¾	13¾	67½	59¾	24½	14¼	18¼	59	64	37½	41½	11¼	48¼	36½
Crigglestone	76½	14¾	17¾	78¼	70½	17½	7¼	27½	69¾	74¾	48¼	52¼	4	59	47¼
Crosby	4¼	92	83¾	6¼	46½	94½	84¼	86¾	45¾	6	41¼	49½	81¼	21¾	41¾
Daisy Field	41¼	75¼	67	43¼	35½	78	67¾	70	34¾	39¾	24½	32¾	64½	23¾	25
Darcy Lever	27¾	59¾	51½	29¾	22	62½	52¼	54½	21¼	26¼	10½	18¾	49¼	10¼	11¼
Darton	80	18¼	21¼	81¾	74	21	10¾	31	73¼	78¼	51¾	55¾	7½	62½	50¾
Denby Dale	78	34¼	26	80	72¼	37	26¾	4¼	71½	76½	49¾	53¾	23¾	60½	49
Dewsbury Junction	...	18½	10¼	71	63	21¼	11	20	62½	67¼	40¾	44¾	7¾	51½	40
Dixon Fold	31½	64½	56¼	33¼	25½	67¼	57	59¼	24¾	29¾	5½	13¾	58¾	14	6
Droylsden	42¼	60¼	52¼	44	36¼	63	52¾	55¼	35½	40½	5½	3	49¾	24¾	4¾
Eastwood	50½	37	28¾	52½	44½	39¾	29½	31¾	43¾	49	22¼	26¼	26½	33	21½
Elland	60¾	26¾	18½	62¾	55	29½	19¼	21½	54¼	59¼	32½	36½	16	43¼	31¾
Entwistle	32¾	66¾	58½	34½	26¾	69½	59	61½	26	31	16	24¼	56	15¼	16½
Euxton	35¾	75¼	67	37½	6½	78	67¾	70	5¾	34	24½	32¾	64½	18¼	25¼
Euxton Junction ...	35¾	75½	67¼	37¾	6¼	78	68	70¼	5½	34¼	24¾	33	64¾	18¼	25¼
Farrington Junction	39	78½	70¼	40¾	3¼	81¼	71	73¼	2½	37¼	27¾	36	67¾	21½	28½
Featherstone	83	4½	24¼	84¾	77	7¼	9	34	76¼	81¼	54¾	58¾	6	65½	53¾
Fleetwood	61½	101	92¾	63¼	19¾	103¾	93½	95¾	20	59¾	50¼	58½	90¼	44	50¾
Formby	9¼	96¾	88½	11¼	51½	99½	89¼	91½	50¾	10¾	46	54¼	86¼	26¾	46¾
Goole	104	16½	45¼	106	98	23	30¼	55	97¼	102½	75¾	79¾	27	86½	75

NOTE.—The Lancashire and Yorkshire Co. are allowed by Act of Parliament double toll between Miles Platting and Victoria; it is not included in this Table.

LANCASHIRE AND YORKSHIRE RAILWAY.—*Continued.*

STATIONS.	Ardwick.	Askern Junction.	Barnsley.	Blackburn.	Bolton.	Bradford.	Burnley.	Burton Salmon Junction.	Bury.	Clifton Junction.	Dewsbury Junc.	Euxton Junction.	Farrington Junc.	Heaton Lodge.	Huddersfield.
Haigh	50¼	27	5	65¼	51¾	21¼	38½	16½	45½	54	9½	66¼	69½	12¼	16
Halifax	33¼	39½	25¼	48	34½	8¼	21½	29	28½	36¾	10¾	49	52¼	8	10
Halshaw Moor	12	73	58½	15¾	2¼	44¾	32¼	62½	8	3¾	44¼	16¾	20	41¼	43
Heaton Lodge	38	31½	17¼	52¾	39½	12	26¼	21	33¼	41¾	2¾	54	57¼	...	3
Hebden Bridge	24½	45	30½	39½	26	16¾	12¾	34½	19¾	28¼	16¼	40½	43¾	13½	16
Heckmondwike	42	33	18½	57	43½	7¾	30½	22¼	37½	45¾	4	58	61¼	4¼	7
Hensall	65¼	16¼	27¾	80¼	66¾	36½	53¾	6¼	60¾	69	22¾	81¼	84½	27¼	31
Heywood	10½	61½	47	23	9½	33¼	20¾	51	3½	14½	32½	24¼	27¼	29¾	32
High Town	48¼	105	90½	47½	34	76¾	64¼	94½	40	40	76¼	43	46¼	73½	76
Hindley	21¼	78	63½	20½	7	49¾	37¼	67½	13	13	49¼	16	19¼	46½	49
Hipperholme	34¾	41¼	26¾	49½	36	6¾	23	30¾	30	38½	12¼	50¾	53¾	9½	12
Holme	25¼	54½	40	40¼	26¾	26¼	8½	44	20¾	29	25¾	41¼	44½	23	25
Holmfirth	46¾	41½	27	61½	48¼	21¾	35	31	42	50½	12¾	62¾	66	10	6
Honley	43¾	38½	24¼	58¾	45¼	19	32¼	28¼	39¼	47½	9¾	59¾	63	7	3
Horbury	44¾	25	10½	59½	46¼	15¾	33	14¼	40	48½	4	60¾	64	6¾	10
Horbury Junction	46¼	23¼	8¾	61¼	47¾	17½	34¾	12¾	41¾	50	5½	62¼	65½	8½	12
Horwich	20¾	77½	63	20	6½	49¼	36¾	67	12½	12½	48¾	8	11¼	46	48
Huddersfield	40½	35¼	20¾	55½	42	15¾	28¾	24¾	36	44¼	6½	56½	59¾	3¾	
Kirkby	36	92¾	78¼	35¼	21¾	64½	52	82¼	27¾	27¾	64	30¾	33¾	61	63
Kirkdale Junction	41¼	97¾	83½	40¼	26¾	69½	57	...	32¾	32¾	...	35¾	39	66¼	68
Kirkham	42½	99	84¾	41½	28	70¾	58¼	88½	34¼	34¼	70¼	13½	10¼	67½	70
Knottingley	59¼	10¼	21¾	74¼	60¾	30½	47½	¼	54¾	63	18½	75¼	78½	21¼	25
Knottingley Junction	59¼	10¼	21¾	74¼	60¾	30½	47½	¼	54¾	63	18½	75¼	78½	21¼	25
Langho	33¼	90	75½	5½	19	61¾	49¼	79½	25	25	61¼	33½	36¾	58¼	61
Lea Road	37½	94¼	79¾	36½	23	65¾	53¼	83½	29¼	29¼	65¼	8½	5¼	62½	65
Leeds, Central	51	39	24¾	66	52½	22¼	39½	28½	46½	54¾	10¼	67	70¼	13	16

NOTE.—The Lancashire and Yorkshire Co. are allowed by Act of Parliament double toll between Miles Platting and Victoria; it is not included in this Table.

LANCASHIRE AND YORKSHIRE RAILWAY—*Continued.*

STATIONS.	Kirkdale Junc.	Knottingley.	Leeds, Central.	Liverpool.	Maudlands.	Methley Junc.	Normanton.	Penistone Junc.	Preston.	Preston Road Junction.	Salford.	Staleybridge Junction.	Wakefield.	Wigan Junc.	Victoria.
aigh	78½	16¾	19¾	80½	72½	19½	9¼	29½	71¾	77	50¼	54¼	6¼	61	49½
alifax	61½	29¼	21	63¼	55½	32	21¾	24	54¾	59¾	33	37¼	18¾	44	32¼
alshaw Moor	29¼	62½	54½	31	23¼	65¼	55	57½	22½	27½	7¾	16	52	11¾	8¼
eaton Lodge	66¼	21¼	13	68	60¼	24	13¾	17¼	59½	64½	38	42	10¾	48¾	37¼
ebden Bridge	52¾	34¾	26½	54¾	47	37½	27¼	29½	46¼	51¼	24½	28½	24¼	35¼	23¾
eckmondwike	70½	22½	14¼	72¼	64½	25¼	15	21½	63¾	68¾	42¼	46	12	52¾	41¼
ensall	93½	6	34¾	95½	87¾	12¾	19¾	44½	87	92	65¼	69¼	16¾	76	64½
eywood	36½	51	43	38¼	30½	53¾	43½	46	29¾	34¾	10½	14½	40½	19	9½
gh Town	7¼	94¾	86½	9	49¼	97½	87¼	89½	48½	8¾	44	52¼	84	24¾	44¾
ndley...............	19¾	67¾	59½	21¾	22¼	70½	60¼	62½	21½	18¼	17	25¼	57	2¼	17¾
pperholme.........	63	30¾	22¾	64¾	57	33½	23¼	25½	56¼	61¼	34¾	38¾	20¼	45½	33¾
lme	53¾	44¼	36	55½	47¾	47	36¾	39	47	52	25½	29½	33½	36¼	24½
lmfirth	75	31¼	23	76¾	69	34	23¾	11	68¼	73¼	46¾	50¾	20½	57½	46
nley	72	28¼	20¼	74	66¼	31	20¾	10¼	65½	70½	44	47¾	17¾	54½	43
rbury	73	14½	14¼	74¾	67	17¼	7	24	66¼	71¼	44¾	48¾	4	55½	44
rbury Junction...	74½	13	16	76½	68¾	15½	5½	25½	68	73	46½	50¼	2¼	57	45½
rwich	27¾	67¼	59	29½	14½	70	59¾	62	13¾	26	16½	24¾	56½	10¼	17
ddersfield	68¾	25	16¾	70¾	63	27¾	17½	13½	62¼	67¼	40½	44½	14¼	51¼	39¾
rkby	5	82½	74¼	7	37	85	74¾	77¼	36¼	3½	31¾	40	71¾	12½	32¼
rkdale Junction...		87½	79¼	2	42¼	90¼	80	82¼	41½	1½	36¾	45	77	...	37½
rkham	49¼	8[illegible]¾	80½	51¼	7½	91½	81¼	83½	8	47¾	38	46¼	78¼	31¾	38¾
ottingley	87½	...	28¾	89½	81¾	6¾	13¾	38½	81	86	59¼	63¼	10¾	70	58½
ottingley Junction	87½	...	28¾	89½	81¾	6½	13¾	38½	81	85¾	59¼	63¼	10¾	70	58½
ngho	45¾	79¾	71½	47¾	39¾	82¼	72	74½	39	44	29	37¼	69	28¼	29½
a Road	44¼	83¾	75½	46¼	2½	86½	76¼	78½	3	42¾	33¼	41¼	73¼	26¾	33¾
eds Central	79¼	28¾	...	81¼	73½	31½	21¼	30¼	72¾	77¾	51	55	18¼	61¾	50¼

NOTE.—The Lancashire and Yorkshire Co. are allowed by Act of Parliament double toll between Miles Platting and Victoria; it is not included in this Table.

orquodale & Co., Printers.

LANCASHIRE AND YORKSHIRE RAILWAY—*Continued.*

STATIONS.	Ardwick.	Askern Junction.	Barnsley.	Blackburn.	Bolton.	Bradford.	Burnley.	Burton Salmon Junction.	Bury.	Clifton Junction.	Dewsbury Junc.	Euxton Junction.	Farrington Junc.	Heaton Lodge.	Huddersfield.
Leeds (Hunslet Ln.)	61½	34¾	23¾	76½	63	32½	19¾	23¼	56¾	65¼	19	77½	80¾	23½	27¼
Leyland	30½	87¼	72¾	29½	16¼	58¾	46¼	76¾	22¼	22¼	58¼	1½	1¾	55½	58
Lightcliffe	35½	40½	26	50½	37	5¾	23¾	30	30¾	39¼	11¾	51½	54¾	10½	13
Littleborough	14¾	55	40½	29½	16	26¾	14¼	44¼	10	18½	26	30¾	33¾	23¼	25¾
Liverpool	43	99¾	85¼	42¼	28¾	71½	59	89¼	34¾	34¾	71	37½	40¾	68¼	70¾
Liversedge	42¼	33¾	19½	57	43½	6¾	30½	23¼	37½	45¾	5	58	61¼	5¼	8¾
Lockwood	41¾	36½	22	56¾	43¼	17	30	26	37	45½	7¾	57¾	61	5	1½
Lostock Lane.........	18¾	75¼	61	17¾	4¼	47	34½	64¾	10½	10½	46½	10¼	13½	43¾	46¼
Lower Darwen	26	82¾	68¼	1¾	11¾	54½	42	72¼	17¾	17¾	54	26¼	29½	51	53½
Low Moor	38¼	37¾	23¼	53¼	39¾	3	26¾	27¼	33¾	42	9	54¼	57½	9	12¾
Luddenden Foot ...	27¼	42¼	27¾	42¼	28¾	14	15¾	31¾	22¾	31	14¼	43¼	46½	10½	13¼
Lytham	48¼	105	90½	47½	34	76¾	64¼	94½	40	40	76½	19¼	16¼	73¼	76
Marsh Lane	42½	99¼	84¾	41¾	28¼	71	58½	88¾	34¼	34¼	70½	37¼	40½	67¾	70¼
Maudlands	35¼	92	77½	34½	21	63¾	51¼	81½	27	27	63	6¼	3¼	60¼	63
Merton Road	42¼	98¾	84½	41½	27¾	70½	58	88¼	34	34	70	36¾	40	67¼	69¾
Methley	61¾	16¾	24¼	76¾	63¼	32¾	50	6¼	57¼	65½	21	77¾	81	23¾	27½
Methley Junction ...	62	17	24½	77	63½	33	50¼	6½	57¼	65¾	21¼	78	81¼	24	27¾
Middleton	6	63½	49	27½	14	35¼	22¾	53	7¾	9¾	34¾	28½	31¾	32	34½
Miles Platting	2¼	67¼	53	25½	12	39	26½	56¾	11¾	6	38½	26¾	29¾	35¾	38¼
Millers Bridge	41¾	98½	84	41	27½	70¼	57¾	88	33¾	33½	69¾	36½	39¾	67	69½
Mirfield	39	30½	16	54	40½	10¾	27½	20	34½	42¾	1¾	55	58¼	1¼	4¾
Moses Gate	12¾	72¼	57¾	15	1¾	44	31½	61¾	7¼	4½	43½	16¼	19½	40½	43¼
Moss Side	46	102¾	88¼	45¼	31¾	74½	62	92¼	37¾	37¾	74	17¼	14	71	73¾
Mumps	9	66½	52	30½	17	38¼	25¾	56	11	12¾	37¾	31½	34¾	35	37½
Mytholmroyd.........	25¾	43¾	29½	40¾	27¼	15½	14	33¼	21	29½	15	41¾	45	12¼	14¾
Normanton	51¾	24	14¼	66¾	53¼	22¾	40	13½	47	55½	11	67¾	71	13¾	17½

NOTE.—The Lancashire and Yorkshire Co. are allowed by Act of Parliament double toll between Miles Platting and Victoria; it is not included in this Table.

LANCASHIRE AND YORKSHIRE RAILWAY—*Continued.*

STATIONS.	Kirkdale Junc.	Knottingley.	Leeds, Central.	Liverpool.	Maudlands.	Methley Junc.	Normanton.	Penistone Junc.	Preston.	Preston Road Junction.	Salford.	Staleybridge Junction.	Wakefield.	Wigan Junc.	Victoria.
Leeds (Hunslet Ln.)	89¾	23½	...	91½	83¾	...	9¾	40¾	83	88	61½	65½	12¾	72¼	60¾
Leyland	87¼	76¾	68¾	89¼	4¾	79½	69¼	71½	4	35¾	26¼	34½	66¼	19¾	26¾
Lightcliffe	63¾	30¼	22	65¾	58	33	22¾	26½	57¼	62¼	35½	39½	19½	46¼	34¾
Littleborough	43	44½	36½	44¾	37	47¼	37	39¼	36¼	41¼	14¾	18¾	34	25½	13¾
Liverpool	2	89½	81¼	...	44	92	82	84¼	43¼	3½	38¾	47	78¾	19½	39¼
Liversedge	70½	23½	15¼	72¼	64½	26¼	16	22¼	63¾	68¾	42¼	46¼	13	53	41¼
Lockwood	70	26¼	18	72	64¼	29	18¾	12¼	63½	68½	41¾	45¾	15½	52½	41
Lostock Lane	25½	65	56¾	27½	16½	67¾	57½	59¾	15¾	24	14¼	22½	54½	8	15
Lower Darwen	38½	72¼	64¼	40¼	32½	75	64¾	67¼	31¾	36¾	21¾	30	61¾	21	22¼
Low Moor	66½	27½	19¼	68½	60¾	30	19¾	26¼	60	65	38¼	42¼	16¾	49	37½
Luddenden Foot	55½	32	23¾	57½	49¾	34½	24¼	26¾	49	54	27½	31¼	21¼	38	26½
Lytham	55¼	94¾	86½	57	13¼	97½	87	89½	13¾	53½	44	52¼	84	37¾	44½
Marsh Lane	1½	89	80¾	3¼	43½	91¾	81½	83¾	42¾	3	38¼	46½	78¼	19	39
Maudlands	42¼	81¾	73½	44	...	84½	74	76½	¾	40½	31	39¼	71	24¾	31½
Merton Road	1	88½	80¼	3	43¼	91¼	81	83¼	42½	2¾	37¾	46	78	18½	38½
Methley	90	6½	31¼	92	84¼	¼	16¼	41	83½	88½	61¾	65¾	13¼	72½	61
Methley Junction	90¼	6¾	31½	92¼	84½	...	16½	41¼	83¾	88¾	62	66	13¼	72¾	61¼
Middleton	40¾	53¼	45	42¾	35	56	45¾	48	34¼	39¼	6	10	42½	23¼	5¼
Miles Platting	39	57	48¾	40¾	33	59¾	49½	51¾	32¼	37¼	2¼	6¼	46¼	21½	1½
Millers Bridge	¾	88¼	80	2¾	43	91	80¾	83	42¼	2¼	37½	45¾	77¾	18¼	38¼
Mirfield	67¼	20¼	12	69¼	61½	22¾	12½	18¼	60¾	65¾	39¼	43	9½	49¾	38¼
Moses Gate	28½	62	53¾	30¼	22½	64½	54½	56¾	21¾	26¾	8½	16½	51¼	11	9
Moss Side	53	92½	84¼	54¾	11	95	84¾	87¼	11½	51¼	41¾	50	81¾	35½	42¼
Mumps	43¾	56¼	48	45¾	38	59	48¾	51	37¼	42¼	9	13	45¾	26¼	8¼
Mytholmroyd	54	33½	25¼	55¾	48	36¼	26	28¼	47¼	52½	25¾	29¾	23	36½	25
Normanton	80	13¾	21¼	81¾	74	16½	...	31	73¼	78½	51¾	55¾	8	62½	51

NOTE.—The Lancashire and Yorkshire Co. are allowed by Act of Parliament double toll between Miles Platting and Victoria; it is not included in this Table.

LANCASHIRE AND YORKSHIRE RAILWAY—*Continued.*

STATIONS.	Ardwick.	Askern Junction.	Barnsley.	Blackburn.	Bolton.	Bradford.	Burnley.	Burton Salmon Junction.	Bury.	Clifton Junction.	Dewsbury Junc.	Euxton Junction.	Farrington Junc.	Heaton Lodge.	Huddersfield.
North Dean	31¾	37¾	23½	46¾	33¼	10	20¼	27¼	27¼	35½	9	47¾	51	6¼	8¾
Norton	66	3¾	28¼	80¾	67½	37	54¼	7	61¼	69¾	25¼	82	85¼	28	31¾
Oldham Road	3¼	68¼	53¾	26½	13	40	27½	57¾	12¾	7	39½	27½	30¾	36¾	39¼
Orrell.................	27½	84¼	69¾	26½	13¼	55¾	43½	73¾	19¼	19¼	55¼	22	25¼	52½	55
Over Darwen	24	80¾	66¼	3¾	9¾	52½	40	70¼	15¾	15¾	52	24¼	27½	49	51¾
Park	2¼	68¼	53¾	26½	13	40	27½	57¾	12¾	7	39½	27¾	30¾	36¾	39¼
Pemberton............	25¾	82½	68	25	11½	54¼	41¾	72	17½	17½	53¾	20½	23¾	51	53½
Pendleton	6	71	56½	21¾	8¼	42¾	30¼	60½	14	2¼	42¼	22¾	26	39½	42
Penistone	54	48¾	34½	69	55½	29¼	42½	38¼	49½	57¾	20	70	73¼	17¼	13½
Pickle Bridge	36½	39½	25	51½	38	4¾	25	29	32	40¼	10½	52½	55¾	10¾	14
Pimbo Lane	28¾	85½	71	28	14½	57¼	44¾	75	20½	20½	56¾	23½	26¾	54	56½
Pontefract	57¼	12¼	19¾	72¼	58¾	28½	45¾	1¾	52¾	61	16½	73¼	76½	19¼	23
Portsmouth	23¼	52½	38	38¼	24¾	24¼	5½	42	18¾	27¼	23¾	39¼	42½	21	23½
Poulton	49	105¾	91¼	48	34¾	77½	64¾	95¼	40¾	40¾	76¾	20	16¾	74	76½
Preston	34½	91¼	76¾	33¾	20¼	63	50½	80¾	26¼	26¼	62½	5¾	2½	59½	62¼
Preston Road.........	39¼	96	81½	38½	25	67¾	55¼	85½	31	31	67¼	34	37	64¼	67
Preston Road Junc.	39½	96¼	81¾	38¾	25¼	68	55½	85¾	31¼	31¼	67½	34¼	37¼	64½	67¼
Rainford	31½	88¼	73¾	30¾	17¼	60	47½	77¾	23¼	23¼	59½	26¼	29½	56¾	59¼
Rawcliffe	71¾	22¾	34¼	86¾	73¼	42¾	60	12¾	67	75½	31	87¾	91	33¾	37½
Ribchester............	31	87¾	73¼	3¼	16¾	59½	47	77¼	22¾	22¾	59	31½	34½	56¼	58¾
Rochdale	11½	58	43½	26½	13	29¾	17¼	47½	7	15¼	29¼	27¾	30¾	26½	29
Salford	4½	69½	55¼	23½	10	41¼	28¾	59	14	4	40¾	24¾	27¾	38	40½
Salwick	39½	96¼	81¾	38¾	25¼	68	55½	85¾	31¼	31¼	67½	10½	7½	64¾	67¼
Seaforth...............	43½	100¼	85¾	42¾	29¼	72	59½	89¾	35¼	35¼	71½	38¼	41½	68¾	71¼
Shepley	47¾	42½	28	62½	49¼	22¾	36	32	43	51½	13¾	63¾	66¾	11	7¼
Snaith	69	20	31¼	83¾	70½	40	57¼	10	64¼	72¾	28¼	85	88¼	81	34¾

NOTE—The Lancashire and Yorkshire Co. are allowed by Act of Parliament double toll between Miles Platting and Victoria; it is not included in this Table.

LANCASHIRE AND YORKSHIRE RAILWAY—*Continued.*

STATIONS.	Kirkdale Junc.	Knottingley.	Leeds, Central.	Liverpool.	Maudlands.	Methley Junc.	Normanton.	Penistone Junc.	Preston.	Preston Road Junction.	Salford.	Staleybridge Junction.	Wakefield.	Wigan Junc.	Victoria.
North Dean	60	27½	19¼	62	54¼	30¼	20	22¼	53½	58½	31¾	35¾	16¾	42½	31
Norton	94¼	6¾	35½	96	88¼	13¼	20¼	45¼	87½	92½	66	70	17¼	76¾	65
Oldham Road	39¾	58	49¾	41¾	34	60¾	50½	52¾	33¼	38¼	3¼	7¼	47¼	22¼	2¼
Orrell	13¾	73¾	65¾	15½	28½	76½	66¼	68¾	27¾	12	23¼	31½	63¼	3¾	23¾
Over Darwen.........	36½	70½	62¼	38¼	30½	73	62¾	65¼	29¾	34¾	19¾	28	59¾	19	20¼
Park	39¾	58	49¾	41¾	34	60¾	50½	52¾	33¼	38¼	3¼	5¼	47¼	22¼	2¼
Pemberton............	15¼	72¼	64	17¼	26¾	75	64¾	67	26	13¾	21½	29¾	61½	2¼	22¼
Pendleton	35¼	60¾	52½	37	29¼	63½	53¼	55½	28½	33½	1¾	10	50	17¾	2¼
Penistone	82¼	38½	30¼	84¼	76½	41¼	31	...	75¾	80¾	54	58	28	64¾	53¼
Pickle Bridge.........	64¾	29	21	66¾	59	31¾	21½	27½	58¼	63¼	36½	40½	18½	47¼	35¾
Pimbo Lane	12¼	75¼	67	14¼	29¾	78	67¾	70	29	10¾	24½	32¾	64½	5¼	25
Pontefract	85½	2	26¾	87½	79¾	4¾	11¾	36½	79	84	57½	61¼	8¾	68	56½
Portsmouth	51½	42¼	34	53½	45¾	44¾	34½	37	45	50	23½	27¼	31½	34	22½
Poulton	55¾	95¼	87¼	57¾	14	98	87¾	90¼	14½	54¼	44¾	53	84¾	38¼	45¼
Preston	41½	81	72¾	43¼	¾	83½	73¼	75¾	...	39¾	30¼	38½	70¼	24	30¾
Preston Road.........	1¾	85¾	77½	3¾	40¼	88¼	78	80½	39½	¼	35	43¼	75	15¼	35½
Preston Road Junc...	1½	86	77¾	3½	40½	88½	78¼	80¾	39¾	...	35¼	43½	75¼	16	35¾
Rainford...............	9½	78	69¾	11½	32½	80¾	70½	72¾	31¾	8	27¼	35½	67¼	8	28
Rawcliffe	100	12½	41¼	102	94¼	19	26¼	51	93½	98½	71¾	75¾	23	82½	71
Ribchester	43½	77½	69¼	45½	37¾	80¼	70	72¼	37	42	26¾	35	66¾	26	27½
Rochdale	39¾	47¾	39½	41¾	34	50½	40¼	42½	33¼	38¼	11½	15½	37	22¼	10¾
Salford	36¾	59¼	51	38¾	31	62	51¾	54	30¼	35¼	...	8½	48¾	19¼	¾
Salwick	46½	86	77¾	48¼	4½	88¾	78½	80¾	5	44¾	35¼	43½	75¼	29	36
Seaforth	2½	90	81¾	4¼	44½	92¾	82½	84¾	43¾	4½	39¼	47½	79¼	20	39¾
Shepley	76	32¼	24	77¾	70	35	24½	6¼	69¼	74¼	47¾	51¾	21½	58½	46¾
Snaith	97¼	9¾	38½	99	91¼	16¼	23½	48¼	90½	95½	69	73	20¼	79¾	68¼

NOTE.—The Lancashire and Yorkshire Co. are allowed by Act of Parliament double toll between Miles Platting and Victoria; it is not included in this Table.

LANCASHIRE AND YORKSHIRE RAILWAY—*Continued.*

STATIONS.	Ardwick.	Askern Junc.	Barnsley.	Blackburn.	Bolton.	Bradford.	Burnley.	Burton Salmon Junction.	Bury.	Clifton Junction.	Dewsbury Junc.	Euxton Junction.	Farrington Junc.	Heaton Lodge.	Huddersfield.
Sough	23	79¾	65¼	4¾	8¾	51½	39	69¼	14¾	14¾	51	23¼	26½	48	50¾
Southport	57¼	114	99½	56½	43	85¾	73¼	103½	49	49	85¼	52	55¼	82½	85
Sowerby Bridge	29	40½	26	44	30½	12¼	17½	30	24½	32¾	11¾	45	48¼	8¾	11½
Staley Bridge	8	73¾	59¼	32	18½	45½	33	63¼	18¾	12½	45	33	36¼	42¼	44¾
Staley Bridge Junc.	7¾	73½	59	31¾	18¼	45¼	32¾	63	18½	12¼	44¾	32¾	36	42	44½
Stocksmoor	46¾	41½	27¼	61¾	48¼	22	35¼	31	42¼	50½	12¾	63	66	10	6¼
Stone Clough	11¼	73½	59	16½	3	45¼	32¾	63	8¾	3	44¾	17¾	20¾	42	44½
The Oakes	16½	73¼	58¾	11¼	2¼	45	32½	62¾	8¼	8¼	44½	16¾	20	41¾	44¼
Thongsbridge	45¾	40¾	26¼	60¾	47¼	21	34¼	30¼	41¼	49½	11¾	62	65	9	5¼
Thornhill	41	28	13½	56½	43	12¾	30	17½	37	45½	1	57¾	60¾	3¾	7½
Todmorden	20	49½	35	35	21½	21¼	8¾	39	15½	23¾	20¾	36	39¼	18	20½
Townley	28¼	57¼	42¾	43	29½	29	¾	46¾	23½	32	28½	44¼	47¼	25¾	28¼
Upholland	27¾	84½	70	27	13½	56¼	43¾	74	19½	19½	55¾	22½	25¾	53	55½
Victoria	3¾	68¾	54¼	24	10¾	40½	28	58¼	13	4½	40	25¼	28½	37¼	39¾
Wakefield	48½	21	11	63½	50	19¾	37	10½	44	52¼	7¾	64¾	67¾	10¾	14¼
Walsden	18¾	51	36½	33½	20	22¾	10¼	40½	14	22½	22	34¾	37¾	19¼	21¾
Waterloo	44¾	101¼	86¾	43¾	30¼	73	60½	90¾	36½	36½	72½	39¼	42½	69¾	72¼
Werneth	8	65½	51	29¼	16	37¼	24¾	55	9¾	11¾	36¾	30½	33½	33¾	36½
Westhoughton	19	75¾	61¼	18	4¾	47½	35	65¼	10¾	10¾	46¾	13¾	16¾	44	46½
Whalley	35¼	92	77½	7½	21	63¾	51¼	81½	27	27	63¼	35½	38¾	60¼	63
Whitley Bridge	63½	14½	26	78½	65	34¾	51¾	4½	59	67¼	22¾	79½	82¾	25½	29¼
Wigan	23¾	80½	66	23	9½	52¼	39¾	70	15½	15½	51¾	18½	21¾	49	51½
Wigan Junction	23¾	80¼	65¾	22¾	9¼	52	39½	...	15¼	15¼	51½	18¼	21½	48¾	51¼
Womersley	63½	6¼	25¾	78¼	64¾	34½	51¾	4¼	58¾	67¼	22¾	79½	82½	25½	29¼
Wray Green	44½	101¼	86¾	43½	30¼	78	60½	90¾	36¼	36¼	72¼	15¾	12¼	69½	72

NOTE.—The Lancashire and Yorkshire Co. are allowed by Act of Parliament double toll between Miles Platting and Victoria; it is not included in this Table.

LANCASHIRE AND YORKSHIRE RAILWAY—*Continued.*

STATIONS.	Kirkdale Junc.	Knottingley.	Leeds, Central.	Liverpool.	Maudlands.	Methley Junc.	Normanton.	Penistone Junc.	Preston.	Preston Road Junction.	Salford.	Staleybridge Junction.	Wakefield.	Wigan Junc.	Victoria.
Sough	35½	69½	61¼	37½	29¾	72	61¾	64¼	29	34	18¾	27	58¾	18	19¼
Southport	16¼	103¾	95½	18	58¼	106½	96¼	98½	57½	17¾	58	61¼	93	33¾	53½
Sowerby Bridge......	57¼	30¼	22	59¼	51½	32¾	22½	25	50¾	55¾	29¼	33	19½	39¾	28¼
Staley Bridge	45¼	63½	55¼	47¼	39½	66¼	56	58¼	38¾	43¾	8¾	...	53	27¾	8
Staley Bridge Junc..	54	63¼	55	47	39¼	66	55¾	58	38½	43½	8½	¼	52½	27½	7¾
Stocksmoor	75	31¼	23	77	69¼	34	23¾	7¼	68½	73½	46¾	50¾	20¾	57½	46
Stone Clough	29¾	63¼	55	31¾	24	66	55¾	58	23¼	28¼	7	15¼	52¾	12¼	7¾
The Oakes...........	29	63	54¾	31	23¼	65¾	55½	57¾	22½	27½	12¼	20½	52¼	11½	12¾
Thongsbridge	74	30¼	22¼	76	68¼	33	22¾	10¼	67½	72½	46	49¾	19¾	56½	45
Thornhill	70	17½	11¼	71¾	63	20¼	10	21	63¼	68¼	41¾	45¾	7	52½	40¾
Todmorden	48¼	39¼	31	50¼	42½	42	31¾	34	41¾	46¾	20	24	28½	30¾	19¼
Townley	56½	47	38¾	58¼	50½	49¾	39½	41¾	49¾	54¾	28¼	32¼	36¼	39	27¼
Upholland	13¼	74¼	66	15¼	28¾	77	66¾	69	28	11¾	23½	31¾	63½	4¼	24¼
Victoria	37½	58½	50¼	39¼	31½	61¼	51	53¼	30¾	35¾	¾	7¾	47¾	20	...
Wakefield	77	10¾	18¼	78¾	71	13¼	3	27¾	70¼	75¼	48¾	52¾	...	59½	47¾
Walsden..............	47	40½	32½	48¾	41	43¼	33	35¼	40¼	45¼	18¾	22¾	30	29½	17¾
Waterloo	3½	91	82¾	5½	45¾	93¾	83½	85¾	45	5	40¼	48½	80½	21	41
Werneth..............	42¾	55¼	47	44½	36¾	57¾	47½	50	36	41	8	12	44½	25¼	7
Westhoughton	22¼	65¼	57¼	24	20	68	57¾	60¼	19¼	20½	14¾	23	54¾	4¾	15¼
Whalley...............	47¾	81¾	73½	49¾	42	84¼	74	76½	41¼	46¼	31	39¼	71	30¼	31½
Whitley Bridge	91¾	4¼	33	93½	86	10¾	18	42¾	85¼	90¼	68½	67½	15	74¼	62¾
Wigan	17¼	70¼	62	19¼	24¾	73	62¾	65	24	15¾	19½	27¾	59½	...	20¼
Wigan Junction ...	...	70	61¾	19½	24¾	72¾	62½	64¾	24	16	19½	27½	59½	...	20
Womersley...........	91¾	4¼	33	93½	86	10¾	17¾	42¾	85¼	90	63½	67½	14¾	74¼	62½
Wray Green	51¼	90¾	82¾	53¼	9½	93½	83¼	85½	10	49¾	40¼	48½	80¼	33¾	40¾

NOTE.—The Lancashire and Yorkshire Co. are allowed by Act of Parliament double toll between Miles Platting and Victoria; it is not included in this Table.

LANCASTER AND CARLISLE RAILWAY.

STATIONS.	Carlisle.	Lancaster.	Oxenholme.	Preston.
Bay Horse	75	5¾	25	15½
Bolton-le-Sands	64¾	4½	14¾	25½
Brisco	3¼	66	46¾	87
Brock	82¾	13½	32¾	7½
Broughton	85½	16¼	35½	5
Burton and Holme	58½	10¾	8½	32
Carnforth	63	6¼	13	27½
Carlisle	...	69¼	50	90¼
Clifton	22¼	47	28	68¼
Galgate	73¼	4¼	23½	16¾
Garstang	80¾	11½	30¾	9½
Grayrigg	45	24¼	5¼	45½
Hest Bank	66	3¼	16	24¼
Lancaster	69¼	...	19¼	21¼
Lowgill	41¾	27½	8¼	48½
Milnthorpe	55¾	13¾	5¾	34¾
Oxenholme	50	19¼	...	40¼
Penrith	17¾	51¼	32¼	72½
Plumpton	13¼	56	37	77¼
Preston	90¼	21¼	40¼	...
Scorton	77¾	8¼	27½	13
Shap	29½	39¾	20½	61
Southwaite	7¾	61¾	42¾	83
Tebay	37	32¼	13	53¼

LEEDS NORTHERN RAILWAY.

STATIONS.	Eaglescliffe Junc.	Harrogate, Starbeck Station.	Knaresboro', E. & W. York Jn.	Leeds.	Northallerton.	Stockton.	Thirsk.
Arthington, or Pool	49¼	8¾	10¾	9¼	35	52¼	29¾
Baldersby	27½	16	18	34	13¾	30½	5
Brompton	12¼	27¾	29¾	45¾	1½	15¼	20¼
Eaglescliffe Junction	...	40	42	58	13¾	3	32½
Harrogate (Starbeck)	40	...	2	18	26¼	43	21
Headingley	55	15	17	3	41¼	58	36
Horsforth	52½	12½	14½	5½	38¾	55½	33½
Knaresboro'	41½	2	½	19½	27¾	44½	22½
Knaresboro', E. & W. Yk. Jn.	42	1½	...	20	28¼	45	23
Leeds	58	18	20	...	44¼	61	39
Leeming-lane	22¾	17¼	19¼	35¼	9	25¾	9¾
Melmerby, or Wath Junction	25¾	14¼	16¼	32¼	12	28¾	6¾
Newby Wiske	17¾	22¼	24¼	40¼	4	20¾	14¾
Northallerton	13¾	26¼	28¼	44¼	...	16¾	18¾
Pannal	43¾	3¼	5¼	14¾	29½	46¾	24¼
Pickhill	21	19	21	37	7¼	24	11½
Picton	4¾	35¼	37¼	53¼	9	7¾	27¾
Pool, or Arthington	49¼	8¾	10¾	9¼	35	52¼	29¾
Ripley	37	3	5	21	23¼	40	18
Ripon	28¾	11¼	13¼	29¼	15	31¾	10¾
Rounton	7	33	35	51	6¾	10	25½
Sinderby	22¾	17¼	19¼	35¼	9	25¾	9¾
Stockton	3	43	45	61	16¾	...	35½
Thirsk	32½	21	23	39	18¾	35½	...
Thirsk Junction	31½	20	22	38	17¾	34½	1
Topcliffe	29½	18	20	36	15¾	32½	3

M'Corquodale & Co., Printers.

LEEDS NORTHERN RAILWAY—*Continued.*

STATIONS.	Eaglescliffe Junc.	Harrogate, Starbeck Station.	Knaresboro', E. & W. York Jn.	Leeds.	Northallerton.	Stockton.	Thirsk.				
Wath Junction, or Melmerby	25¾	14¼	16¼	32¼	12	28¾	6¾				
Weeton	47	6½	8½	11½	32¾	50	27½				
Welbury	9	31	33	49	4¾	12	23½				
Wormald Green	34	6	8	24	20¼	37	15				
Yarm	1¼	38¾	40¾	56¾	12½	4¼	31¼				

LIVERPOOL, CROSBY, & SOUTHPORT RAILWAY.

STATIONS.	Kirkdale Junc.	Liverpool.									
Ainsdale	13	14¾									
Birkdale	15	17									
Bootle Village	1	3									
Crosby	4¼	6¼									
Formby and Altcar	9¼	11¼									
Hightown	7	9									
Kirkdale Junction	...	2									
Liverpool	2	...									
Marsh Lane	1½	3¼									
Millers Bridge	¾	2¾									
Seaforth	2½	4¼									
Southport	16½	18½									
Waterloo	4	5½									

LONDON & NORTH WESTERN RAILWAY.

STATIONS.	Ardwick.	Banbury.	Bedford.	Bescot Junction.	Birmingham, B. and B.	Birmingham, Mid.	Birmingham, Stour Val. Junc.	Bletchley.	Bolton.	Bushbury Junc.	Camden.	Chester.
Acton	44½	156	141	58¾	69	68¼	68	124¾	28½	52¾	170¼	35½
Adlington	12½	169	154	71¾	82	81¼	81	137¾	70	65¾	183¼	48½
Alderley	13	159	144	61¾	72	71¼	71	127¾	60	55¾	173¼	38½
Allesley Lane	99¼	82	67	24½	14¼	15	14¾	50¾	111¾	30½	96¼	90¼
Ampthill	151	41½	6	85½	75¼	76	75¾	10¼	163½	91½	55¾	142
Ardwick	...	172	157	74¼		84¼		140¾	73		186¼	57½
Armitage	67¼	104¾	89¾	32	42¼	41½	41¼	73½	79¾	26	119	58¼
Astley	8¾	179	164	81¾	92	91¼	91	147¾	14	75¾	193¼	58½
Atherstone	85¾	86¼	71¼	43¼	33¼	34	33¾	55	98¼	44½	100½	76¾
Atherton	17¾	179¾	164¾	82½	92¾	92	91¾	148½	4¾	76½	194	59¼
Aylesbury	158¼	48¾	33¾	93	82¾	83½	83¼	17½	170¾	99	42	149¼
Banbury	172	...	47½	106½	96¼	97	96¾	31¼	184½	112½	76¾	163
Barnwell	156	79	64	90½	80¼	81	80¾	47¾	168½	96½	93¼	147
Barton Moss	8	179¾	164¾	82½	92¾	92	91¾	148½	14¾	76½	194	59¼
Basford	32¾	139¼	124¼	42	52¼	51½	51¼	108	45¼	36	153½	23¾
Batley	33¼	201	186	103¾	114	113¼	113	169¾	56¼	97¾	215¼	80½
Bedford	157	47½	...	91½	81¼	82	81¾	16¼	169½	97½	61¾	148
Bedworth	94½	85¼	70¼	34¾	24½	25¼	25	54	107	40¾	99½	85½
Beeston	40¾	152¾	137¾	55½	65¾	65	64¾	121½	53¾	49½	167	10¼
Berkhampstead	159½	50	35	94	83¾	84½	84¼	18¾	172	100	26¾	150½
Berkswell	97¼	84	69	22½	12¼	13	12¾	52¾	109¾	28½	98¼	88¼
Bescot Sta. and Jn.	74¼	106½	91½	...	10¼	9	9¾	75¼	87¼	6	120¾	65¾
Bicester		11½	36	95	84¾	85½	85¼	19¾	173	101	65¼	151½
Billing Road		56¼	41¼	67¾	57½	58¼	58	25	145¾	73¾	70½	124¼
Bilstone	71¼	109½	95	8½	13¾	13	12¾	78¼	81¾	2½	124	62¼
Birmingham, Curzon Street	84¼	97	82	9	¾	...	¼	65¾	96¾	15½	111¼	75¼

LONDON & NORTH WESTERN RAILWAY—*Continued.*

STATIONS.	Clifton Junction.	Colwich.	Crewe.	Dewsbury Junc.	Dudley Port.	Guide Bridge.	Hampton.	Heaton Lodge.	Huddersfield.	Leamington.	Leeds.
Acton	30	45	14¼	71	60¼	36¾	77½	61	56¼	94¼	75¼
Adlington	71½	58	27¼	39	73¼	12½	90½	36½	32¾	107¼	49½
Alderley	61½	48	17¼	39½	63¼	13	80½	37	33¼	97¼	50
Allesley Lane	113¼	50¼	69	125¾	23	99¼	5¾	123¼	119½	12½	136¼
Ampthill	165	90	120¾	177½	84	151	66¾	175	171¼	62	188
Ardwick		61	80¼	30¾	76¼	4¼	93½	28¼	24½	111¾	41¼
Armitage	81¼	6¼	37	93¾	36½	67¼	50¾	28¼	87½	43	104¼
Astley	7	68	37¼	39¾	83¼	13¼	100½	38¼	33½	117¼	50¼
Atherstone	99¾	24¾	55½	112¼	52	85¾	24¾	111	106	24½	122¾
Atherton	16¼	68¾	38	49	84	22½	101¼	47	42¾	118	59½
Aylesbury	172¼	97¼	128	184¾	91½	158¼	74	182¼	178½	69¼	195¼
Banbury	186	111	141¾	198½	105	172	87¾	196	192¼	83	209
Barnwell	170	95	125¾	182½	89	156	71¾	180	176¼	67	193
Barton Moss	6¼	68¾	38	39	84	13¼	101¼	37¼	32¾	118	49½
Basford	46¾	28¼	2½	59¼	43½	32¾	60¾	57	53	77½	69¾
Batley	42¼	90	59¼	2½	105¼	28¼	122½	5	8¾	139¼	8
Bedford	171	96	126¾	183½	90	157	72¾	181	177¼	68	194
Bedworth	108½	33½	64¼	121	33¼	94½	16	118½	114¾	15¾	131½
Beeston	55¼	41¾	11	67¾	57	41¼	74¼	65	61½	91	78¼
Berkhampstead	173½	98½	129¼	186	92½	159½	75¼	183½	179¾	70½	196½
Berkswell	111¼	48¼	67	123¾	21	97¼	3¾	121¼	117½	14½	134¼
Bescot Station and Junction	88¾	2[illegible]¾	44½	101¼	13¼	74¾	18¾	98¾	95	37	111¾
Bicester	174½	99½	130½	187	93½	160½	76¼	184½	180¾	71½	197½
Billing Road	147¼	72¼	103	159¾	66¼	1[illegible]3¼	49	157¼	153½	44¼	170¼
Bilstone	85¼	22¼	41	97¾	5	71¼	22½	95½	91½	40½	108¼
Birmingham, Curzon Street	98¼	35¼	54	110¾	8	84¼	9¼	108¼	104½	27½	121¼

LONDON & NORTH WESTERN RAILWAY—*Continued.*

STATIONS.	Lichfield.	Luffenham.	Macclesfield.	Manchester, Liverpool Road.	Manchester, London Road.	Manchester, Victoria.	North and South Western Junc.	Norton Bridge.	Oxford.	Parkside.	Patricroft.
Acton	55¾	124¼	49¼	30¾	45¼	31½	166	33¼	156¼	16½	26½
Adlington	68¾	137¼	4¼	72¼	13¼	15¾	179	46¼	169¼	58	68
Alderley	58¾	127¼	14¾	62¼	13¾	16¼	169	36¼	159¼	48	58
Allesley Lane	33	50¼	100½	114	100	114¾	92	50	82¼	99¾	109¾
Ampthill	79¼	81¾	152¼	165¾	151¾	166½	51½	101¾	41¾	151½	161½
Ardwick	71¾	140¼	16¾	75¼	¾			49¼	172¼	61	71
Armitage	4½	73	68½	82	68	82¾	114¾	18	105	67¾	77¾
Astley	78¾	147¼	68¾	7¾	68¼	8½	189	56¼	179¼	6½	3½
Atherstone	14	54½	87	100½	86½	101¼	96¼	36½	86½	86¼	96¼
Atherton	79½	148	69½	17	69	17¾	189¾	57¼	180	7¼	12¾
Aylesbury	86½	89	159½	173	159	173¾	87¾	109	49	158¾	168¾
Banbury	100¼	102¾	173¼	186¾	172¾	187½	72½	122¾	43¼	172½	182½
Barnwell	84¼	86¾	157¼	170¾	156¾	171½	89	106¾	51¼	156½	166½
Barton Moss	79½	148	69½	7	69	7¾	189¾	57	180	7¼	2¾
Basford	89	107½	34	47½	33½	48¼	149¼	16½	139½	33¼	43¼
Batley	100¾	169¼	45¾	34½	34	34½	211	78¼	201¼	48¾	38¾
Bedford	85¼	87¾	158¼	171¾	157¾	172½	57½	107¾	47¾	157½	167½
Bedworth	22¾	53½	95¾	109¼	95¼	110	95¼	45¼	85½	95	105
Beeston	52½	121	42½	56	42	56¾	162¾	30	153	41¾	51¾
Berkhampstead	87¾	90¼	160¾	174¼	160¼	175	22½	110¼	50¼	160	170
Berkswell	34½	52¼	98½	112	98	112¾	94	48	84¼	97¾	107¾
Bescot Station and Junction	36½	74¾	76	89½	75½	90¼	116½	25½	106¾	75¼	85¼
Bicester	88¾	91¼	161¾	175¼	161¼	176	61	111¼	11¾	161	171
Billing Road	61½	64	134½	148	134	148¾	66¼	84	56½	133¾	143¾
Bilstone	33	77¾	73½	86	72	86¾	119¾	23	109¾	71¾	81¾
Birmingham, Curzon St.	46	65¼	85½	99	85	99¾	107	35	97¼	84¾	94¾

LONDON & NORTH WESTERN RAILWAY—*Continued.*

STATIONS.	Peterboro'.	Preston Junc.	Rugby.	St. Helens Junc.	Sandbach.	Stafford.	Staleybridge.	Tamworth.	Walton Junction.	Warrington.	West London Junction.
Acton	155¾	16½	88¾	17¾	20	39	48¼	62	9	10	166¼
Adlington	168¾	58	101¾	59¼	22½	52	15	75	50½	51½	179¼
Alderley	158¾	48	91¾	49¼	12½	42	15½	65	40½	41½	169¼
Allesley Lane	81¾	99¾	14¾	101	73¾	44¼	101¾	26¾	92¼	93¼	92¼
Ampthill	73¾	151½	46¼	152¾	125½	96	153½	73	144	145	51¾
Ardwick	171¾	61	104¾	62¼	25½	55	6¾	78		21	182¼
Armitage	104½	67¾	37½	69	41¾	12¼	69¾	10¾	60¼	61¼	115
Astley	178¾	6¾	111¾	11¼	42	62	15¾	85	14	13	189¼
Atherstone	86	86¼	19	87½	60¼	30¾	88¼	7¾	78¾	79¾	96½
Atherton	179½	7½	112¼	12	42¾	63¾	25	85¾	14¾	13¾	190
Aylesbury	81	158¾	53½	160	132¾	103¼	160¾	80¼	151¼	152¼	38
Banbury	94¾	172½	67¼	173¾	146½	117	174½	94	165	166	72¾
Barnwell	15¾	156½	51¼	157¾	130½	101	158½	78	149	150	89¼
Barton Moss	179½	7½	112½	12	42¾	62¾	15	85¾	14¾	13¾	190
Basford	139	33¼	72	34½	7¼	22¼	35¼	45¼	25¾	26¾	149½
Batley	200¾	49	133¾	53½	54½	84	26½	107	56¼	55¼	211¼
Bedford	79¾	157½	52¼	158¾	131½	102	159½	79	150	151	57¾
Bedworth	77	95	18	96¼	69	39½	97	16½	87½	88½	95½
Beeston	152½	41¾	85½	43	15¾	35¾	43¾	58¾	34¼	35¼	163
Berkhampstead	82¼	160	54¾	161¼	134	104½	162	81½	152½	153½	22¾
Berkswell	83¾	97¾	16¾	99	71¾	42¼	99¾	28¼	90¼	91¼	94¼
Bescot Station and Junction	106¼	75¼	39¼	76½	49¼	19¾	77¼	42¾	67¾	68¾	116¾
Bicester	83¼	161	55¾	162¼	135	105½	163	82½	153½	154½	61¼
Billing Road	38½	133¾	28½	135	107¾	78¼	135¾	55¼	126¼	127¼	66½
Bilstone	109¼	71¾	42¼	73	45¾	16¼	73¾	39¼	64¼	65¼	120
Birmingham, Curzon Street	96¾	84¾	29¾	86	58¾	29¼	86¾	41¾	77¼	78¼	107¼

LONDON & NORTH WESTERN RAILWAY —*Continued.*

STATIONS.	Ardwick.	Banbury.	Bedford.	Bescot Junction.	Birmingham, B. and B.	Birmingham, Mid.	Birmingham, Stour Val. Junc.	Bletchley.	Bolton.	Bushbury Junc.	Camden.	Chester.
Birmingham, B. & B.		96¼	81¼	10¼	...	¾		65	97½		110½	76
Birmingham, Stour Valley Junction		96¾	81¾	9¾		¼	...	65½	96½		111	75
Birmingham, Stour Valley Station	83¼	97½	83	10½	1¼	1	¾	66¼	95¾	14½	111¾	74¼
Birstall												
Blackwall	196½	87	72	131	120¾	121½	121¼	55¾	209	137	10¼	187½
Bletchley	140¾	31¼	16¼	75¼	65	63¾	65½	...	153¼	81¼	45½	131¾
Blisworth	124½	47½	32½	59	48¾	49½	49¼	16¼	137	65	61¾	115½
Bolton	73	184½	169½	87¼	97½	96¾	96½	153¼	...	81¼	198¾	64
Boxmoor	163	53½	38½	97½	87¼	88	87¾	22¼	175½	103½	23¼	154
Brackley	162¼	9¾	37¾	96¾	86½	87¼	87	21½	174¾	102¾	66¾	153¼
Bradley	27¼	195	180	97¾	108	107¼	107	163¾	50¼	91¾	209¼	74½
Bradshaw Leach ...	64¾	176¼	161¼	79	89¼	88½	88¼	145	8¼	73	190½	55¾
Bramhall	9	166	151	68¾	79	78¼	78	134¾	77¼	62¾	180¼	45½
Brandon...............	107½	73¾	58¾	32¾	22½	23¼	23	42½	123¾	38¾	88	98½
Broad Green	70½	182	167	84¾	95	94¼	94	150¾	25	78¾	196¼	61½
Bromford	77¾	103	88	16	6¾	6½	6¼	71¾	90¼	9	117¼	68¾
Buckingham	155	17	30½	89½	79¼	80	79¾	14¼	167½	95½	59¾	146
Bulkington............	94¾	77¼	62¼	42	31¾	32½	32¼	46	107¼	48	91½	85¾
Bury Lane............	65½	176¾	161¾	79½	89¾	89	88¾	145½	11¾	72½	191	56¼
Bushbury Junction		112½	97½	6		15½		81¼	81¼	...	126¾	59¾
Bushey	171¼	61¾	46¾	105¾	95½	96¼	96	30½	183¾	111¾	15	162¼
Calveley...............	38½	150	135	52¾	63	62¼	62	118¾	51	46¾	164¼	13
Camden	186¼	76¾	61¾	120¾	110½	111¼	111	45½	198¾	126¾	...	177¼
Castle Ashby	136¼	59¼	44¼	70¾	60½	61¼	61	28	148¾	76¾	73½	127¼
Castor	166½	89½	74½	101	90¾	91½	91¼	58¼	179	107	103¾	157½
Cheadle	7½	164½	149½	67¼	77½	76¾	76½	133¼	65½	61¼	178¾	44

LONDON & NORTH WESTERN RAILWAY—*Continued.*

STATIONS.	Clifton Junction.	Colwich.	Crewe.	Dewsbury Junc.	Dudley Port.	Guide Bridge.	Hampton.	Heaton Lodge.	Huddersfield.	Leamington.	Leeds.
Birmingham, B. & B.		36	54¾	111½	8¾	85	8½	109	105¼	26¾	122
Birmingham, Stour Valley Junction		35	53¾	110½	7¾	84	9	108	104¼	27¼	121
Birmingham, Stour Valley Station	97¼	34¼	53	109¾	7	83¼	9¾	107¼	103½	28	120¼
Birstall											
Blackwall	210½	135½	166¼	223	129½	196½	110¼	220½	216¾	107½	233½
Bletchley	154¾	79¾	110½	167½	73¾	140¾	56½	164¾	161	51¾	177¾
Blisworth	138½	63½	94¼	151	57½	124½	40¼	148½	144¾	35½	161½
Bolton	21	78½	42¾	53¾	88¾	27¼	106	51¼	47½	124¼	64¼
Boxmoor	177	102	132¾	189½	96	163	78¾	187	183½	74	200
Brackley	176¼	101¼	132	188¾	95½	162½	77¾	186¼	182½	73¼	199½
Bradley	36¼	84	53¼	3½	115¼	22¼	116½	1	2¾	133¼	14
Bradshaw Leach	12¾	65¼	34½	45	80½	19	97¾	43	39¼	114½	56
Bramhall	68¾	55	24¼	35½	70¼	9	87½	33	29¼	104¼	46
Brandon.......................	121½	50¼	77¼	137¾	31¼	107½	14	131½	127¾	13¾	144½
Broad Green	26½	71	40¼	58¾	86¼	32¾	103½	56¾	53	120¼	69¾
Bromford	91¾	28¾	47½	104¼	1½	77¾	15¾	101¾	98	34	114¾
Buckingham	169	94	124¾	181½	88	155	70¾	179	175¼	66	192
Bulkington	108¾	33¾	64½	121¼	40	94¾	23¼	118¾	115	23	131¾
Bury Lane.....................	9¼	65¾	35	41½	81	15½	98¼	39½	35¾	115	52½
Bushbury Junction		19¾	38½	95¼	7½	68¾	24¾	93¾	89	43	105¾
Bushey	185¼	110¼	141	197¾	104¼	171¼	87	195¼	191½	82¼	208¼
Calveley.......................	52½	39	8¼	65	54¼	38½	71½	62½	58¾	88¼	75½
Camden	206¼	125¼	156	212¾	119¼	186¼	102	210¼	206½	97¼	223¼
Castle Ashby.................	150¼	75¼	106	162¾	69¼	136¼	52	160¼	156½	47¼	173¼
Castor	180½	105½	136¼	193	99½	166½	82¼	190½	186¾	77½	203½
Cheadle	67¼	53½	22¾	31	68¾	7½	86	31½	27¾	102¾	44½

LONDON & NORTH WESTERN RAILWAY—*Continued.*

STATIONS.	Lichfield.	Luffenham.	Macclesfield.	Manchester, Liverpool Road.	Manchester, London Road.	Manchester, Victoria.	North and South Western Junc.	Norton Bridge.	Oxford.	Parkside.	Patricroft.
Birmingham, B. & B.	46¾	64½	85¾	99¾	85¾	100½		35¾	96½	85½	95¼
Birmingham, Stour Valley Junction	45¾	65	85¼	98¾	84¾	98¾		34¾	97	84½	94½
Birmingham, Stour Valley Station	45	65¾	84½	98	84	98¾	107½	34	97¾	83¾	93¾
Birstall											
Blackwall	124¾	127¼	197¾	211¼	197¼	212	14½	147¼	87¼	197	207
Bletchley	69	71½	142	155½	141½	156¼	41¼	91½	31½	141¼	151¼
Blisworth	52¾	55¼	125¾	139¼	125¼	140	57½	75¼	47¾	125	135
Bolton	84¼	152¾	74¼	21¾	73¾	22½	194½	61¾	184¾	12	17½
Boxmoor	91¼	93¾	164¼	177¾	163¾	178½	19	113¾	53¾	163½	173¼
Brackley	90½	93	163½	177	168	177¾	62¾	113	83½	162¾	172¾
Bradley	94¾	163¼	39¾	28½	28	28½	205	72¼	195¼	42¾	32¾
Bradshaw Leach	76	144½	66	13½	65½	14¼	186¼	53½	176½	3¾	9¼
Bramhall	65¾	134¼	7¾	10¼	9¾	12¼	176	43¼		24½	14½
Brandon	39½	42	108	122¼	107¾	123	83¾	56¾	74	106½	116½
Broad Green	81¾	150¼	71¾	27¼	71¼	28	192	59¼	182¼	13	23
Bromford	39½	71¼	79	92½	78½	93¼	113	28½	103¼	78¼	88¼
Buckingham	83¼	85¾	156¼	169¾	155¾	170½	50	105¾	26¼	155½	165½
Bulkington	23	45½	96	109½	95½	110¼	87¼	45½	77½	95¼	105¼
Bury Lane	76½	145	66½	10	66	10¾	186¾	54	177	4¼	5¾
Bushbury Junction	30	80¾	70½	83½	69½	84¼		19½	112¾	69¼	79¼
Bushey	99½	102	172½	186	172	186¾	10¾	122	62	171¾	181¾
Calveley	49¾	124¼	39¾	53¼	89¼	54	160	27¼	150¼	39	49
Camden	114½	117	187½	201	187	201¾	4½	137	77	186¾	196¾
Castle Ashby	64½	67	137½	151	137	151¾	22½	87	59½	136¾	146¾
Castor	94¾	97¼	167¾	181¼	167¼	182	99½	117¼	89¾	167	177
Cheadle	64¼	182¾	9¼	67¾	8¼	10¾	174½	41¾	164¾	53½	63½

LONDON & NORTH WESTERN RAILWAY—*Continued.*

STATIONS.	Peterboro'.	Preston Junction.	Rugby.	St. Helens Junc.	Sandbach.	Stafford.	Staleybridge.	Tamworth.	Walton Junction.	Warrington.	West London Junction.
Birmingham, B. & B.	96	85½	29	86¾	59½	30	87½	41		79	106½
Birmingham, Stour Valley Junction	96½	84½	29½	85¾	58½	29	86½	41¾		78	107
Birmingham, Stour Valley Station	97¼	83¾	30¼	85	57¾	28¼	85¼	42¾	76¼	77¼	107¾
Birstall											
Blackwall	119¼	197	91¾	198¼	171	141½	199	118½	189½	190½	14¼
Bletchley	63½	141¼	36	142½	115¼	85¾	143¼	62¾	133¾	134¾	41½
Blisworth	47¼	125	19¾	126¼	99	69½	127	46½	117½	118½	57¾
Bolton	184¼	12¼	117¼	16¾	47½	67½	30¼	90½	19½	18½	194¾
Boxmoor	85¾	163½	58¼	164¾	137½	108	165½	85	156	157	19¼
Brackley	85	162¾	57½	164	136¾	107¼	164¾	84¼	155¼	156¼	63
Bradley	194¾	43	127¾	47½	48½	78	20½	101	50¼	49¼	205¼
Bradshaw Leach	176	4	109	8½	39¼	59¼	22	82¼	11¼	10¼	186½
Bramhall	165¾	24¾	98¾	29¼	19	49	11½	72	32	31	176¼
Brandon........................	73½	106½	6½	107¾	80½	51	108½	28	99		84
Broad Green	181¾	13	114¾	8¼	45	65	35¾	88	17	16	192¼
Bromford	102¾	78¼	35¾	79½	52¼	22¾	80¼	45¾	70¾	71¾	113¼
Buckingham	77¾	155½	50¼	156¾	129½	100	157½	77	148	149	50¾
Bulkington	77	95¼	10	96½	69¼	39¾	97¼	16¾	87¾	88¾	87½
Bury Lane........................	176½	4½	109½	9	39¼	59¾	18½	82¾	11¾	10¾	187
Bushbury Junction	112¼	69¼	45¼	70½	43¼	13¾	71¼	36¾		62¾	122¾
Bushey	94	171¾	66½	173	145¾	116¼	173¾	93¼	164¼	165¼	11
Calveley	149¾	39	82¾	40¼	13	33	41	56	31½	32½	160¼
Camden........................	109	186¾	81½	188	160¾	131¼	188¾	108¼	179¼	180¼	4
Castle Ashby..................	35½	136¾	31½	138	110¾	81¼	138¾	58¼	129¼	130¼	22¾
Castor	5¼	167	61¾	168¼	141	111½	169	88½	159½	160½	99¾
Cheadle	164¼	53½	97¼	54¾	18	47½	10	70½	46	47	174¾

LONDON & NORTH WESTERN RAILWAY—*Continued.*

STATIONS.	Ardwick.	Banbury.	Bedford.	Bescot Junction.	Birmingham, B. and B.	Birmingham, Mid.	Birmingham, Stour Val. Junc.	Bletchley.	Bolton.	Bushbury Junc.	Camden.	Chester.
Cheddington	151¼	41¾	26¾	85¾	75½	76¼	76	10½	163¾	91¾	35	142¼
Chelford..............	16¼	155¾	140¾	58½	68¾	68	67¾	124½	56¾	52½	170	35¼
Chequerbent	69½	181	166	83¾	94	93¼	93	149¾	16	76¾	195¼	60½
Chester	57½	163	148	65¾	76	75¼	75	131¾	64	59¾	177¼	...
Chillington............	71¼	110	95	3½	13¾	13	13¼	78¾	83¾	2½	124¼	62¼
Chilvers Coton	92¼	87½	72½	37	26¾	27½	27¼	56¼	97	43	101¾	83¼
Churwell	38¼	206	191	108¾	119	118¼	118	174¾	61¼	102¾	220¼	85½
Claydon...............	152¼	19¾	27¾	86¾	76½	77¼	77	11½	164	92¾	56¾	143¼
Clifton Junction		186	171	88¾		98¼		154¾	21		200¼	65½
Collins Green..........	60½	172	157	74¾	85	84¼	84	140¾	15	68¾	186¼	51½
Colwich	61	111	96	25¾	36	35¼	35	79¾	73½	19¾	125½	52
Counden Road	100	80	65	29½	19¼	19¾	19¾	48¾	116¾	35½	94¼	95¼
Coventry	102¾	78½	63½	28	17¾	18½	18¼	47¼	115¼	34	92¾	93¾
Crewe..................	30¼	141¾	126¾	44½	54¾	54	53¾	110½	42¾	38½	156	21¼
Crick	112¼	59¾	44¾	46¾	36½	37¼	37	28½	124¾	52¾	74	103¼
Cross Lane............	74¼	185¾	170¾	88½	98¾	98	97¾	154½	20¾	82½	200	65¼
Darlaston	73¼	108	93	1½	11¾	11	10¾	76¾	85¾	4½	122¼	64¼
Daubhill...............	71¾	183¼	168¼	86	96¼	95½	95¼	152	1¼	80	197½	62¾
Delph..................	14¾	181¾	166¾	104¼	94¾	94	93¾	150½	37	78½	196	61¼
Denton	7½	170½	155½	98¼	83½	82¾	82½	139¼	30½	67¼	184¾	50
Deepfields	73¼	107½	92½	10½	11¼	11	10¾	76¼	85¾	4½	121¾	64¼
Dewsbury	32¼	200	185	123	113	112¼	112	168¾	55¼	96¾	214¼	79½
Dewsbury Junction..	30¾	198½	183½	101¼	111½	110¾	110½	167¼	53¾	95¼	212¾	78
Diggle	14½	181½	166½	104½	94½	93¾	93½	150¼	36¾	78¼	195¾	61
Ditchford	142¼	65¼	50¼	76¾	66½	67¼	67	34	154¾	82¾	79½	133¼
Dudley Port	76¼	105	90	13½	8¾	8	7¾	73¾	88¾	7½	119¼	67¼

LONDON & NORTH WESTERN RAILWAY—*Continued.*

STATIONS.	Clifton Junction.	Colwich.	Crewe.	Dewsbury Junc.	Dudley Port.	Guide Bridge.	Hampton.	Heaton Lodge.	Huddersfield.	Leamington.	Leeds.
Cheddington	165¼	90¼	121	177¾	84¼	151¼	67	175¼	171½	62¼	188¼
Chelford	58½	44¾	14	42¾	60	16¼	77¼	40¼	36½	94	53¼
Chequerbent	17½	70	39¼	50¼	85¼	23¼	102½	47¾	44	119¼	60¾
Chester	65½	52	21¼	78	67¼	51½	84½	75½	71¾	102¾	88½
Chillington	85¼	22¼	41	97¾	10	71¼	22¼	95¼	91½	40½	108¼
Chilvers Coton	106¼	31¼	62	118¾	35½	92¼	18¼	116¼	112½	18	129¼
Churwell	47¼	95	64¼	7½	110¼	33¼	127½	10	13¾	144¼	3
Claydon	166¼	91¼	122	178¾	85¼	152¼	68	176¼	172½	63¼	189¼
Clifton Junction	...	75	44¼	64	90¼	21	107½	37¼	33½	125¾	50¼
Collins Green	16½	61	30¼	49¼	76¼	22¼	93½	46¾	43	110¼	59¾
Colwich	75	...	30¾	87½	27¼	61	44½	85	81¼	49¼	98
Counden Road	118	38¾	69¾	126½	28	100	10¾	124	120¼	10½	137
Coventry	116¾	40¼	71	127¾	26½	101¼	9¼	125½	123	9	139¾
Crewe	44¼	30¾	...	56¾	46	30¼	63¼	54¼	50½	80¼	67¼
Crick	126¼	51¼	82	138¾	45¼	112¼	28	136¼	132½	23¼	149¼
Cross Lane	6¾	74¾	44	33	90	6	107¼	30½	26¾	124	43½
Darlaston	87¼	24¼	43	99¾	12	73¼	20¼	97¼	93½	38½	110¼
Daubhill	19¾	72¼	41½	52½	87½	26	104¾	50	46½	121½	63
Delph	23	70¾	40	19¾	86	9¾	103¼	17¼	13½	120	30¼
Denton		59½	28¾	28	74¾	1½	92	25½	21¾	108¾	38½
Deepfields	87¼	24¼	43		3		20¼	97¼	93½	38½	110¼
Dewsbury	65½	89	58¼	1½	104¼	28	121½	4	7¾	138¼	9
Dewsbury Junction	64	87½	56¾	...	102¾	26½	120	2½	6½	136¾	10½
Diggle	22¾	70½	39¾	16½	85¾	9½	103	14	10¼	119¾	27
Ditchford	156¼	81¼	112	168¾	75¼	142¼	58	166¼	162½	53¼	179¼
Dudley Port	90¼	27¼	46	102¾	...	76¼	17¼	100¼	96½	35½	113¼

LONDON & NORTH WESTERN RAILWAY—*Continued.*

STATIONS.	Lichfield.	Luffenham.	Macclesfield.	Manchester, Liverpool Road.	Manchester, London Road.	Manchester, Victoria.	North and South Western Junc.	Norton Bridge.	Oxford.	Parkside.	Patricroft.
Cheddington	79½	82	152½	166	152	166¾	30¾	102	42	151¾	161¾
Chelford	55½	124	17	59	17	19½	165¾	33	156	44¾	54¾
Chequerbent	80¾	149¼	70¾	18¼	70¼	19	191	58¼	181¼	8½	14
Chester	62¾	131¼	52¾	66¼	52¼	67	173	40¼	163¼	52	62
Chillington	33	78¼	72½	86	72	86¾	120	22	110¼	71¾	81¾
Chilvers Coton	20½	55¾	93½	107	93	107¾	97½	43	87¾	92¾	102¾
Churwell	105¾	174¼	50¾	39½	39	39½	216	83¼	206¼	53¾	43¾
Claydon	80½	83	153½	167	153	167¾	52¾	103	23½	152¾	162¾
Clifton Junction	85¾	154¼	76¼	7¾	75½	8½	...	63¼	186¼	13½	3½
Collins Green	71¾	140¼	61¾	17¼	61¼	18	182	49¼	172¼	3	13
Colwich	10¾	79¼	62¼	75¾	61¾	76½	121	11¾	111¼	61½	71½
Counden Road	20½	48¼	101¼	114¾	100¾	115½	90	50¾	80¼	100½	110½
Coventry	29½	46¾	102½	116	102	116¾	88½	52	78¾	101¾	111¾
Crewe	41½	110	31½	45	31	45¾	151¾	19	142	30¾	40¾
Crick	40½	43	113½	127	113	127¾	31¾	63	60	112¾	122¾
Cross Lane	85½	154	74½	1	75	1¾	195¾	63	186	13¼	3¼
Darlaston	35	76¼	74½	88	74	88¾	118	24	108¼	73¾	83¾
Daubhill	83	151½	38½	20½	21	21¼	193¼	60½	183½	10¾	16¼
Delph	81½	150	26½	15¼	14¾	16	191¾	59	182	29½	19¼
Denton	70¼	138¾	15¼	8¾	8¼	9½	180½	47¾	170¾	23	13
Deepfields	35	75¾	74½	88	74	88¾	117½	24	107¾	73¾	83¾
Dewsbury	99¾	168¼	44¾	33½	33		210	77¼	200¼	47¾	37¾
Dewsbury Junction	98¼	166¾	43¼	32	31½		208½	75¾	198¾	46¼	36¼
Diggle	81¼	149¾	26¼	15	14½	15¾	191½	58¾	181¾	29¼	19
Ditchford	70½	73	143½	157	143	157¾	75¼	93	65½	142¾	152¾
Dudley Port	38	73¼	77½	91	77	91¾	115	27	105¼	76¾	86¾

LONDON & NORTH WESTERN RAILWAY—*Continued.*

STATIONS.	Peterboro'.	Preston Junction	Rugby.	St. Helens Junc.	Sandbach.	Stafford	Staleybridge.	Tamworth.	Walton Junction.	Warrington.	West London Junction.
Cheddington	74	151¾	46½	153	125¾	96¼	153¾	73¼	144¼	145¼	31
Chelford	155½	44¾	88½	46	9¼	38¾	18¾	61¾	60¾	38¼	166
Chequerbent	180¾	8¾	113¾	13¼	44	64	26¾	87	16	15	191¼
Chester	162¾	52	95¾	53¼	26	46	54	69	44½	45½	173¼
Chillington	109¾	71¾	42¾	73	45¾	16¼	73¾	39¼	64¼	65¼	120¼
Chilvers Coton	87¼	92¾	20¼	94	66¾	37¼	94¾	14¼	85¼	86¼	97¾
Churwell	205¾	54	138¾	58½	59½	89	31½	112	61¼	60¼	216¼
Claydon	75	152¾	47½	154	126¾	97¼	154¾	74¼	145¼	146¼	53
Clifton Junction	165¼	13¾	118¾	18¼	49	69	15¾	92		20	196¼
Collins Green	171¾	3	104¾	1¾	35	55	25¾	78	7	6	182¼
Colwich	110¾	61½	43¾	62¾	35½	6	63½	17	54	55	121¼
Coundon Road	79¾	100½	12¾	101¾	74½	45	102½	22	93	94	90¼
Coventry	78¼	101¾	11¼	103	75¾	46¼	103¾	23¼	94¼	95¼	88¾
Crewe	141½	30¾	74½	32	4¾	24¾	32¾	47¾	23¼	24¼	152
Crick	59½	112¾	7½	114	86¾	57¼	114¾	34¼	105¼	106¼	32
Cross Lane	185½	13½	118½	18	37¾	68¾	9½	91¾	20¾	19¾	196
Darlaston	107¾	73¾	40¾	75	47¾	18¼	75¾	41¼	66¼	67¼	118¼
Daubhill	183	11	116	15½	46¼	66¼	28½	89¼	18¼	17¼	193½
Delph	181½	29¾	114½	34¼	35¼	64¾	7¼	87¾	37	36	192
Denton	170¼	23¼	103¼	27¾	24	53½	4	76½	30½	29½	180¾
Deepfields	107¼	73¾	40¼	75	47¾	18½	75¾	41½	66¼	67¼	117¾
Dewsbury	199½	48	132¾	52½	53½	83	25½	106	55¼	54¼	210¼
Dewsbury Junction	198¼	46½	131¼	51	52	81½	24	104½	54¾	52¾	208¾
Diggle	181¼	29½	114¼	34	35	64½	7	87½	36¾	35¾	191¾
Ditchford	29½	142¾	37½	144	116¾	87¼	144¾	64¼	135¼	136¼	75½
Dudley Port	104¾	76¾	37¼	78	50¾	21¼	78¾	44¼	69¼	70¼	115¼

LONDON & NORTH WESTERN RAILWAY—*Continued.*

STATIONS.	Ardwick.	Banbury.	Bedford.	Bescot Junction.	Birmingham, B. and B.	Birmingham, Mid.	Birmingham, Stour Val. Junc.	Bletchley.	Bolton.	Bushbury Junc.	Camden.	Chester.
Dunstable	154	37½	29½	88½	78¼	79	78¾	13¼	166½	94½	46¼	145
Eccles	72	183½	168½	86¼	96½	95¾	95½	152¼	18½	78¼	197¾	63
Edge Hill	72½	184	169	86¾	97	96½	96	152¾	27	80¾	198¼	63½
Elton	162¾	85¾	70¾	97¼	87	87¾	87½	54½	175¼	103¼	100	153¾
Euston	187½	78	63	122	111¾	112½	112¼	46¾	200	128	1¼	178½
Farthinghoe	168	58½	43½	102½	92¼	93	92¾	27¼	180½	108½	72¾	159
Fenny Stratford	142	32½	17½	76½	66¼	67	66¾	1¼	154½	82½	46¾	133
Foleshill	98¼	81½	66½	31	20¾	21½	21¼	50¼	110¾	37	95¾	96¾
Four Ashes	64¼	117	102	10½	20¾	20	19¾	85¾	76¾	4½	131¼	55¼
Golcar	21½	189¼	174¼	112¼	102¼	101½	101¼	158	44½	86	203½	68¾
Great Western Jun.	182¾	73¼	58½	117¼	107	107¾	107½	42	195¼	123¼	4½	173¾
Greenfield	11½	179¼	164¼	82	92¼	91½	91¼	148	35	76	193½	58¾
Guide Bridge	4¼	172	157	74¾	85	84¼	84	140¾	27¼	68¾	186¼	51½
Hampton	93½	87¾	72¾	18¾	8½	9¼	9	56½	106	24¾	102	84½
Handforth	9¾	162¼	147¼	65	75¼	74½	74¼	131	63¼	59	176½	41¾
Harrow	176	66½	51½	110½	100¼	101	100¾	35¼	188½	116½	10¼	167
Hartford	41¾	153¼	138¼	56	66¼	65½	65¼	122	31¼	50	167½	32¾
Hawkesbury	96	83¾	68¾	33¼	23	23¾	23½	52½	108½	39¼	98	87
Haydon Square	195¾	86¼	71¼	130¼	120	120¾	120½	55	208¼	136¼	9½	186
Heaton Chapel	3¾	168¼	153¼	71	81¼	80½	80¼	137	69¼	65	182½	48¾
Heaton Lodge	28¼	196	181	98¾	109	108¼	108	164¾	51¼	93¾	210¼	75½
Heaton Norris	4½	167½	152½	68¼	80½	79¾	79½	136¼	68½	64¼	181¾	47
Higham Ferrers	144½	67½	52½	79	68¾	69½	69¼	36¼	157	85	81¾	135½
Holmes Chapel	22	160	145	53	65	64¼	64	128¾	51	46¾	174¼	29½
Huddersfield	24½	192¼	177¼	95	105¼	104½	104¼	161	47½	89	206½	71¾
Huyton Lane	26	180	165	82¾	93	92¼	92	148¾	23	76¾	194½	59½

LONDON & NORTH WESTERN RAILWAY—*Continued.*

STATIONS.	Clifton Junction.	Colwich.	Crewe.	Dewsbury Junc.	Dudley Port.	Guide Bridge.	Hampton.	Heaton Lodge.	Huddersfield.	Leamington.	Leeds.
Dunstable	168	93	123¾	180½	87	154	69¾	178	174¼	65	191
Eccles	4½	72½	41¾	38¼	87¾	8¾	105	32¾	29	121¾	45¾
Edge Hill	28½	73	42¼	61¼	88¼	34¾	105½	58¾	55	122¼	71¼
Elton	176¾	81¼	132½	189¼	95¾	162¾	78½	186¾	183	73¾	199¾
Euston	201½	126½	157¼	214	120½	187½	103¼	211½	207¾	98½	224½
Farthinghoe	182	107	137	194½	101	168	83¾	192	188¼	79	205
Fenny Stratford	156	81	111¾	168½	75	142	57¾	166	162¼	53	179
Foleshill	119¾	37¼	68	124¾	20½	98¼	12¼	122¼	118½	12	135¼
Four Ashes	78¼	15¼	34	90¾	12	64¼	29¼	88½	84½	47½	101¼
Golcar		68¾	47½	9¼	93½	17¼	110¾	6¾	3	127½	19¾
Great Western Junction	196¾	121¾	152½	209¼	115¾	182¾	98½	206¾	203	39¾	219¾
Greenfield	21	68¼	37½	19¼	83½	6½	100¾	16¾	13	117½	29¾
Guide Bridge	21	61	30¼	26½	76¼	...	93½	23¼	19½	110¼	36¼
Hampton	107½	44½	63¼	120	17¼	93½	...	117½	113¾	18¼	130½
Handforth	64¾	51¼	20½	36¼	66½	9¾	83¾	33¾	30	100½	46¾
Harrow	190	115	145¾	202½	109	176	91¾	200	196¼	87	213
Hartford	32¾	42¼	11½		57½	39	74¾	63	59¼	91½	76
Hawkesbury	110	35	65¾	122½	31¾	96	14½	120	116¼	14¼	133
Haydon Square	209¾	134¾	165½	222¼	128¾	195¾	111½	219¾	216	106¾	232¾
Heaton Chapel	70¾	57¼	26½	31¾	72½	5¼	89¾	29¼	25½	106½	42¼
Heaton Lodge	37¼	85	54¼	2½	100¼	23¼	117½	...	3¾	134½	13
Heaton Norris	70	56½	25¾	31	71¾	4½	89	28½	24¾	105¾	41½
Higham Ferrers	158½	83½	114¼	171	77½	144½	60¼	168½	164¾	55½	181½
Holmes Chapel	52½	39	8¼	48½	54¼	22	73½	46	42¼	98¼	59
Huddersfield	33½	81¼	50½	6¼	96½	19½	113¾	3¾	...	130½	16¾
Huyton Lane	24½	69	38¼		84¼		101½	54¾	51	118¼	67¾

M'Corquodale & Co., Printers.

LONDON & NORTH WESTERN RAILWAY—*Continued.*

STATIONS.	Lichfield.	Luffenham.	Macclesfield.	Manchester, Liverpool Road.	Manchester, London Road.	Manchester, Victoria.	North & South Western Junc.	Norton Bridge.	Oxford.	Parkside.	Patricroft.
Dunstable	82¼	84¾	155¼	168¾	154¾	169½	35	104¾	44¾	154½	164½
Eccles	83¼	151¾	21¼	3¼	3¾	4	193½	60¾	183¾	11	1
Edge Hill	83¾	152¼	47¼	29¼	29¾	30	194	61¼	184¼	15	25
Elton	91	93½	164	177½	163½	178¼	95¾	113½	86	163¼	173¼
Euston	115¾	118¼	188¾	202¼	188¼	203	5½	138¼	78¼	188	198
Farthinghoe	96¼	98¾	169¼	182¾	168¾	183½	68½	118¾	39¼	168½	178½
Fenny Stratford	70¼	72¾	143¼	156¾	142¾	157½	42½	92¾	32¾	142½	152½
Foleshill	26½	49¾	99½	113	99	113¾	91½	49	81¾	98¾	108¾
Four Ashes	26	85¼	65½	79	65	79¾	127	15	117¼	64¾	74¾
Golcar	89	157½	34	22¾	22¼		199¼	66	189½	37	27
Great Western Junction	111	113½	184	197½	183½	198¼	¾	133½	73½	183¼	193¼
Greenfield	79	147½	23¼	13¼	12¾		189¼	56½	179½	28½	17½
Guide Bridge	71¾	140¼	16¾	5½	5		182	49¼	172¼	19¾	9¾
Hampton	38¾	56	94¾	108¼	94¼	109	97¾	44¼	88	94	104
Handforth	62	130½	10½	11	10½		172¼	39½	162½	25¼	15¼
Harrow	104¼	106¾	177¼	190¾	176¾	191½	6	126¾	66¾	176½	186½
Hartford	53	121½	43	33½	42½	34¼	163¼	30½	153½	19¼	29¼
Hawkesbury	24¼	52	97¼	110¾	96¾	111½	93¾	46¾	84	96½	106½
Haydon Square	124	126½	197	210½	196½	211¼	13¾	146½	86½	196¼	206¼
Heaton Chapel	68	136½	13	71½	4½		178¼	45½	168½	57¼	67¼
Heaton Lodge	95¾	164¼	40¾	29½	29		206	73¼	196¼	43¾	33¾
Heaton Norris	67¼	135¾	12¼	74¾	5¼		177½	44¾	167¾	56½	66½
Higham Ferrers	72¾	75¼	145¾	159¼	145¼	160	77½	95¼	67¾	145	155
Holmes Chapel	49¾	128¼	23¾	53¼	22¾		170	27¼	160¼	39	49
Huddersfield	92	160½	37	25¾	25¼		202¼	69½	192½	40	30
Huyton Lane	79¾	148¼	69¾	25¼	69¼	26	190	57¼	180¼	11	21

LONDON & NORTH WESTERN RAILWAY—*Continued.*

STATIONS.	Peterboro'.	Preston Junc.	Rugby.	St. Helens Junc.	Sandbach.	Stafford.	Staley Bridge.	Tamworth.	Walton Junc.	Warrington.	West London Jun.
Dunstable	76¾	154½	49¼	155¾	128½	99	156½	76	147	148	35¼
Eccles	183¼	11¼	116¼	15¾	46½	66½	11¼	89½	18½	17½	193¾
Edge Hill	183¾	15	116¾	10¼	47	67	37¼	90	19	18	194¼
Elton	9	163¼	58	164½	137¼	107¾	165¼	84¾	155¾	156¾	96
Euston	110¼	188	82¾	189¼	162	132½	190	109½	180½	181½	5¼
Farthinghoe	90¾	168½	63¼	169¾	142½	113	170½	90	161	162	68¾
Fenny Stratford	64¾	142½	37¼	143¾	116½	87	144½	64	135	136	42¾
Foleshill	81¼	98¾	14¼	100	72¾	43¼	100¾	20¼	91¼	92¼	91¾
Four Ashes	116¾	64¾	49¾	66	38¾	9¼	66¾	32¼	57¼	58¼	127¼
Golcar	189	37¼	122	41¾	42¾	73¼	14¾	95¼	44½	43½	199½
Great Western Junction	105½	183¼	78	184½	157¼	127¾	185¼	104¾	175¾	176¾	½
Greenfield	179	28¾	112	32¼	32¾	62¼	4¾	85¼	35	34	189½
Guide Bridge	171¾	20	104¾	24½	25½	55	1¾	78	27¼	26¼	182¼
Hampton	87½	94	20½	95¼	68	38½	96	32½	86½	87½	98
Handforth	162	25½	95	30	15¾	45¼	12¼	68¼	32¾	31¾	172½
Harrow	98¾	176½	71¼	177¾	150½	121	178½	98	169	170	6¼
Hartford	153	19¼	86	20½	16¼	36¼	44¼	59¼	11¾	12¾	163½
Hawkesbury	83½	96½	16½	97¾	70½	41	98½	18	89	90	94
Haydon Square	45	196¼	91	197½	170¼	140¾	198¼	117¾	188¾	189¾	13½
Heaton Chapel	168	57¼	101	58½	21¾	60¼	7¾	74¼	49¾	50¾	178½
Heaton Lodge	195¾	44	128¾	48½	49½	79	21½	102	51¼	50¼	206¼
Heaton Norris	167¼	56½	100¼	57¾	21	50½	7	73½	49	50	177¾
Higham Ferrers	27¼	145	39¾	146¼	119	89½	147	66½	137½	138½	77¾
Holmes Chapel	159¾	39	92¾	40¼	3½	33	25	56	31½	32½	170¼
Huddersfield	192	40¼	125	44¾	45¾	75¼	17¾	98¼	47½	46½	202½
Huyton Lane	179¾	11	112¾	6¼	43	63	71	86	15	14	190¼

LONDON & NORTH WESTERN RAILWAY—*Continued.*

STATIONS.	Ardwick.	Banbury.	Bedford.	Bescot Junc.	Birmingham, B. & B.	Birmingham, Mid.	Birmingham, Stour Val. Junc.	Bletchley.	Bolton.	Bushbury Junc.	Camden.	Chester.
Huyton Quarry	25¼	179	164	81¾	92	91¼	91	147¾	22	75¾	193¼	58½
Islip	166½	5½	42	101	90¾	91½	91¼	25¾	179	107	71	157½
Kenilworth	106½	83¾	68¾	33¼	23	23¾	23½	52½	120¼	39¼	98	99
Kensington	185¼	75¾	60¾	119¾	109½	110¼	110	44½	197¾	125¾	7	176¼
Kenyon Junction	13	174¾	159¾	77½	87¾	87	86¾	143½	9¾	71½	189	54¼
Kilburn	184½	75	60	119	108¾	109½	109¼	43¾	197	125	1¾	175½
Kings Langley	166½	57	42	101	90¾	91½	91¼	25¾	179	107	19¾	157½
Launton	158¼	13¾	33¾	92¾	82½	83¼	83	17½	170¾	98¾	63	149¼
Leamington	110¼	83	68	37	26¾	27½	27¼	51¾	124¼	43	97¼	102¾
Leeds	41¼	209	194	111¾	122	121¼	121	177¾	64¼	105¾	223¼	88½
Leigh	15½	177¼	162¼	80	90¼	89½	89¼	146	7¼	74	191½	56¾
Leighton	147	37½	22½	81½	71¼	72	71¾	6¼	159½	87½	39¼	138
Levenshulme	2¼	169¾	154¾	72½	82¾	82	81¾	138½	70¾	66½	184	49¼
Lidlington	149½	40	25	84	73¾	74½	74¼	8¾	162	90	54¼	140½
Lichfield	71¾	100¼	85¼	36½	46¾	46	45¾	69	84¼	30	114½	62¾
L'pool, Lime Street	74	185½	170½	88¼	98½	97¾	97½	154¼	28½	82¼	199¾	65
L'pool, Park Lane	74¼	185¾	170¾	88½	98¾	98	97¾	154½	28¾	82½	200	65¼
Liverpool, Waterloo	75	186½	171½	89¼	99½	98¾	98½	155¼	29½	83¼	200¾	66
Longford and Exhall	96¾	83	68	32½	22¼	23	22¾	51¾	109¼	38½	97¼	87¾
Longsight	1	171	156	73¾	84	83¼	83	139¾	72	67¾	185¼	50½
Longwood	22¾	190½	175½	93¼	103½	102¾	102½	159¼	96	87¼	204¾	70
Luffenham	140¼	102¾	87¾	74¾	64½	65¼	65	71½	152¾	80¾	117	131¼
Lyddington	134¼	96¾	81¾	68¾	58½	59¼	59	65½	146¾	74¾	111	125¼
Macclesfield	16¾	173¼	158¼	76	85¾	85½	85¼	142	74¼	70½	187½	52¾
Madeley	38¼	134	119	36¾	47	46¼	46	102¾	50½	30¾	148¼	29
Manchester, Liverpool Road	75¼	186¾	171¾	89½	99¾	99	98¾	155½	21¾	83½	201	66¼

LONDON & NORTH WESTERN RAILWAY—*Continued.*

STATIONS.	Clifton Junc.	Colwich.	Crewe.	Dewsbury Junc.	Dudley Port.	Guide Bridge.	Hampton.	Heaton Lodge.	Huddersfield.	Leamington.	Leeds.
Huyton Quarry	23½	68	37¼		83¼		100½	53¾	50	117¼	66¾
Islip	180½	105½	136¼	193	99½	166½	82¼	190½	186¾	77½	203½
Kenilworth	122	50¾	77¾	133	31¾	106½	14½	130¾	126¾	3¾	145
Kensington	199¼	124¼	155	211¾	118¼	185¼	101	209¼	205½	96¼	222¼
Kenyon Junction	11¼	63¾	33		79		96¼	41½	37¾	113	54½
Kilburn	198½	123½	154¼	211	117½	184½	100¼	208½	204¾	95½	221½
Kings Langley	180½	105½	136¼	193	99½	166½	82¼	190½	186¾	77½	203½
Launton	172¼	97¼	128	184¾	91¼	158¼	74	182¼	178½	69¼	195¼
Leamington	125¾	49¼	80¼	136¾	35½	110¼	18¼	134½	130½	...	147¼
Leeds	50¼	98	67¼	10½	113¼	36¼	130½	13	16¾	147¼	...
Leigh	13¾	66¼	35½	46½	81½	20	98¾	44	40¼	115½	57
Leighton	161	86	116¾	174	80	147	62¾	171	167¼	58	184
Levenshulme	72¼	58¾	28	33¼	74	6¾	91¼	30¾	27	108	43¾
Lidlington	163½	88½	119¼	176	82½	149½	65¼	173½	169¾	60½	186½
Lichfield	85¾	10¾	41½	98¼	38	71¾	38¾	95¾	92	38½	108¾
Liverpool, Lime Street	30	74½	43¾	62¾	89¾	36¼	107	60¼	56½	134	73¼
Liverpool, Park Lane	30¼	74¾	44	63	90	36½	107¼	60½	56¾	134¼	73½
Liverpool, Waterloo	31	75½	44¾	63¾	90¾	37¼	108	61¼	57½	135	74¼
Longford and Exhall	110¾	35¾	66½	123¼	31	96¾	13¾	120¾	117	13½	133¾
Longsight	73½	60	29¼	34½	75¾	8	92½	32	28¼	109¼	45
Longwood	31¾	79½	48¾	8	94¾	17¾	112	5½	1¾	128¾	18½
Luffenham	154¼	79¼	110	166¾	73¼	140¼	56	164¼	160½	51¼	177¼
Lyddington	148¼	73¼	104	160¾	67¼	134¼	50	158¼	154½	45¼	171¼
Macclesfield	76¼	62¼	31½	43¼	77½	16¾	94¾	40¾	37	111½	53¾
Madeley	59	23	7¾	64½	38¼	38	55½	62	50¼	72¼	75
Manchester, Liverpool Road	7¾	75¾	45	32	91	5½	108¼	29½	25¾	125	42½

LONDON & NORTH WESTERN RAILWAY—*Continued.*

STATIONS.	Lichfield.	Luffenham.	Macclesfield.	Manchester, Liverpool Road.	Manchester, London Road.	Manchester, Victoria.	North & South Western Junc.	Norton Bridge.	Oxford.	Parkside.	Patricroft.
Huyton Quarry	78¾	147¼	68¾	24¼	68¼	25	189	56¼	179¼	10	20
Islip	94¾	97¼	167¾	181¼	167¼	182	67	117¼	5½	167	177
Kenilworth	34¾	52	107¾	121¼	107¼	122	93¾	57¼	84	107	117
Kensington	113½	116	186½	200	186	200¾	3½	136	76	185¾	195¾
Kenyon Junction	74½	143	64½	12	64	12¾	184¾	52	175	2¼	7¾
Kilburn	112¾	115¼	185¾	199¼	185¼	200	2½	135¼	75¼	185	195
Kings Langley	94¾	97¼	167¾	181¼	167¼	182	15½	117¼	57¼	167	177
Launton	86½	89	159½	173	159	173¾	58¾	109	14	158¾	168¾
Leamington	38½	51¼	111½	125	111	125¾	93	61	83¼	110¾	120¾
Leeds	108¾	177¼	53¾	42½	42		219	86¼	209¼	56¾	46¾
Leigh	77	145½	67	14½	15	15¼	187¼	54½	177½	4¾	10¼
Leighton	75¼	77¾	148¼	161¾	147¾	162½	35	97¾	37¾	147½	157½
Levenshulme	69½	138	14½	69½	3		179¾	47	170	58¾	68¾
Lidlington	77¾	80¼	150¾	164¼	150¼	165	50	100¼	40¼	150	160
Lichfield	...	68½	73	86½	72½	87¼	110¼	22½	100½	72¼	82¼
Liverpool, Lime Street	85¼	153¾	75¼	30¾	31¼	31½	195½	62¾	185¾	16½	26½
Liverpool, Park Lane	85½	154	75½	31	31½	31¾	195¾	63	186	16¾	26¾
Liverpool, Waterloo	86¼	154¾	76¼	31¾	32¼	32½	196½	63¾	186¾	17½	27½
Longford and Exhall	25	51¼	98	111½	97½	112¼	93	47½	83¼	97¼	107¼
Longsight	70¾	139¼	15½	74¼	1¾		181	48¼	171¼	60	70
Longwood	90¼	158¾	35¼	24	23½		200½	67¾	190¾	38¼	28¼
Luffenham	68½	...	141½	155	141	155¾	112¾	91	103	140¾	150¾
Lyddington	62½	6	135½	149	135	149¾	106¾	85	97	134¾	144¾
Macclesfield	73	141½	...	73½	17½		183¾	50½	173½	62¼	72¾
Madeley	33¾	102¼	39¼	52¾	38¾	53½	144	11¼	134¼	38½	48½
Manchester, Liverpool Road	86½	155	73½	...	76	1¾	196¾	64	187	14¼	4¼

LONDON & NORTH WESTERN RAILWAY—*Continued.*

STATIONS.	Peterboro'.	Preston Junc.	Rugby.	St. Helens Junc.	Sandbach.	Stafford.	Staley Bridge.	Tamworth.	Walton Junc.	Warrington.	West London Junction.
Huyton Quarry	178¾	10	111¾	5¼	42	62	70	85	14	13	189¼
Islip	89¼	167	61¾	168¼	141	111½	169	88½	159½	160½	67¼
Kenilworth	83½	107	16½	108¼	81	51½	109	28½	99½	100½	94
Kensington	108	185¾	80½	187	159¾	130¼	187¾	107¼	178¼	179¼	3¼
Kenyon Junction	174½	2½	107½	7	37¾	57¾	65¾	80¾	9¾	8¾	185
Kilburn	107¼	185	79¾	186¼	159	120½	187	106½	177½	178½	2¼
Kings Langley	89¼	167	61¾	168¼	141	111½	169	88½	159½	160½	15¾
Launton	80¾	158¾	53½	160	132¾	103¼	160¾	80¼	151¼	152¼	59
Leamington	82¾	110¾	15¾	112	84¾	55¼	112¾	32¼	103¼	104¼	93¼
Leeds	208¾	57	141¾	61½	62½	92	34½	115	64¼	63¼	219¼
Leigh	177	5	110	9½	40¼	60¼	22½	83¼	12¼	11¼	187½
Leighton	69¾	147½	42¼	148¾	121½	92	149½	69	140	141	35¼
Levenshulme	169½	58¾	102½	60	23¼	52¾	9¼	75¾	51¼	52¼	180
Lidlington	72¼	150	44¾	151¼	124	94½	152	71½	142½	143½	50¼
Lichfield	100	72¼	33	73½	46¼	16¾	74¼	6¼	64¾	65¾	110½
Liverpool, Lime Street	185¼	16½	118¼	11¾	48½	68½	38¾	91½	20½	19½	195¾
Liverpool, Park Lane	185½	16¾	118½	12	48¾	68¾	39	91¾	20¾	19¾	196
Liverpool, Waterloo	186¼	17¼	119¼	12¾	49½	69½	39¾	92½	21½	20½	196¾
Longford and Exhall	82¾	97¼	15¾	98½	71¼	41¾	99¼	18¾	89¾	90¾	93¼
Longsight	170¾	60	103¾	61¼	24½	54	10½	77	52½	53½	181¼
Longwood	190¼	38½	123¼	43	44	73½	16	96½	45¾	44¾	200¾
Luffenham	102½	140¾	35½	142	114¾	85¼	142¾	62¼	133¼	134¼	113
Lyddington	96½	134¾	29½	136	108¾	79¼	136¾	56¼	127¼	128¼	107
Macclesfield	173	62¼	106	63½	27¼	56¼	19¼	79¼	55¼	55¾	183½
Madeley	133¾	38½	66¾	39¾	12½	17	40½	40	31	32	144¼
Manchester, Liverpool Road	186½	14½	119½	19	49¾	69¾	8	92¾	21¾	20¾	197

LONDON & NORTH WESTERN RAILWAY—*Continued.*

STATIONS.	Ardwick.	Banbury.	Bedford.	Bescot Junc.	Birmingham, B. & B.	Birmingham, Mid.	Birmingham, Stour Val Junc.	Bletchley.	Bolton.	Bushbury Junc.	Camden.	Chester.
Manchester, London Road	¾	172¾	157¾	75½	85¾	85	84¾	141½	73¾	69½	187	52¼
Manchester, Victoria		187½	172½	90¼	100½	99¾	98¾	156¼	22½	84¼	201¾	67
Market Harbro	122½	85	70	57	46¾	47½	47¼	58¾	135	63	99¼	113½
Marsden...............	17½	185¼	170¼	88	98¼	97½	97¼	154	92	82	199½	64¾
Marston Gate	154	44½	29½	88½	78¼	79	78¾	13¼	166½	94½	37¾	145
Marston Green	90¼	91	76	15½	5¼	6	5¾	59¾	102¾	21½	105¼	81¼
Marton	113	75½	60½	47½	37¼	38	37¾	44¼	125½	53½	89¾	104
Medbourne Bridge...	127½	90	75	62	51¾	52½	52¼	58¾	140	68	104¼	118½
Minshull Vernon ...	35¼	146¾	131¾	49½	59¾	59	58¾	115½	37¾	43½	161	26¼
Moore	51	162½	147½	65¼	75½	74¾	74½	131¼	22	59¼	176¾	42
Morley	36¼	204	189	106¾	117	116¼	116	172¾	110¾	100¾	218¼	83½
Mossley	9¼	177	162	79¾	90	89¼	89	145¾	83¾	73¾	191¼	56½
Nantwich	34	145½	130½	48¼	58½	57¾	57½	114¼	46½	42¼	159¾	17½
Newton Bridge	60¼	171¾	156¾	74½	84¾	84	83¾	140½	12¾	68½	186	51¼
Newton Road	77¼	104	89	2½	7¾	7	7¼	72¾	89¾	8½	118¼	68¼
Newton, or Warrington Junctn.	59¼	170¾	155¾	73½	83¾	83	82¾	139½	13¾	67½	185	50¼
Northampton.........	129¼	52¼	37¼	63¾	53½	54¼	54	21	141¾	69¾	66½	120¼
North and South Western Junc.		72½	57½	116½		107		41¼	194½		4¼	173
Norton Bridge	49¼	122¾	107¾	25½	35¾	35	34¾	91½	61¾	19½	137	40¼
Nuneaton	91	77½	62½	38¼	28	28¾	28½	46¼	108½	44¼	95¼	82
Ordsall Lane	74¾	186¼	171¼	89	99¼	98½	98¼	155	21¼	83	200½	65¾
Oundle	158¾	81¾	66¾	93¼	83	83¾	83½	50½	171¼	99¼	96	149¾
Overton	169	92	77	103½	93¼	94	93¾	60¾	181½	109½	106¼	160
Oxford	172¼	43¼	47¾	106¾	96½	97¼	97	31½	184¾	112¾	77	163¼
Parkside	61	172½	157½	75¼	85½	84¾	84½	141¼	12	69¼	186¾	52
Patricroft	71	182½	167½	85¼	95½	94¾	94½	151¼	17½	79¼	196¾	62

LONDON & NORTH WESTERN RAILWAY—*Continued.*

STATIONS.	Clifton Junction.	Colwich.	Crewe.	Dewsbury Junc.	Dudley Port.	Guide Bridge.	Hampton.	Heaton Lodge.	Huddersfield.	Leamington.	Leeds.
Manchester, London Road.	75½	61¾	31	31½	77	5	94¼	29	25¼	111	42
Manchester, Victoria	8½	76½	45¾		91¾		109			125¾	
Market Harbro	136½	61½	92¼	149	55½		38¼	146½	142¾	33½	159½
Marsden.......................	26½	74¼	43½	13¼	89½	12½	106¾	10¾	7	123½	23¾
Marston Gate	168	93	123¾	180½	87	154	69¾	178	174¼	65	191
Marston Green	104¼	41¼	60	116¾	14	90¼	3¼	114¼	110½	21½	127¼
Marton	127	52	82¾	139½	46	113	28¾	137	133¼	7½	150
Medbourne Bridge	141½	66½	97¼	154	60½	127½	43¼	151½	147¾	38½	164½
Minshull Vernon	39¼	35¾	5	72	51	45½	68¼	69½	65¾	85	82½
Moore	23½	51½	20¾	56¼	66¾	29¾	84	53¾	50	100¾	66¾
Morley	44¾	93	62¼	5½	108¼	31¼	125½	8	12½	142¼	5
Mossley	17¾	66	35¼	21½	81¼	4¼	98½	19		115¼	32
Nantwich	48	34½	3¾	60½	49¾	34	67	58	54¼	83¾	71
Newton Bridge	14¼	60¾	30	47	76	20½	93¼	44½	40¾	110	57½
Newton Road	91¼	28¼	47	103¾	14¾	77¼	16¼	101¼	97¼	34½	114¼
Newton, or Warrington Jn.	15¼	59¾	29	48	75	21½	91¼	45½	41¾	109	58½
Northampton..................	143¼	99	99	155¾	62¼	129¼	45	153¼	149½	40¼	166¼
North & South Western Jn.		121	151¾	208½	115	182	97¾	206	202¼	93	219
Norton Bridge	63¼	11¾	19	75¾	27	49¼	44¼	73¼	69½	61	86¼
Nuneaton	105	30	60¾	117½	36¼	91	19½	115	111¼	19¼	128
Ordsall Lane.................	7¼	75¼	44½	32½	90½	6	107¾	30	26¼	124½	43
Oundle	172¾	97¾	128½	185¼	91¾	158¾	74½	182¾	179	69¾	195¾
Overton	183	108	138¾	195½	102	169	84¾	193	189¼	80	206
Oxford	186¼	111¼	142	198¾	105¼	172¼	88	196¼	192½	83¼	209¼
Parkside	13½	61½	30¾	46¼	76¾	19¾	94	43¾	40	110¾	56¾
Patricroft	3½	71½	40¾	36¼	86¾	9¾	104	33¾	30	120¾	46¾

M'Corquodale & Co., Printers.

LONDON & NORTH WESTERN RAILWAY—*Continued.*

STATIONS.	Lichfield.	Luffenham.	Macclesfield.	Manchester, Liverpool Road.	Manchester, London Road.	Manchester, Victoria.	North and South Western Junc.	Norton Bridge.	Oxford.	Parkside.	Patricroft.
Manchester, London Road	72½	141	17½	76	...		182¾	50	173	61¾	71¾
Manchester, Victoria	87¼	155¾		1¾		...	197½	64¾	187¾	15	5
Market Harbro	50¾	17¾	123¾	137¼	123¼		95	73¼	85¼	123	133
Marsdon........................	85	153½	29½	18¾	18¼		195¼	62½	185½	33	23¼
Marston Gate	82¼	84¾	155¼	168¾	154¾		54½	104¾	44¾	154½	164½
Marston Green	42	59¼	91½	105	91		101	41	91¼	90¾	100¾
Marton	41¼	43¾	114¼	127¾	113¾		85½	63¾	75¾	113½	123½
Medbourne Bridge	55¾	12¾	128¾	142¼	128¼		100	78¼	90¼	128	138
Minshull Vernon	46½	115	36½	40	36	40¾	156¾	24	147	25¾	35¾
Moore	62¼	130¾	52¼	24¼	51¾	25	172½	39¾	162¾	10	20
Morley	103¾	172¼	48¼	37½	37		214	81¼	204¼	51¾	42
Mossley	76¾	145¼	40	10½	10		187	54¼	177¼	24¾	15
Nantwich	45¼	113¾	35¼	48¾	34¾	49½	155½	22¾	145¾	34½	44½
Newton Bridge	71½	140	61½	15	61	15¾	181¾	49	172	¾	10¾
Newton Road	39	72¼	78½	92	78	92¾	114	28	104¼	77¾	87¾
Newton, or Warrington Jun.	70½	139	60½	16	60	16¾	180¾	48	171	1¾	11¾
Northampton..................	57½	60	130½	144	130		62¼	80	52½	129¾	139¾
North & South Western Jn.	110¼	112¾	183¾	196¾	182¾	197½	...	132¾	72¾	182½	192½
Norton Bridge	22½	91	50½	64	50	64¾	132¾	...	123	49¾	59¾
Nuneaton	19¼	49¼	92¼	105¾	91¾	106½	91	41¾	81¼	91½	101½
Ordsall Lane.................	86	154½	76	½	75½	1¼	196¼	63½	186½	13¾	3¾
Oundle	87	89½	160	173½	159½	174¼	91¾	109½	82	159¼	169¼
Overton........................	97¼	99¾	170¼	183¾	169¾	184½	102	119¾	92¼	169½	179½
Oxford	100½	103	173½	187	173	187¾	72¾	123	...	172¾	182¾
Parkside	72¼	140¾	62¼	14¼	61¾	15	182½	49¾	172¾	...	10
Patricroft	82¼	150¾	72¾	4¼	71¾	5	192½	59¾	182¾	10	...

LONDON & NORTH WESTERN RAILWAY—*Continued.*

STATIONS.	Peterboro'.	Preston Junc.	Rugby.	St. Helens Junc.	Sandbach.	Stafford.	Staleybridge.	Tamworth.	Walton Junction.	Warrington.	West London Junction.
Manchester, London Road	172½	61¾	105½	63	26¼	55¾	7½	78¾	54¼	55¼	183
Manchester, Victoria	187¼	15¼	120¼	19¾		70½	8¾	93½	22½	21½	197¾
Market Harbro	84¾	123	17¾	124¼	97	67½	125	44½	115½	116½	95¼
Marsden	185	33¼	118	37¾	38¾	68¼	10¾	91¼	40½	39¾	195½
Marston Gate	76¾	154½	49¼	155¾	128½	99	156½	76	147	148	54¾
Marston Green	90¾	90¾	23¾	92	64¾	35¼	92¾	35¾	83¼	84¼	101¼
Marton	75¼	113½	8¼	114¾	87½	58	115½	35	106	107	85¾
Medbourne Bridge	89¾	128	22¾	129¼	102	72½	130	49½	120½	121½	100¼
Minshull Vernon	146½	25¾	79½	27	9¾	29¾	48½	52¾	18¼	19¼	157
Moore	162¼	10	95¼	11¼	25½	45½	32¾	68½	2½	3½	172¾
Morley	203¾	52	136¾	56½	57½	87	29½	110	59¼	58¼	214¼
Mossley	176¾	25	109¾	29½	30½	60	2½	83	32¼	31¼	187¼
Nantwich	145¼	34½	78¼	35¾	8½	28½	36½	51½	27	28	155¾
Newton Bridge	171½	¾	104½	4	34¾	54¾	23½	77¾	6¾	5¾	182
Newton Road	103¾	77¾	36¾	79	51¾	22¼	79¾	45¼	70¼	71¼	114¼
Newton, or Warrington Jun.	170½	1¾	103½	3	33¾	53¾	24½	76¾	5¾	4¾	181
Northampton	42½	129¾	24½	131	103¾	74¼	131¾	51¼	122¼	123¼	62½
North & South Western Jn.	104¾	182½	77¼	183¾	156½	127	184½	104		176	¼
Norton Bridge	122½	49¾	55½	51	23¾	5¾	51¾	28¾	42¼	43¼	133
Nuneaton	80¾	91½	13¾	92¾	65½	36	93½	13	84	85	91¼
Ordsall Lane	186	14	119	18½	49¼	69¼	9	92¼	21¼	20¼	196½
Oundle	13	159¼	54	160½	133¼	103¾	161¼	80¾	151¾	152¾	92
Overton	2¾	169½	64¼	170¾	143½	114	171½	91	162	163	102¼
Oxford	95	172¾	67½	174	146¾	117¼	174¾	94¼	165¼	166¼	73
Parkside	172¼	¼	105¼	4¾	35½	55½	22¾	78½	7½	6½	182¾
Patricroft	182¼	10¼	115¼	14¾	45½	65½	12¾	88½	17½	16½	192¾

LONDON & NORTH WESTERN RAILWAY—*Continued.*

STATIONS.	Ardwick.	Banbury.	Bedford.	Bescot Junction.	Birmingham, B. and B.	Birmingham, Mid.	Birmingham, Stour Val. Junc.	Bletchley.	Bolton.	Bushbury Junc.	Camden.	Chester.
Penkridge	60¼	121	108	14½	24¾	24	23¾	89¾	72¾	8½	135¼	51¼
Perry Bar	80¾	100½	85½	6	4¼	3½	3¼	69¼	93¼	12	114¾	71¾
Peterboro'	171¾	94¾	79¾	106¼	96	96¾	96½	63½	184¼	112¼	109	162¾
Pinner	174	64½	49½	108½	98¼	99	98¾	33¼	186½	114½	12¼	165
Polesworth	81¾	90¼	75¼	46½	53½	52¾	52½	59	94¼	40½	104½	72¾
Poynton	10½	167½	152½	69¾	80½	79¾	79½	136¼	68½	64¼	181¾	47½
Poynton (Coal)	9¾	166¾	151¾	69	79¾	79	78¾	135½	67¾	63½	181	46½
Poplar	194¾	85¼	70¼	129¼	119	119¾	119½	54	207¼	135¼	8½	185¾
Prestbury	14½	171½	156½	73¾	84½	83¾	83½	140¼	72½	68¼	185¾	51¼
Preston Brook	48¾	160¼	145¼	63	73¼	72½	72¼	129	24¼	57	174½	39¾
Preston Junction ...	61	172½	157½	75¼	85½	84¾	84½	141¼	12¼	69¼	186¾	52
Rainhill	65	176½	161½	79¼	89½	88¾	88½	145¼	19½	73¼	190¾	56
Ridgemount	147¾	38¼	9¼	82¼	72	72¾	72½	7	160¼	88¼	52½	138¾
Ringstead	147¼	70¼	55¼	81¾	71½	72¼	72	39	159¾	87¾	84½	138¼
Roade..................	127½	44½	29½	62	51¾	52½	52¼	13¼	140	68	58¾	118½
Roby Lane	68¾	180¼	165¼	83	93¼	92½	92¼	149	23¼	77	194½	59¾
Rockingham Castle..		95	80	67	56¾	57½	57¼	63¾	145	73	109¼	123½
Rookery Bridge......	26¼	145¾	130¾	48½	58¾	58	57¾	114½	46¾	42½	160	25¼
Rudgeley	64	108	93	28¾	39	38¼	38	76¾	76½	22¾	122¼	55
Rugby	104¾	67¼	52¼	39¼	29	29¾	29½	36	117¼	45¼	81½	95¾
Saddleworth	12½	180¼	165¼	83	93¼	92½	92¼	149	35½	77	194½	59¾
St. Helens Junction	62¼	173¾	158¾	76½	86¾	86	85¾	142½	16¾	70½	188	53¼
Sandbach	25½	146½	131½	49¼	59½	58¾	58½	115¼	47½	43¼	160¾	26
Seaton	136½	99	84	71	60¾	61½	61¼	67¾	149	77	113¼	127½
Shepherds Bush	184¼	74¾	59¾	118¾	108½	109¼	109	43½	196¾	124¾	6	175¼
Shilton	97	76	61	47	34	34¾	34½	44¾	109½	50¼	90¼	38

LONDON & NORTH WESTERN RAILWAY—*Continued.*

STATIONS.	Clifton Junction.	Colwich.	Crewe.	Dewsbury Junc.	Dudley Port.	Guide Bridge.	Hampton.	Heaton Lodge.	Huddersfield.	Leamington.	Leeds.
Penkridge	74¼	11¼	30	86¾	16	60¼	33¼	84¼	80½	51½	97¼
Perry Bar	94¾	31¾	50½	107¼	11¼	80¾	12¾	104¾	101	31	117¾
Peterboro'	165¼	110¾	141½	198¼	104¾	171¾	87½	195¾	192	82¾	208¾
Pinner	188	113	143¾	200½	107	174	89¾	198	194¼	85	211
Polesworth	95¾	20¾	51½	108¼	48	81¾	28¾	105¾	102	28½	118¾
Poynton	70	56½	25¾	37	71¾	10½	89	33¾	30	104¾	46¾
Poynton (Coal)	69¼	55¾	25	36¼	71	9¾	88¼	33	29¼	105	46
Poplar	208¾	133¾	164½	221¼	127¾	194¾	110½	218¾	215	105¾	231¾
Prestbury	74	60½	29¾	41	75¾	14½	93	37¾	34	109¾	50¾
Preston Brook	25¾	49¼	18½	58½	64½	32	81¾	56	52¼	98½	69
Preston Junction	13¾	61½	30¾	46½	76¾	20	94	44	40¼	110¾	57
Rainhill	21	65½	34¾	53¾	80¾	27¼	98	51¼	47½	114¾	64¼
Ridgemount	161¾	86¾	117½	174¼	80¾	147¾	63½	171¾	168	58¾	184¾
Ringstead	161¼	86¼	117	173¾	80¼	147¼	63	171¼	167½	58¼	184¼
Roade	141½	66½	97¼	154	60½	127½	43¼	151½	147¾	38½	164½
Roby Lane	24¾	69¼	38½	57½	84½	31¾	101¾	55	51¼	118½	68
Rockingham Castle	146½	71½	102¼	159	65½	132½	48¼	156½	152¾	43½	169½
Rookery Bridge	48¼	34¾	4	52¾	50	26¼	67¼	50¼	46½	84	63¼
Rudgeley	78	3	33¾	90½	30¼	64	47½	88	84¼	46¼	101
Rugby	118¾	43¾	74½	131¼	37¼	104¾	20½	128¾	125	15¾	141¾
Saddleworth	21½	69¼	38½	18¼	84½	7½	101¾	15¾	12	118½	28¾
St. Helen's Junction	18¼	62¾	32	51	78	24½	95¼	48½	44¾	112	61½
Sandbach	49	35½	4¾	52	50¾	25½	68	49½	45¾	84¾	62½
Seaton	150½	75½	106¼	163	69½	136½	52¼	160½	156¾	47½	173½
Shepherds Bush	198¼	123¼	154	210¾	117¼	184¼	100	208¼	204½	95¼	221¼
Shilton	111	36	66¾	123½	42¼	97	29¼	121	117¼	24½	134

LONDON & NORTH WESTERN RAILWAY—*Continued.*

STATIONS.	Lichfield.	Luffenham.	Macclesfield.	Manchester, Liverpool Road.	Manchester, London Road.	Manchester, Victoria.	North & South Western Junc.	Norton Bridge.	Oxford.	Parkside.	Patricroft.
Penkridge	22	89¼	61½	75	61	75¾	131	11	121¼	60¾	70¾
Perry Bar	42½	68¾	82	95½	81½	96¼	110½	31½	100¾	81½	91¼
Peterboro'	100	102½	173	186½	172½	187¼	104¾	122½	95	172¼	182¼
Pinner	102¼	104¾	175¼	188¾	174¾	189½	8	124¾	64¾	174½	184½
Polesworth	10	58½	83	96½	82½	97¼	100¼	32½	90½	82¼	92¼
Poynton	67¼	135¾	6¼	70¾	11¼		177½	44¾	167¾	56½	66½
Poynton (Coal)	66½	135	7	70	10½		176¾	44	167	55¾	65¾
Poplar	123	125½	196	209½	195	210¼	12¾	145½	85½	195¼	205¼
Prestbury	71¼	139¾	2¼	15¾	15¼		181½	48¾	171¾	30	20
Preston Brook	60	128½	50	26½	49½	27¼	170¼	37½	160½	12¼	22¼
Preston Junction	72¼	140¾	62¼	14½	61¾	15¼	182½	49¾	172¾	¼	10¼
Rainhill	76¼	144¾	66¼	21¾	65¾	22½	186½	53¾	176¾	7½	17½
Ridgemount	76	78½	149	162½	148½	163¼	48¼	98½	38½	148¼	158¼
Ringstead	75½	78	148½	162	148	162¾	80¼	98	70½	147¾	157¾
Roade	55¾	58¼	128¾	142¼	128¼	143	54½	78¼	44¾	128	138
Roby Lane	80	148½	70	25½	69½	26¼	190¼	57½	180½	11¼	21¼
Rockingham Castle	60¾	7¾	133¾	147¼	133¼	148	105	83¼	95¼	133	143
Rookery Bridge	45½	114	28	49	27		155¾	23	146	34¾	44¾
Rudgeley	7¾	76¼	65¼	78¾	64¾	79½	118	14¾	108¼	64½	74½
Rugby	33	35½	106	119½	105½	120¼	77¼	55½	67½	105¼	115¼
Saddleworth	80	148½	25	13¾	13¼		190¼	57½	180½	28	18
St. Helens Junction	73½	142	63½	19	63	19¾	183¾	51	174	4¾	14¾
Sandbach	46¼	114¾	27¼	49¾	26¼		156½	23¾	146¾	35½	45½
Seaton	64¾	3¾	137¾	151¼	137¼	152	109	87¼	99¼	137	147
Shepherds Bush	112½	115	185½	199	185	199¾	2¼	135	75	184¾	194¾
Shilton	25¼	44¼	98½	111¾	98	112½	86	47¾	76¼	97½	107½

LONDON & NORTH WESTERN RAILWAY—*Continued.*

STATIONS.	Peterboro'.	Preston Junc.	Rugby.	St. Helen's Junc.	Sandbach.	Stafford.	Staley Bridge.	Tamworth.	Walton Junc.	Warrington.	West London Junction.
Penkridge	120¾	60¾	53¾	62	34¾	5¼	62¾	28¼	53¼	54¼	131¼
Perry Bar	100¼	81¼	33¼	82½	55¼	25¾	83¼	48¾	73¾	74¾	110¾
Peterboro'	...	172¼	67	173½	146¼	116¾	174¼	93¾	164¾	165¾	105
Pinner	96¾	174½	69¼	175¾	148½	119	176½	96	167	168	8¼
Polesworth	90	82¼	23	83½	56¼	26¾	84¼	3¾	74¾	75¾	100½
Poynton	167¼	56½	100¼	57¾	21	50½	13	73½	49	50	177¾
Poynton (Coal)	166½	55¾	99½	57	20¼	49¾	12¼	72¾	48¼	49¼	177
Poplar	117½	195¼	90	196½	169¼	139¾	197¼	116¾	187¾	188¾	12½
Prestbury	171¼	30¼	104¼	34¾	25	54½	17	77½	37½	36½	181¾
Preston Brook	160	12¼	93	13½	28¼	43¼	35	66¼	4¾	5¾	170½
Preston Junction	172¼	...	105¼	4¾	35½	55½	23	78½	7½	6½	182¾
Rainhill	176¼	7½	109¼	2¾	39½	59½	30¼	82½	11½	10½	186¾
Ridgemount	70½	148¼	43	149½	122¼	92¾	150¼	69¾	140¾	141¾	48½
Ringstead	24½	147¾	42½	149	121¾	92¼	149¾	69¼	140¼	141¼	80½
Roade	50¼	128	22¾	129¼	102	72½	130	49½	120½	121½	54¾
Roby Lane	180	11¼	113	6½	43¼	63¼	33½	86¼	15¼	14¼	190½
Rockingham Castle	94¾	133	27¾	134¼	107	77½	135	54½	125½	126½	105¼
Rookery Bridge	145½	34¾	78½	36	¾	28¾	28¾	51¾	27¼	28¼	156
Rudgeley	107¾	64½	40¾	65¾	38½	9	66½	14	57	58	118¼
Rugby	67	105¼	...	106½	79¼	49¾	107¼	26¾	97¾	98¾	77½
Saddleworth	180	28¼	113	32¾	36¼	63¼	5¾	86¼	60¼	59¼	190½
St. Helens Junction	173½	4¾	106½	...	36¾	56¾	27	79¾	8¾	7¾	184
Sandbach	146¼	35½	79¼	36¾	...	29½	28	52½	28	29	156¾
Seaton	98¾	137	31¾	138¼	111	81½	139	58½	129½	130½	109¼
Shepherds Bush	107	184¾	79½	186	158¾	129¼	186¾	106¼	177¼	178¼	2
Shilton	75¾	97½	8¾	98¾	71½	42	99½	19	90	91	86¼

LONDON & NORTH WESTERN RAILWAY—*Continued.*

STATIONS.	Ardwick.	Banbury.	Bedford.	Bescot Junction.	Birmingham, B. and B.	Birmingham, Mid.	Birmingham, Stour Val. Junc.	Bletchley.	Bolton.	Bushbury Junc.	Camden.	Chester.
Slaithwaite	20	187¾	172¾	90½	100¾	100	99¾	156½	48	84½	202	67¼
Smethwick............	79¾	101	86	14	4¾	4½	4¼	69¾	92¼	11	115¼	70¾
Spon Lane............	79	102	87	15	5¾	5½	5¼	70¾	91¼	10	116¼	69¾
Spread Eagle.........	62½	118¾	103¾	12¼	22½	21¾	21½	87½	75	6¼	133	53½
Stafford	55	117	102	19¾	30	29¼	29	85¾	67½	13¾	131¼	46
Staley Bridge	6¾	174½	159½	77¼	87½	86¾	86½	143¼	29¾	71¼	188¾	54
Stamford	146	108½	93½	80½	70¼	71	70¾	77¼	158	86½	122¾	137
Stanbridge Ford												
Standon Bridge	45¼	126¾	111¾	29½	39¾	39	38¾	95½	57¾	23½	141	36¼
Stanford Hall.........	110¼	72¾	57¾	44¾	34½	35¼	35	41½	122¾	50¾	87	101¼
Stetchford	87½	93½	78½	12¾	2½	3¼	3	62¼	100	18¾	108	78½
Stockport	5	167	152	69¾	80	79¼	79	135¾	68	63¾	181¼	46½
Stretton	100½	71¾	56¾	43¾	33½	34¼	34	40½	112¾	49¾	86	91¼
Sudbury	179¼	69¾	54¾	113¾	103½	104¼	104	38½	191¾	119¾	7	170¼
Sutton, or Lea Green	21¼	175¼	160¼	78	88¼	87½	87¼	144	18¼	72	189½	54¾
Swanbourne	146¼	25¾	21¾	80¾	70½	71¼	71	5½	158¾	86¾	51	137¼
Sykes Junction	5¼	166¾	151¾	69½	79¾	79	78¾	135½	67¾	63½	181	46¼
Tamworth	78	94	79	42¾	41	41¾	41¾	62¾	90½	36¾	108¼	69
Tattenhall	44¾	156¼	141¼	59	69¼	68½	68¼	125	57¼	53	170½	6¾
Theddingworth	117½	80	65	52	41¾	42½	42¼	48¾	130	58	94¼	108½
Thorpe	153	76	61	87½	77¼	78	77¾	44¾	165½	93½	90¼	144
Thrapstone	150½	73½	58	85	74¾	75½	75¼	42¼	163	91	87¾	141½
Tipton	75¼	105½	90½	12½	9¼	9	8¾	74¼	87¾	6½	119¾	66¼
Tring	155¾	46¼	31¼	90¼	80	80¾	80½	15	168¼	96¼	30½	146¾
Walton		165	150	67¾		77¼		133¾	19½		179¼	44½
Wansford	165½	88½	73½	100	89¾	90½	90¼	57¼	178	106	102¾	156½

LONDON & NORTH WESTERN RAILWAY—*Continued.*

STATIONS.	Clifton Junction.	Colwich.	Crewe.	Dewsbury Junc.	Dudley Port.	Guide Bridge.	Hampton.	Heaton Lodge.	Huddersfield.	Leamington.	Leeds.
Slaithwaite	29	76¾	46	10¾	92	15	109¼	8¼	4½	126	21¼
Smethwick	93¾	30¾	49½	106¼	3½	79¾	13¾	103¾	100	32	116¾
Spon Lane	92¾	29¾	48¾	105½	2½	79	14¾	103	99¼	33	116
Spread Eagle	76½	13½	32¼	89	13¾	62½	31	86½	82¾	49¼	99½
Stafford	69	6	24¾	81½	21¼	55	38½	79	75¼	55¼	92
Staleybridge	15¾	63½	32¾	24	78¾	1¾	96	21½	17¾	112¾	34½
Stamford	160	85	115¾	172½	79	146	61¾	170	166¼	57	183
Stanbridge Ford											
Standon Bridge	59¼	15¾	15	71¾	31	45¼	48¼	69¼	65½	65	82¼
Stanford Hall	124¼	49¼	80	136¾	43¼	110¼	26	134¼	130½	21¼	147¼
Stetchford	101½	38½	57¼	114	11¼	87½	6	111½	107¾	24¼	124½
Stockport	69½	56	25¼	31½	71¼	5	88½	29	25¼	105¼	42
Stretton	114¼	39¼	70	126¼	41¾	100½	25	124¼	120½	20¼	137¼
Sudbury	193¼	118¼	149	205¾	112¼	179¼	95	203¼	199½	90¼	216¼
Sutton, or Lea Green	19¾	64¼	33½	53¼	79½	25½	96¾	87¾	84	113½	63
Swanbourne	160¼	85¼	116	172¾	79¼	146¼	62	170¼	166½	57¼	183¼
Sykes Junction	69¼	55¾	25	31¾	71	5¼	88¼	29¼	25½	105	42¼
Tamworth	92	17	47¾	104½	44¼	78	32½	102	98¼	32¼	115
Tattenhall	58¾	45¼	14½	71¼	60½	44¾	77¾	69	65	94½	81¾
Theddingworth	131½	56½	87¼	144	50¼	117½	33¼	141½	137¾	28½	154½
Thorpe	167	91½	122¾	179½	86	153	68¾	177	173¼	64	190
Thrapstone	164½	89½	120¼	177	83½	150½	66¼	174½	170¾	61½	187½
Tipton	89¼	26¼	45	101¾	1	75¼	18¼	99¼	95½	36½	112¼
Tring	169¾	94¾	125½	182¼	88¾	155¾	71½	179¾	176	66¾	192¾
Walton		54	23¼	54¾	69¼	27¼	86½	51¼	47½	103¼	64¼
Wansford	179½	104½	135¼	192	98½	165½	81¼	189½	185¾	76½	202½

M'Corquodale & Co., Printers.

LONDON & NORTH WESTERN RAILWAY—*Continued.*

STATIONS.	Lichfield.	Luffenham.	Macclesfield.	Manchester, Liverpool Road.	Manchester, London Road.	Manchester, Victoria.	North and South Western Junc.	Norton Bridge.	Oxford.	Parkside.	Patricroft.
Slaithwaite	87½	156	32½	21¼	20¾		197¾	65	188	36½	25½
Smethwick	41½	69¼	81	94½	80½	95¼	111	30½	101¼	80¼	90¼
Spon Lane	40½	70¼	80¼	93½	79¾	94¼	112	29½	102¼	79¼	89¼
Spread Eagle	24¼	87	63¾	77¼	63¼	78	128¾	13¼	119	63	73
Stafford	16¾	85¼	56¼	69¾	55¾	70½	127	5¾	117¼	55½	65½
Staleybridge	74¼	142¾	19¼	8	7½	8¾	184½	51¾	174¾	22¾	12¾
Stamford	74¼	5¾	147¼	160¾	146¾	161½	118½	96¾	108¾	146½	156½
Stanbridge Ford											
Standon Bridge	26½	95	46½	60	46	60¾	136¾	4	73	45¾	55¾
Stanford Hall	38½	30	111½	125	111	125¾	82¾	61	127	110¾	120¾
Stetchford	44¾	62	88¾	102¼	88¼	103	103¾	38¼	93¾	88	98
Stockport	66¾	135¼	11¾	6¼	5¾		177	44¼	167¼	56	66
Stretton	28½	40	101½	115	101	115¾	81¾	51	72	100¾	110¾
Sudbury	107½	110	180½	194	180	194¾	2¾	130	70	179¾	189¾
Sutton, or Lea Green	75	143½	105¾	20½	64½	21¼	185¼	52½	175½	6¼	16¼
Swanbourne	74½	77	147½	161	147	161¾	46¾	97	37	146¾	156¾
Sykes Junction	66½	135	11½	6½	6		176¾	44	167	55¾	65¾
Tamworth	6¼	62¼	79¼	92¾	78¾	93½	104	28¾	94¼	78½	88½
Tattenhall	56	124½	46	59½	45½	60¼	166¼	33½	156½	45¼	55¼
Theddingworth	45¾	22¾	118¾	132¼	118¼	133	90	33½	80¼	118	128
Thorpe	81¼	83¾	154¼	167¾	153¾	168½	86	103¾	76¼	153½	163½
Thrapstone	78¾	81¼	151¾	165¼	151¼	166	83	101¼	73¾	151	161
Tipton	37	73¾	76½	90	76	90¾	115½	26	105¾	75¾	85¾
Tring	84	86½	157	170½	156½	171¼	26¼	106½	46½	156¼	166¼
Walton	64¾	133¼	55¼	21¾	54¼	22½		42¼	165¼	7½	17½
Wansford	93¾	96¼	166¾	180¼	166¼	181	98½	116¼	88¾	166	176

LONDON & NORTH WESTERN RAILWAY—*Continued.*

STATIONS.	Peterboro'.	Preston Junction.	Rugby.	St. Helens Junc.	Sandbach.	Stafford.	Staleybridge.	Tamworth.	Walton Junction.	Warrington.	West London Junction.
Slaithwaite	187½	36¾	120½	40¼	43¾	70¾	13¼	93¾	67¾	66¾	198
Smethwick	100¾	80¼	33¾	81½	54¼	24¾	82¼	47¾	72¾	73¾	111¼
Spon Lane	101¾	79¼	34¾	80½	53½	23¾	81½	46¾	71¾	72¾	112¼
Spread Eagle	118½	63	51½	64¼	37	7½	65	30½	55½	56½	129
Stafford	116¾	55½	49¾	56¾	29½	...	57½	23	48	49	127¼
Staleybridge	174¼	23	107¼	27	28	57½	...	80½	54½	28¾	184¾
Stamford	108¼	146½	41¼	147¾	120½	91	148½	68	139	140	118¾
Stanbridge Ford											
Standon Bridge	126½	45¾	59½	47	19¾	9¾	47¾	32¾	38¼	39¼	137
Stanford Hall	72½	110¾	5½	112	84¾	55¼	112¾	32¼	103¼	104¼	83
Stetchford	93½	88	26½	89¼	62	32½	90	38½	80½	81½	104
Stockport	166¾	56	99¾	57¼	20½	50	7½	73	48½	49½	177¼
Stretton	71½	100¾	4½	102	74¾	45¼	102¾	22¼	93¼	94¼	82
Sudbury	102	179¾	74½	181	153¾	124¼	181¾	101¼	172¼	173¼	3
Sutton, or Lea Green	175	6¼	108	1½	38¼	58¼	28½	81¼	10¼	9¼	185½
Swanbourne	69	146¾	41½	148	120¾	91¼	148¾	68¼	139¼	140¼	47
Sykes Junction	166½	55¾	99½	57	20¼	49¾	7¾	72¾	48¼	49¼	177
Tamworth	93¾	78½	26¾	79¾	52½	23	80½	...	71	72	104¼
Tattenhall	156	45¼	89	46½	19¼	39¼	47¼	62¼	37¾	38¾	166½
Theddingworth	79¾	118	12¾	119¼	92	62½	120	39½	110½	111½	90¼
Thorpe	18¾	153½	48¼	154¾	127½	98	155½	75	146	147	86¼
Thrapstone	21¼	151	45¾	152¼	125	95½	153	72½	143½	144½	83¾
Tipton	105¼	75¾	38¼	77	49¾	20¼	77¾	43¼	68¼	69¼	115¾
Tring	78½	156¼	51	157½	130¼	100¾	158¼	77¾	148¾	149¾	26½
Walton	164¾	7½	97¾	8¾	28	48	54½	71	...	1	175¼
Wansford	6¼	166	60¾	167¼	140	110½	168	87½	158½	159½	98¾

LONDON & NORTH WESTERN RAILWAY—*Continued:*

STATIONS.	Ardwick.	Banbury.	Bedford.	Bescot Junction.	Birmingham, B. and B.	Birmingham, Mid.	Birmingham, Stour Val. Junc.	Bletchley.	Bolton.	Bushbury Junc.	Camden.	Chester.
Warrington	21	166	151	68¾	79	78¼	78	134¾	18½	62¾	180¼	45½
Watford	169¾	60¼	45¼	104¼	94	94¾	90½	29	182¼	110¼	16½	160¾
Waverton	47½	159	144	61¾	72	71¼	71	127¾	60	55¾	173¼	4
Weaste Lane.........	3	184½	169½	87¼	97½	96¾	96½	153¼	19½	79¼	198¾	64
Wednesfield Heath...	70	111¼	96¼	4¾	15	14¼	14½	80	82½	1¼	125½	61
Weedon	117¾	54¼	39¼	52¼	42	42¾	42½	23	130¼	58¼	68½	108¾
Welford	114¼	76¾	61¾	48¾	38½	39¼	39	45½	126¾	54¾	91	105¼
Wellingboro'	140¼	63¼	48¼	74¾	64½	65¼	65	32	152¾	80¾	77½	131¼
West London Junc..	182¼	72¾	57¾	116¾	106½	107¼	107	41½	194¾	122¾	4	173¼
Whitmore	41	131	116	33¾	44	43¼	43	99¾	53½	27¾	145¼	32
Willenhall	72¼	109	94	2½	12¾	12	11¾	77¾	84¾	3½	123¼	63½
Willesden	181¼	71¾	56¾	115¾	105½	106¼	106	40½		121¾	5	172¼
Wilmslow	11¼	160¾	145¾	63½	73¼	73	72¾	129½	61¾	57½	175	40¼
Winsford	37½	149	134	51¾	62	61¼	61	117¾	35½	45¾	163¼	28½
Winslow	148¼	38¾	23¾	82¾	72½	73¼	73	7½	160¾	88¾	53	139¼
Woburn	145	35½	21	79½	69¼	70	69¾	4¼	157½	85½	49¾	136
Wolverhampton, Stour Valley, ...	70¼	110½	95½	7½	14¼	14	13¾	79¼	82¾	1½	124¾	61¼
Wolverton	135	37	22	69½	59¼	60	59¾	5¾	147½	75½	51¼	126
Wortley	39¾	207½	192½	110¼	120½	119¾	119½	176¼	114¾	104¼	221¾	87

LONDON & NORTH WESTERN RAILWAY—*Continued.*

STATIONS.	Clifton Junction.	Colwich.	Crewe.	Dewsbury Junc.	Dudley Port.	Guide Bridge.	Hampton.	Heaton Lodge.	Huddersfield.	Leamington.	Leeds.
Warrington	20	55	24¼	52¾	70¼	26¼	87½	50¼	46½	104¼	63¼
Watford	185¾	108¾	189½	196¼	102¾	169¾	85½	193¾	190	80¾	206¾
Waverton	61½	48	17¼	74	63¼	47½	80½	71½	67¾	97¼	84½
Weaste Lane	5½	78½	42¾	35½	88¾	6¾	106	97	93¼	122¾	44¾
Wednesfield Heath	84	21	39¾	70	8¾	74¼	23½	94	110½	41¾	126¾
Weedon	131¾	56¾	87½	144¼	50¾	117¾	33½	141¾	138	28¾	154¾
Welford	128¼	53¼	84	140¾	47¼	114¼	30	138¼	134½	25¼	151¼
Wellingboro'	154¼	79¼	110	166¾	73¼	140¼	56	164¼	160½	51¼	177¼
West London Junction	196¼	121¼	152	208¾	115¼	182¼	98	206¼	202½	93¼	219¼
Whitmore	55	20	10¾	67½	35¼	41	52½	65	61¼	69¼	78
Willenhall	86¼	23¼	42	98¾	12	72¼	21¼	96¼	92½	39½	109¼
Willesden	195¼	120¼	151	207¾	114¼	181¼	97	205¼	201½	92¼	218¼
Wilmslow	63¼	49¾	19	37¾	65	11¼	82¼	35¼	31½	99	48¼
Winsford	37	38	7¼	68	53¼	41¾	70½	67¼	63¾	87¼	79¾
Winslow	162¼	87¼	118	174¾	81¼	148¼	64	172¼	168½	59¼	185¼
Woburn	159	84	114¾	171½	78	145	60¾	169	165¼	56	182
Wolverhampton, Stour Valley	84¼	21¼	40	70¼	6	74½	23¼	94¼	110¾	41½	127
Wolverton	149	74	104¾	161½	68	135	50¾	159	155¼	46	172
Wortley	48¾	96½	65¾	9	111¾	34¾	129	11½	15¼	145¾	1½

LONDON & NORTH WESTERN RAILWAY—*Continued.*

STATIONS.	Lichfield.	Luffenham.	Macclesfield.	Manchester, Liverpool Road.	Manchester, London Road.	Manchester, Victoria.	North and South Western Junc.	Norton Bridge.	Oxford.	Parkside.	Patricroft.
Warrington	65¾	134¼	55¾	20¾	55¼	21½	176	43¼	166¼	6½	16½
Watford	98	100½	171	184½	170½	185¼	12¼	120½	60½	170¼	180¼
Waverton	58¾	127¼	48¾	62¼	48¼	63	169	36¼	159¼	48	58
Weaste Lane	84¼	152¾	74¼	2¼	73¾	3	194½	61¾	184¾	12	2
Wednesfield Heath	31¾	79½	71¾	84¾	70¾	85½	121¼	20¾	111½	70½	80½
Weedon'	46	48½	119	132½	118½		64¼	68½	54½	118¼	128¼
Welford	42½	26	115½	129	115	129¾	86¾	65	77	114¾	124¾
Wellingboro'	68½	70½	141½	155	141	155¾	73¼	91	63½	140¾	150¾
West London Junction	110½	113	183½	197	183	197¾	½	133	73	182¾	192¾
Whitmore	30¾	99¼	42¼	55¾	41¾	56½	141	8¼	131¼	41½	51½
Willenhall	34	77¼	73½	87	73	87¾	119	23	109¼	72¾	82¾
Willesden	109½	112	182½	196	182	196¾	¾	132	72	181¾	191¾
Wilmslow	60½	129	12		12		170¾	38	161	49¾	59¾
Winsford	48¾	117¼	44¼	37¾	38¼	38½	159	26¼	149¼	23½	33½
Winslow	76½	79	149½	163	149	163¾	48¾	99	24	148¾	158¾
Woburn	73¼	75¾	146¼	159¾	145¾	160½	45½	95¾	35¾	145½	155½
Wolverhampton, Stour Valley	32	78¾	72	85	71	85¾	120½	21	110¾	70¾	80¾
Wolverton	63¼	65¾	136¼	149¾	135¾	150½	47	85¾	37¼	135½	145½
Wortley	127½	175¾	52¼	41	40½		217½	84¾	207¾	55½	45½

LONDON & NORTH WESTERN RAILWAY—*Continued.*

STATIONS.	Peterboro'.	Preston Junction.	Rugby.	St. Helens Junc.	Sandbach.	Stafford.	Staleybridge.	Tamworth.	Walton Junction.	Warrington.	West London Junction.
Warrington	165¾	6½	98¾	7¾	29	49	28¾	72	1	...	176½
Watford	92½	170¼	65	171½	144¼	114¾	172¼	91¾	162¾	163¾	12½
Waverton	158¾	48	91¾	49¼	22	42	50	65	40½	41½	169½
Weaste Lane	184¼	12¼	117¼	16¾	27½	67½	10¼	90½	19½	18½	194¾
Wednesfield Heath	111	70½	44	71¾	44½	15	72½	38	63	64	121½
Weedon	54	118¼	13	119½	92¼	62¾	120¼	39¾	110¾	111¾	64½
Welford	76½	114¾	9½	116	88¾	59¼	116¾	36¼	107¼	108¼	87
Wellingboro'	81½	140¾	35½	142	114¾	85¼	142¾	62¼	133¼	134¼	78½
West London Junction	105	182¾	77½	184	156¾	127½	184¾	104¼	175¼	176¼	...
Whitmore	130¾	41½	63¾	42¾	15½	14	43½	37	34	35	141¼
Willenhall	108¾	72¾	41¾	74	46¾	17¼	74¾	40¼	65¼	66¼	119¾
Willesden	104	181¾	76½	183	155¾	126¼	183¾	103¼	174¼	175¼	1
Wilmslow	160½	49¾	93½	51	14¼	43¾	13¾	66¾	42¼	43¼	171
Winsford	148¾	23½	81¾	24¾	12	32	40	55	16	17	159¼
Winslow	71	148¾	43½	150	122¾	93¼	150¾	70¼	141¼	142¼	49
Woburn	67¾	145½	40¼	146¾	119½	90	147½	67	138	139	45¾
Wolverhampton, Stour Valley	110¾	70¾	43¼	72	44¾	15½	72¾	38¼	63¼	64¼	120¾
Wolverton	57¾	135½	30¼	136¾	109½	80	137½	57	128	129	47¼
Wortley	207¼	55½	140¼	60	61	90½	33	113½	62¾	61¾	217¾

LONDON & SOUTH WESTERN RAILWAY.

STATIONS.	Basingstoke.	Dorchester.	Guildford.	Kew Junction.	Portsmouth.	Waterloo.	Windsor.				
Addlestone	30	122½	12¾	26¾	76¼	21	38¼				
Alton	48¼	140¾	18¾	55	95	49	71				
Andover Road	10½	82	39¾	64	35¾	58¼	75½				
Ash	35	127½	6	42	81¼	36¼	53½				
Ashford	57	149½	39¾	8¾	103¼	17½	8				
Barnes	46¾	139¼	29½	2¾	93	7¼	18¼				
Basingstoke	...	92½	29¼	53¾	46¼	47¾	65				
Beaulieu Road	41¾	50¾	71	95½	37	89½	106¼				
Bishopstoke	25½	67	54¾	79¼	20¾	73¼	90½				
Blechynden	34	59½	62¼	86¼	28¼	80¾	98				
Botley	31¼	72¾	60½	84¾	15	79	96¼				
Brentford	50¼	142¾	33	¾	96½	10¾	15				
Brockenhurst	46½	46	75¾	100	41¾	94¼	111½				
Chandlers Ford	27½	69	56¾	81¼	22¾	75¼	92½				
Chertsey	31½	124	14½	28¼	78	22¼	39½				
Chiswick	48¼	140¾	31	1¼	94½	8¾	17				
Christchurch Road	51½	41	80¾	105	46¾	99¼	116½				
Clapham Common	43½	136	26¼	10½	89¾	4¼	21½				
Cosham	42¼	83¾	71½	96	4	90	107¼				
Datchet	63¼	155¾	46	15	109½	23¾	1¾				
Dean	40½	82	69¾	94	35¾	88¼	105½				
Dorchester	92½	...	121¾	146¼	87¾	140¼	157½				
Dunbridge	36½	78	65¾	90¼	31¾	84¼	101½				
Esher	33¼	125¾	16	20½	79½	14½	31¾				
Eling	36½	56	66	90¼	32¼	84¼	109¾				
Fareham	36½	78	65¾	90¼	9¾	84¼	101½				

LONDON & SOUTH WESTERN RAILWAY—*Continued.*

STATIONS.	Basingstoke.	Dorchester.	Guildford.	Kew Junction.	Portsmouth.	Waterloo.	Windsor.
Farnboro'	14½	107	14¾	39¼	60¾	33¼	50½
Farnham	39¼	131¾	10	46½	85½	40½	57¾
Feltham	54¼	146¾	37	6	100½	14¾	10¾
Fleetpond	11	103½	18¼	42¾	57¼	36¾	54
Godalming	32¾	125¼	3½	39½	79	34	51¼
Gosport	41½	83	70¾	95	14¾	89¼	106½
Guildford	29¼	121¾	...	36½	75½	30½	47¾
Hampton Court	36	128½	18¾	21	82¼	15	32¼
Hounslow	53	145½	35¾	3½	99¼	13½	12¼
Isleworth	51¾	144¼	34½	2	98	12¼	13½
Kew	49¼	141¾	32	¼	95½	9¾	16
Kew Junction	53¾	146¼	36½	...	100½	9¾	16¾
Kingston	35¾	128¼	18½	18	82	12	29¼
Lyndhurst Road	39¼	53¼	68½	92¾	34½	87	104¼
Malden	37¾	130¼	20½	15¾	84	10	27¼
Moreton	86¾	5¾	116	140½	82	134½	151¾
Mortlake	47¾	140¼	30½	9	94	8¼	17¼
Nine Elms	46	137¾	29	8	92	2	24
Poole	74½	21½	103¾	128	69¾	122¼	139½
Poole Junction	72¾	19¾	102	126¼	68	120½	137¾
Porchester	39¾	81¼	69	93¼	6½	87½	104¾
Portsmouth	46¼	87¾	75½	100½	...	94	111¼
Putney	45½	138	28¼	4	91¾	6	19½
Redbridge	35¾	56¾	65	89¼	31	83½	100¾
Richmond	49¼	141¾	32	7½	95½	9¾	15¾
Ringwood	57½	35	86¾	111	52¾	105¼	122½

M'Corquodale and Co., Printers.

LONDON & SOUTH WESTERN RAILWAY—*Continued.*

STATIONS.	Basingstoke.	Dorchester.	Guildford.	Kew Junction.	Portsmouth.	Waterloo.	Windsor.
Romsey	32¾	74¼	62	86½	28	80½	97¾
Salisbury	47½	89	76¾	101	42¾	95¼	112½
Southampton	31¼	61¼	60½	85	26½	79	96¼
Staines	58½	151	41¼	10¼	104¾	19	6½
Twickenham	51	143½	33¾	6	97¼	11½	14
Vauxhall	46¼	138¾	29	8¼	92½	1½	24
Walton	30¾	123¼	13½	23	77	17	34¼
Wandsworth	44½	137	27¼	5	90¾	5	20½
Wareham	77½	15	106¾	131	72¾	125¼	142½
Waterloo (London)	47¾	140¼	30½	9¾	94	...	25½
Weybridge	28¾	121¼	11½	25	75	19	36¼
Wimbledon	40¼	132¾	23	13½	86½	7½	24¾
Wimborne	66¾	25¾	90	120½	62	114½	131¾
Winchester	18¾	73¾	48	72½	27½	66½	83¾
Winchfield	8½	101	20¾	45	54¾	39¼	56½
Windsor	65	157½	47¾	16¾	111¼	25½	...
Woking	23¼	115¾	6	30½	69½	24½	41¾
Wool	82½	10	111¾	136	77¾	130¼	147½
Wraysbury	61¼	153¾	44	13	107½	21¾	3¾

LOWESTOFT RAILWAY.

STATIONS.	Reedham.										
Haddiscoe	3½										
Lowestoft	11¼										
Mutford	9¾										
Reedham	...										
Somerleyton	5¾										

MALTON & DRIFFIELD JUNCTION RAILWAY.

STATIONS.	Driffield.	Malton.									
Burdale	11	9									
Driffield	...	20									
Fimber	8½	11½									
Garton	3	17									
Malton	20	...									
North Grimston	15	5									
Settrington	16½	3½									
Wetwang	6½	13½									
Wharram	13	7									

MANCHESTER, SHEFFIELD, & LINCOLN RAILWAY.

STATIONS.	Ardwick.	Ashton.	Beighton.	Gainsboro'.	Great Grimsby.	Guide Bridge.	Hull.	Lincoln.	Manchester.	New Holland.	Penistone.	Retford.	Sheffield.	Staleybridge.
Ardwick	...	5½	47½	73¾	109½	4¼	109¼	83¾	¾	106¼	27¼	64¼	40½	6¾
Ashton	5½	...	44½	70¾	106½	1¼	106¼	80¾	6¼	103¼	24¼	61¼	37½	1¼
Barnetby	94	91	48¾	20¼	15½	89¾	15¼	29½	94¼	12¼	66¾	29¾	53½	92¼
Barrow Haven	108	105	62¾	34¼	18	103¾	4¾	43½	108¾	1¾	80¾	43¾	67½	106¼
Barton	110	107	64¾	36¼	20	105¾	6¾	45½	110¾	3¾	82¾	45¾	69½	108¼
Beighton	47½	44½	...	28½	64¼	43¼	64	39	48½	61	20¼	19	7	45¾
Blyton	78½	75½	33¼	4¾	31	74¼	30¾	45	79¼	27¾	51¼	14¼	38	76¾
Brigg	90¼	87¼	45	16½	19¼	86	19	33¼	91	16	63	26	49¾	88½
Broadbottom	9¼	6¼	38¼	64½	100¼	5	100	74½	10	97	18	55	31¼	7½
Brocklesby	98¾	95¾	53½	25	10¾	94½	10½	34¼	99½	7½	71½	34½	58¼	97
Checker House	60¼	57¼	15	13½	49¼	56	49	23¾	61	46	33	4	19¾	58½
Cottam	72¼	69¼	27	10½	46¼	68	46	12	73	43	45	8	31¾	70½
Darnall	43	40	4½	30¾	66½	38¾	66¼	40½	43¾	63¼	15¾	21¼	2½	41¼
Deepcar	32¾	29¾	14¾	41	76¾	28½	76½	51	33½	73½	5½	31½	7¾	31
Dinting	11¼	8¼	36¼	62½	98¼	7	98	72½	12	95	16	53	29¼	9½
Dog Lane	4¾	1¾	42¾	69	104¾	½	104½	79	5½	101½	22½	59½	35¾	3
Dukinfield	5	½	44	70¼	106	¾	105¾	80¼	5¾	102¾	23¾	60¾	37	1¾
Dunford Bridge	21¾	18¾	25¾	52	87¾	17½	87½	62	22½	84½	5½	42½	18¾	20
Fairfield	2¾	2¾	44¾	71	106¾	1½	106½	81	3½	103½	24½	61½	37¾	4
Gainsboro'	73¾	70¾	28½	...	35¾	69½	35½	49¾	74½	32½	46½	9½	33¼	72
Glossop	12¼	9¼	37¼	63½	99¼	8	99	73½	13	96	17	54	30¼	10½
Gorton	1¾	3¾	45¾	72	107¾	2½	107½	82	2½	104½	25½	62½	38¾	5
Goxhill	104	101	58¾	30¼	14	99¾	5¼	39½	104¾	2¼	76¾	39¾	63½	102¼
Greatcoates	107½	104½	62¼	33¾	2	103¼	17¼	43	108¼	14¼	80¼	43¼	67	105¾
Great Grimsby	109½	106½	64¼	35¾	...	105¼	19¼	45	110¼	16¼	82¼	45¼	69	107¾
Great Grimsby Docks	111	108	65¾	37¼	1½	106¾	20¾	46½	111¾	17¾	83¾	46¾	70½	109¼

In this Table, only the actual distance of the Ferry between New Holland and Hull is included.

MANCHESTER, SHEFFIELD, & LINCOLN RAILWAY—*Continued.*

STATIONS.	Ardwick.	Ashton.	Beighton.	Gainsboro'.	Great Grimsby.	Guide Bridge.	Hull.	Lincoln.	Manchester.	New Holland.	Penistone.	Retford.	Sheffield.	Staleybridge.
Guide Bridge.........	4¼	1¼	43¼	69½	105¼	...	105	79½	5	102	23	60	36¼	2½
Haboro'...............	101½	98½	56¼	27¾	8	97¼	11¼	37	102¼	8¼	74¼	37¼	61	99¾
Hadfield...............	12	9	35½	61¾	97½	7¾	97¼	71¾	12¾	94¼	15¼	52¼	28½	10¼
Hazlehead Bridge ...	24¼	21¼	23¼	49½	85¼	20	85	59½	25	82	3	40	16¼	22½
Holton	103	100	57¾	29¼	24½	98¾	24¼	20½	103¾	21¼	75¾	38¾	62½	101¼
Howsham	98	95	52¾	24¼	19½	93¾	19¼	25½	98¾	16¼	70¾	33¾	57½	96¼
Hull	109¼	106¼	64	35½	19¼	105	...	44¾	110	3	82	45	68¾	107½
Kirton Lindsay	84	81	38¾	10¼	25½	79¾	25¼	39½	84¾	22¼	56¾	19¾	43½	82¼
Kiveton Park.........	51¼	48¼	6	22½	58¼	47	58	32¾	52	55	24	13	10¾	49½
Langworth............	90¼	87¼	45½	23¼	38½	86	38¼	6½	91	35¼	63	26¼	49½	88½
Leverton	70	67	24¾	8	43¾	65¾	43½	14	70¾	40½	42¾	5½	29½	68¼
Lincoln	83¾	80¾	39	49¾	45	79½	44¾	...	84½	41¾	56½	19¾	43	82
Manchester	¾	6¼	48¼	74½	110¼	5	110	84½	...	107	28	65	41¼	7½
Market Rasen	98¾	95¾	54	31¾	30	94½	29¾	15	99½	26¾	71½	34¾	58	97
Melton Ross Siding	95¾	92¾	50½	22	13¾	91½	13½	31¼	96½	10½	68½	31½	55¼	94
Moortown	101¼	98¼	56	27½	22¾	97	22½	22¼	102	19½	74	37	60¾	99½
Mottram...............	9¼	6¼	38¼	64½	100¼	5	100	74½	10	97	18	55	31¼	7½
New Holland.........	106¼	103¼	61	82½	16¼	102	3	41¾	107	...	79	42	65¾	104½
Newton	6¾	3¾	40¾	67	102¾	2½	102½	77	7½	99½	20½	57½	33¾	5
Northorpe	81½	78½	36¼	7¾	28	77¼	27¾	42	82¼	24¾	54¼	17¼	41	79¾
North Kelsey.........	99¾	96¾	54½	26	21¼	95½	21	23¾	100½	18	72½	35½	59¼	98
Openshaw	¾	4¾	46¾	73	108¾	3½	108½	83¼	1¼	105½	26½	63½	39¾	6
Oxspring	29¼	26¼	18¼	44½	80¼	25	80	54½	30	77	2	35	11¼	27½
Oughty Bridge	35¾	32¾	11¾	38	73¾	31½	73½	48	36½	70½	8½	28½	4¾	34
Penistone	27¼	24¼	20¼	46½	82¼	23	82	56½	28	79	...	37	13¼	25½
Reepham	88¾	85¾	44	21¾	40	84½	39¾	5	89½	36¾	61½	24¾	48	87

In this Table, only the actual distance of the Ferry between New Holland and Hull is included.

MANCHESTER, SHEFFIELD, & LINCOLN RAILWAY—*Continued.*

STATIONS.	Ardwick.	Ashton.	Beighton.	Gainsboro'.	Great Grimsby.	Guide Bridge.	Hull.	Lincoln.	Manchester.	New Holland.	Penistone.	Retford.	Sheffield.	Staleybridge.
ord	64¼	61¼	19	9½	45¼	60	45	19¾	65	42	37	...	23¾	62½
ey Inn Siding.	60¼	57¼	15	13½	49½	56	49	23¾	61	46	33	4	19¾	58½
by	87½	84½	42¼	13¾	22	83¼	21¾	36	88¼	18¾	60¼	23¼	47	85¾
field............	40½	37½	7	33¼	69	36¼	68¾	43	41¼	65¾	13¼	23¾	...	38¾
Oaks	54¼	51¼	9	19½	55¼	50	55	29½	55	52	27	10	13¾	52½
land	93¼	90¼	48½	26¼	35½	89	35¼	9½	94	32¼	66	29¼	52½	91
ybridge	6¾	1¼	45¾	72	107¾	2½	107½	82	7½	104½	25½	62½	38¾	...
ingbro'	105¼	102¼	60	31½	4¼	101	15	40¾	106	12	78	41	64¾	103½
ton	70	67	24¾	3¾	39½	65¾	39¼	20½	70¾	36¼	42¾	5¾	29½	68¼
nton Curtis	102¼	99¼	57	28½	12¼	98	7	37¾	103	4	75	38	61¾	100½
goland..........	30¾	27¾	16¾	43	78¾	26½	78½	53	31½	75½	3½	33½	9¾	29
sey............	73½	70½	28¼	11¾	47½	69¼	47¼	10½	74¼	44¼	46¼	9¼	33	71¾
by	99¾	96¾	54½	26	9¾	95½	9½	35¼	100½	6½	72½	35½	59¼	98
lby	101½	98½	56¾	32	27¼	97¼	27	17¾	102¼	24	74¼	37½	60¾	99¾
sley Bridge ...	37¾	34¾	9¾	36	71¾	33½	71½	46	38½	68½	10½	26½	2¾	36
kenby	94¾	91¾	50	27¾	34	90½	33¾	11	95½	30¾	67½	30¾	54	93
dhead............	18¾	15¾	28¾	55	90¾	14½	90½	65	19½	87½	8½	45½	21¾	17
dhouse	46¼	43¼	1¼	27½	63¼	42	63	37½	47	60	19	18	6	44½
ksop	56¼	53¼	11	17½	53¼	52	53	27½	57	50	29	8	15¾	54½
tley	31¾	28¾	15¾	42	77¼	27½	77½	52	32½	74½	4½	32½	8¾	30

In this Table, only the actual distance of the Ferry between New Holland and Hull is included.

MANCHESTER, SOUTH JUNCTION, & ALTRINCHAM RAILWAY.

STATIONS.	Castlefield Junc.	Liverpool Road.	London Road.
Altrincham	7¼	7¾	8½
Bowdon	7¾	8¼	9
Knot Mill	¼	½	1
Liverpool Road	½	...	1½
London Road	1¼	1½	...
Old Trafford	1½	1¾	2½
Oxford Road	½	¾	¾
Sale Moor	4½	5	5¾
Stretford	3	3¼	4
Timperley	6¼	6¾	7½

NOTE.—South Junction Traffic from London Road to Liverpool Road, and vice versa, calculated as three miles, in accordance with three mile clause in the Act of Parliament, Manchester, South Junction, and Altrincham Railway Act, 8 and 9 Victoria, Session, 1845.

MARYPORT & CARLISLE RAILWAY.

STATIONS.	Carlisle Double Switches, N. and C. Junc.	Maryport.
Arkleby Depots..............	21	6¾
Arkleby Station..............	20¾	7
Aspatria..........................	19¾	8
Brayton Domain Branch, Brayton Domain Colliery	21¼	6½
Brayton Station..............	17¾	10
Bullgill Depots, Gilcrux Colliery	23½	4¼
Bullgill Quarry Points	24	3¾
Bullgill Station	23¼	4½
Carlisle Double Switches, N. and C. Junction ...	...	27¾
Carlisle, Crown St. Station..	¼	28
Carthwaite Depots...........	6¾	21
Carthwaite Station	6¾	21
Dalston Depots	4	23¾
Dalston Station	4	23¾
Dearham Bridge Station, Dearham Colliery	25¼	2½
Fletcher's Points	25	2¾
Heathfield Lime Depots	17¼	10½
Kirkhaugh's Drops, Oughterside Colliery	22¾	5
Leegate Station	15	12¾
Maryport	27¾	...
Warthole Guards Aspatria Coal Co., F. L. B. Dykes	21½	6¼
Wigton Goods Shed & Depots	11½	16¼
Wigton Station	11½	16¼
Wood, Steel, & Co., Siding.	25	2¾

McCorquodale & Co. Printers.

MIDLAND RAILWAY.

STATIONS.	Abbott's Wood.	Altofts Junction.	Beighton Junc.	Birmingham, Lawley Street.	Birmingham, L. & N. W.	Bristol.	Burton.	Colne.	Colwick.	Doncaster.	Gloucester.	Hampton.	Leeds, Northern Junction.	Leeds and Dewsbury Junc.	Lincoln.
Abbott's Wood	...	135	105¼	29¾	28½	64	60¼	183½	89¼	125	24½	47¼	146¾	146½	119¾
Altofts	135	...	87¾	105¼	105½	199	74¾	48½	82¼	28	159½	102¼	11¾	11½	112¾
Ambergate	81½	53½	23¾	51¾	52	145½	21¼	102	28¾	43½	106	48¾	65¼	65	59¼
Apperley Bridge.....	153¾	18¾	56½	124	124¼	217¾	93½	29¾	101	46¾	178¼	121	7	7¼	131½
Armley	147¾	12¾	50½	118	118¼	211¾	87½	35¾	95	40¾	172¼	115	1	1¼	125¼
Ashby	70¼	84¾	55	40½	40¾	134¼	10	133¼	89	74¾	94¾	37½	96½	96¼	69½
Ashchurch	10½	145½	115¾	40¼	39	53½	70¾	194	99¾	135½	14	57¾	157¼	157	130¼
Ashwell	115	107½	77¾	85¼	85½	179	54¾	156	44	97½	139½	82¼	119¼	119	74½
Bagworth	78½	93	63¼	48¾	49	142½	18¼	141½	42½	83	103	45¾	104¾	104½	73
Bardon Hill	76½	91	61¼	46¾	47	140½	16¼	139½	44½	81	101	43¾	102¾	102½	75
Barnt Green	17	118	88¼	12¾	11¼	81	43¼	166½	72¼	108	41½	30¼	129¾	129½	102¾
Barrow	90½	83½	53¾	60¾	61	154½	30¼	132	20	73½	115	57¾	95¼	95	50½
Barton and Walton..	56¼	78¾	49	26½	26¾	120¼	4	127¼	33	68¾	80¾	23½	90½	90¼	63¼
Basford	90¼	83¼	53½	60½	60¾	154¼	30	131¾	6½	73¼	114¾	57½	95	94¾	37
Beeston	83½	76½	46¾	53¾	54	147½	23¼	125	5¾	66½	108	50¾	88¼	88	36¼
Beighton Junction ...	105¼	37¾	...	75½	75¾	169¼	45	86¼	52½	27¾	129¾	72½	49½	49¼	83
Belper	78¼	56¾	27	48½	48¾	142¼	18	105¼	25¼	46¾	102¾	45½	68½	68¼	56
Berkley Road	41¾	176¾	147	71½	70¼	22¼	102	225¼	131	166¾	15¼	89	188½	188¼	161½
Bingley	160	25	62¾	130¼	130½	224	99¾	23½	107¼	53	184½	127¼	13¼	13½	137¾
Birmingham, Lawley Street...	29¾	105¼	75½	...	2¼	93¾	30½	153¾	59½	95¼	54¼	17½	117	116¾	90
Birmingham, L. & N. W..........	28½	105½	75¾	2¼	...	92½	30¾	154	59¾	95½	53	17¾	117¼	117	90¼
Blackwell	15½	119½	89¾	14¼	13	79½	44¾	168	73¾	109½	40	31¾	131¼	131	104¼
Borrowash	75	68	38¼	45¼	45½	139	14¾	116½	14¼	58	99½	42¼	79¾	79½	44¾
Bradford	159¾	24¾	62½	130	130¼	223¾	99½	29¾	107	52¾	184¼	127	13	13¼	137½
Braunston	85¾	100¼	70½	56	56¼	149¾	25½	148¾	35¼	90¼	110¼	53	112	111¾	65¾
Breedon	8½	143½	113¾	38¼	37	55½	68¾	192	97¾	133½	16	55¾	155¼	155	128¼

NOTE.—In this Table, the distance between Woodhouse Mill and Beighton Junction, from Junctions North of those points, is twice include
The Midland Company are allowed two miles for break of gauge to all Stations on B. and B. Branch beyond Gloucester; it is included in this Table.

MIDLAND RAILWAY—*Continued.*

STATIONS.	Luffenham.	Methley, G. N. Junction.	Methley, Y. N. M. Junc.	Newark.	Normanton.	Nottingham, (Goods.)	Peterboro'.	Rugby.	Sheffield.	Skipton.	Stoke Works.	Swinton.	Tamworth.	Willington June.	Wichnor June.
Abbott's Wood	125½	136½	136¼	104¼	134	86½	144¼	120½	116	172	11	116	47¼	65¾	54½
Altofts	118	1½	1¼	97¼	1	79½	136¾	113½	29	37	124	19	87¾	69¼	80½
Ambergate	64½	55	54¾	43¾	52½	26	83¼	60	34½	90½	70¼	34½	34¼	15¾	27
Apperley Bridge	136¾	17¼	17½	116	19¾	98¼	155½	132¼	47¾	18¼	142¾	37¾	106½	88	99¼
Armley	130¾	11¼	11½	110	13¾	92¼	149½	126¼	41¾	24¼	136¾	31¾	100½	82	93¼
Ashby	55¼	86¼	86	54	83¾	36¼	74	40¼	65¾	121¾	59¼	65¾	23	15½	15¾
Ashchurch	136	147	146¾	114¾	144½	97	154¾	131	126½	182½	21½	126½	57¾	76¼	65
Ashwell	10½	109	108¾	59	106½	41¼	29¼	44	88½	144½	104	88½	67¾	48¾	60½
Bagworth	47	94½	94¼	57½	92	39¾	65¾	82	74	130	67½	74	31¼	23¾	24
Bardon Hill	49	92½	92¼	59½	90	41¾	67¾	34	72	128	65½	72	29¼	21¾	22
Barnt Green	108½	119½	119¼	87¼	117	69½	127¼	103½	99	155	6	99	30½	48¾	37½
Barrow	34½	85	84¾	35	82½	17¼	53¼	30	64½	120½	79½	64½	43¼	24¾	36
Barton and Walton...	69¼	80¼	80	48	77¾	30¼	88	64¼	59¾	115¾	45¼	59¾	9	9½	1¾
Basford	55½	84¾	84½	21½	82¼	3¾	74¼	51	64¼	120¼	79¼	64¼	43	24½	35¾
Beeston	48¾	78	77¾	20¾	75½	3	67½	44¼	57½	113½	72½	57½	36¼	17¾	29
Beighton Junction...	88¼	39¼	39	67½	36¾	49¾	107	83¾	18¾	74¾	94¼	18¾	58	39½	50¾
Belper	61¼	58¼	58	40½	55¾	22¾	80	56¾	37¾	93¾	67¼	37¾	31	12½	23¾
Berkley Road	167½	178¼	178	146	175¾	128¼	186	162¼	157¾	218¾	52¾	157¾	89	107½	96¼
Bingley	143	23½	23¾	122¼	26	104½	161¾	138½	54	12	149	44	112¾	94¼	105½
Birmingham, Lawley Street...	95¾	106¾	106½	74½	104¼	56¾	114½	90¾	86¼	142¼	18¾	86¼	17½	36	24¾
Birmingham, L. & N. W.............	96	107	106¾	74¾	104½	57	114¾	82	85½	142½	17½	86½	17¾	36¼	25
Blackwell	110	121	120¾	88¾	118½	71	128¾	105	100½	156½	4½	100½	31¾	50¼	39
Borrowash	50	69½	69¼	29¼	67	11½	68¾	45½	49	105	64	49	27¾	9½	20½
Bradford	142¾	23¼	28½	122	25¾	104¼	161½	138¼	53¾	18¼	148¾	43¾	112½	94	105¼
Braunston	39¾	101¾	101½	50¼	99¼	32½	58½	24¾	81¼	137¼	74¾	81¼	38½	31	31¼
Breedon	134	145	144¾	112¾	142½	95	152¾	129	124½	180½	19½	124½	55¾	74¼	63

NOTE.—In this Table, the distance between Woodhouse Mill and Beighton Junction, from Junctions North of those points, is twice included. The Midland Company are allowed two miles for break of gauge to all Stations on B. and B. Branch beyond Gloucester; is is included in is Table.

MIDLAND RAILWAY—*Continued.*

STATIONS.	Abbott's Wood.	Altofts Junction.	Beighton Junc.	Birmingham, Lawley Street.	Birmingham, L. & N. W.	Bristol.	Burton.	Colne.	Colwick.	Doncaster.	Gloucester.	Hampton.	Leeds, Northern Junc.	Leeds and Dewsbury Junc.	Lincoln.
Brightsides	114	27	16¾	83¼	83½	178	53¾	75	61¼	17	138½	81¼	38¾	38½	91¾
Bristol	64	199	169¼	93¾	92½	...	124¼	247½	153¼	189	37½	111¼	210¾	210½	[illegible]
Bromsgrove	13½	121½	91¾	16¼	15	77½	46¾	170	75¾	111½	38	33¾	133¼	133	105¾
Brooksby	100½	93	63¼	70¾	71	164½	40¼	141½	29½	83	125	67¾	104¾	104½	60
Broughton	100½	102½	72¾	70¾	71	164½	40¼	151	39	92½	125	67¾	114¼	114	69½
Bulwell	91¾	84¾	55	62	62¼	155¾	31½	133¼	8	74¾	116¼	59	96½	96¼	38½
Burton	60¼	74¾	45	30½	30¾	124¼	...	123¼	29	64¾	84¾	27½	86½	86½	59¼
Burton Joyce	92	85	55¼	62¼	62½	156	31¾	133½	2¾	75	116½	59¼	96¾	96½	27¾
Calverley	151¾	16¾	54½	122	122¼	215¾	91½	31¾	99	44¾	176¼	119	5	5¼	129¼
Camp Hill	26¾	108¼	78½	3½	2¼	90¾	33½	156¾	62½	98¼	51¼	20½	120	119¾	93
Carlton	90	83	53¼	60¼	60½	154	29¾	181½	¾	78	114½	57¼	94¾	94½	29¾
Castle Bromwich	34¼	100¾	71	4½	4¾	98¼	26	149¼	55	90¾	58¾	13	112½	112¼	85½
Charfield	47	182	152¼	76¾	75½	17	107¼	230½	136¼	172	20½	94¼	193¾	193½	166¾
Cheltenham	17¾	152¾	123	47½	46¼	46¼	78	201¼	107	142¾	6¾	65	164½	164¼	137½
Chesterfield	95	40	10¼	65¼	65½	159	34¾	88½	42¼	30	119½	62¼	51¾	51½	72¾
Clay Cross	91	44	14¼	61¼	61½	155	30¾	92½	38¼	34	115½	58¼	55¾	55½	68¾
Cleeve	14	149	119¼	43¾	42½	50	74¼	197½	103¼	139	10½	61¼	160¾	160½	133¾
Coalville	75	89½	59¾	45¼	45½	139	14¾	138	43¾	79½	99½	42¼	101¼	101	74¼
Codnor Park	93	86¼	56½	63½	63¾	157¼	33	134¾	21½	76¼	117¾	60½	98	97¾	52
Coleshill	42½	97½	67¾	12¾	13	106½	22¾	146	51¾	87½	67	4¾	109¼	109	82¼
Collingham	109¼	102¼	72½	79½	79¾	173¼	49	150¾	20	92¼	183¾	76½	114	113¾	10½
Colne	183½	48½	86¼	153¾	154	247½	123¼	...	130¾	76½	208	150¾	36¾	37	161¼
Colwick	89¼	82¼	52½	59½	59¾	153¼	29	130¾	..	72¼	113¾	56½	94	93¾	30½
Conisbro'	119¾	22¾	22½	90	90¼	183¾	59½	71¼	67	5¼	144¼	87	34½	34¼	97½
Cononley	169¼	34¼	72	139½	139¾	233¼	109	14¼	116½	62¼	193¾	136½	22½	22¾	147
Cossington	97	87½	57¾	67¼	67½	161	36¾	136	24	77½	121½	64¼	101¼	101	54½

NOTE.—In this Table, the distance between Woodhouse Mill and Beighton Junction, from Junctions North of those points, is twice included. The Midland Company are allowed two miles for break of gauge to all Stations on B. and B. Branch beyond Gloucester; it is included in

MIDLAND RAILWAY—*Continued.*

STATIONS.	Luffenham.	Methley, G. N. Junction.	Methley, Y. N. M. June.	Newark.	Normanton.	Nottingham (Goods).	Peterboro'.	Rugby.	Sheffield.	Skipton.	Stoke Works.	Swinton.	Tamworth.	Willington Junc.	Wichnor Junc.
Brightsides	97	28½	28¼	76¼	26	58½	115¾	92½	2	64	103	8	66¾	48¼	59¼
Bristol	189½	200¼	200¼	168¼	198	150½	208¼	184½	180	236	75	180	111¼	129¾	118¼
Bromsgrove	112	123	122¾	90¾	120½	73	130¾	107	102½	158½	2½	102½	33¾	52¼	41
Brooksby	25	94¼	94¼	44½	92	26¾	43¾	29½	74	130	89½	74	58½	34¼	46
Broughton	43½	104	103¾	54	101½	36¼	62¼	11	83½	139½	89½	83½	53½	43¾	46
Bulwell	57	86½	86	23	83¾	5¼	75¾	52½	65½	121¾	80½	65½	44½	26	37½
Burton	65¼	76¼	76	44	73¾	26¼	84	51¼	55¾	111¾	49¼	55¾	13	5¼	5¾
Burton Joyce	57¼	86¼	86¼	12¼	84	5¼	76	52¾	66	122	81	66	44¾	26¼	37½
Calverley	134¾	15½	15½	114	17¾	96½	153½	130½	45¾	20¼	140¾	35½	104½	86	97¼
Camp Hill	98¾	109¾	109½	77½	107½	59¾	117½	93¾	89½	145¼	15½	89½	20½	39	27¾
Carlton	55¼	84½	84½	14¼	82	3½	74	50¾	64	120	79	64	42¾	24¼	35½
Castle Bromwich	91¼	102¼	102	70	99¾	52¼	110	86¼	81½	137¼	23¼	81¾	13	31½	20¼
Charfield	172½	183½	183½	151½	181	133½	191¼	167½	163	219	58	163	94½	112¾	101¼
Cheltenham	143¼	154¼	154	122	151¾	104¼	162	138¼	133¾	189¾	28¾	133¾	65	83½	72¼
Chesterfield	78	41½	41½	57¼	39	39½	96¾	73½	21	77	84	21	47¾	29¼	40¼
Clay Cross	74	45¼	45¼	53¼	43	35½	92¾	69½	25	81	80	25	48¾	25¼	36¼
Cleeve	139½	150½	150½	118½	148	100½	158½	134½	130	186	25	130	61¼	79¾	68¼
Coalville	50½	91	90¾	58¾	88½	41	69½	35½	70½	126½	64	70½	27¾	20¼	20¼
Codnor Park	58½	87½	87½	36½	85¼	18¾	77¼	54	67½	123½	82½	67½	46	27½	38¾
Coleshill	88	99	98¾	66¾	96½	49	106¾	83	78½	134½	31½	78½	9¾	28¼	17
Collingham	74½	103¾	103½	5	101¼	22¾	93¼	70	88½	139½	98½	83½	62	43½	54¾
Colne	166½	47	47¼	145¾	49½	128	185½	162	77¼	11½	172½	67½	136¼	117¾	129
Colwick	54½	83¾	83½	15	81¼	2¾	73¼	50	63½	119¼	78½	63½	42	23½	34¾
Conisbro'	102¾	24¼	24	82	21¼	64¼	121¼	98¼	13¾	59¾	108¾	3¾	72½	54	65¼
Cononley	152¼	32¾	33	131¼	35¼	113¾	171	147¾	63¼	2¾	158¼	53¼	122	103½	114¾
Cossington	30½	89	89¾	39	86½	21¼	49½	26	68½	124½	86	70½	49¾	30¼	42¼

NOTE—In this Table, the distance between Woodhouse Mill and Beighton Junction, from Junctions North of those points, is twice included. The Midland Company are allowed two miles for break of gauge to all Stations on B. and B. Branch beyond Gloucester; it is included in

MIDLAND RAILWAY—*Continued.*

STATIONS.	Abbott's Wood.	Altofts Junction.	Beighton Junc.	Birmingham, Lawley Street.	Birmingham, L. & N. W.	Bristol.	Burton.	Colne.	Colwick.	Doncaster.	Gloucester.	Hampton.	Leeds, Northern Junction.	Leeds and Dewsbury Junc.	Lincoln.
Countesthorpe	97	99	69¼	67¼	67½	161	36¾	147½	35½	89	121½	64¼	110¾	110½	66
Cromford	86½	58½	28¾	56¾	57	150½	26¼	107	33¾	48½	111	53¾	70¼	70	64¼
Cudworth	124	11	26¾	94¼	94½	188	63¾	59½	71¼	17	148½	91¼	22¾	22½	101¾
Darfield	119¾	15¼	22½	90	90¼	183¾	59½	63¾	67	12¾	144¼	87	27	26¾	97¼
Darley	90¾	62¾	33	61	61¼	154¾	30½	111¼	38	52¾	115¼	58	74	74¼	68½
Defford	4½	139½	109¾	34¼	33	59½	64¾	188	93¾	129½	20	51¾	151¼	151	124¼
Derby..................	71	64	34¼	41½	41½	135	10¾	112½	18¼	54	95½	38¼	75¾	75½	48¾
Desford	83	97½	67¾	53¼	53½	147	22¾	146	38	87½	107½	50¼	109¼	109	68½
Doncaster	125	28	27¾	95¼	95½	189	64¼	76½	72¼	...	149½	92¼	39¾	39½	102¾
Draycote	76¾	69¾	40	47	47¼	140¾	16½	118¼	12½	59¾	101¼	44	81½	81¼	43
Droitwich Road......	8½	126½	96¾	21¼	20	72½	51¾	175	80¾	116½	33	38¾	138¼	138	111¼
Duffield	76¼	58¾	29	46½	46¾	140¼	16	107¼	23½	48¾	100¾	43½	70½	70¼	54
Dunhampstead	6½	128½	98¾	23¼	22	70½	53¾	177	82¾	118½	31	40¾	140¼	140	113¼
Earby...................	178½	43½	81¼	148¾	149	242½	118¼	5	125¾	71½	203	145¾	31¾	32	156¼
Eckington	101¼	33¾	4	71½	71¾	165¼	41	82¼	48½	23¾	125¾	68½	45½	45¼	79
Eckington, B. and B.	5¾	140¾	111	35½	34¼	58¼	66	189¼	95	130¾	18¾	53	152½	152¼	125¼
Elslack	176	41	78¾	146¼	146½	240	115¾	7½	123¼	69	200½	143¼	29¼	29½	153¾
Fiskerton	99½	92½	52¾	69¾	70	163½	39¼	141	10¼	82½	124	66¾	104¼	104	20¼
Forge Mills	38	97	67¼	8¼	8½	102	22¼	145½	51¼	87	62½	9¼	108¾	108½	81¾
Foulridge	181¼	46¼	84	151½	151¾	245¼	121	2¼	128½	74¼	205¾	148½	34½	34¾	159
Frisby	102½	95	65¼	72¾	73	166½	42¼	143½	31½	85	127	69¾	106¾	106½	62
Frocester	37¼	172¼	142½	67	65¾	26¾	97½	220¾	126½	162¼	10¾	84½	184	183¾	157
Glenfield	87¼	101¾	72	57½	57¾	151¼	27	150¼	40¾	91¾	111¾	54½	113½	113¼	71¼
Gloucester...........	24½	159½	129¾	54¼	53	37½	84¾	208	113¾	149½	...	71¾	171¼	171	144¼
Gloucester Docks ...	26¼	161¼	131½	56	53¾	39¼	86½	209¾	115½	151¼	1¾	73½	173	172¾	146
Gresley	65¼	79¾	50	35½	35¾	129¼	5	128¼	34	69¾	89¾	82½	91½	91¼	64½

NOTE.—In this Table, the distance between Woodhouse Mill and Beighton Junction, from Junctions North of those points, is twice included. The Midland Company are allowed two miles for break of gauge to all Stations on B. and B. Branch beyond Gloucester; it is included in this Table.

MIDLAND RAILWAY—*Continued.*

STATIONS.	Luffenham.	Methley, G. N. Junction.	Methley, Y. N. M. Junc.	Newark.	Normanton.	Nottingham, (Goods.)	Peterboro'.	Rugby.	Sheffield.	Skipton.	Stoke Works.	Swinton.	Tamworth.	Willington Junc.	Wichnor Junc.
ountesthorpe	40	100½	100¼	50½	98	32¾	58¾	14½	80	136	86	80	49¾	40¼	42½
romford	69½	60	59¾	48¾	57½	31	88¼	65	39½	95½	75½	39½	39¼	20¾	32
udworth	107	12½	12¼	86¼	10	68½	125¾	102½	18	48	113	8	76¾	56¼	69½
arfield	102¾	16¾	16½	82	14¼	64¼	121½	98¼	13¾	52¼	108¾	8¾	72½	54	65¼
arley	73¾	64¼	64	53	61¾	35¼	92½	69¼	43¾	99¾	79¾	43¾	43½	25	36¼
efford	130	141	140¾	108¾	138½	91	148¾	125	120½	176½	15½	120½	51¾	70¼	59
erby..................	54	65½	65¼	33¼	63	15½	72¾	49½	45	101	60	45	23¾	5¼	16½
esford	42½	99	98¾	53	96½	35¼	61¼	27½	78½	134½	72	78½	35¾	28¼	28½
oncaster	108	29½	29¼	87¼	27	69½	126¾	103½	19	65	114	9	77¾	59¼	70½
raycote	48¼	71¼	71	27½	68¾	9¾	67	43¾	50¾	106¾	65¾	50¾	29½	11	22¼
roitwich Road......	117	128	127¾	95¾	125½	78	135¾	112	107½	163½	2½	107½	38¾	57¼	46
uffield	59¼	60¼	60	38½	57¾	20¾	78	54¾	39¾	95¾	65¼	39¾	29	10½	21¾
unhampstead	119	130	129¾	97¾	127½	80	137¾	114	109½	165½	4½	109½	40¾	59¼	48
arby..................	161½	42	42¼	140¾	44½	123	180¼	157	72½	6½	167½	62½	131¼	112¾	124
ckington	84¼	35¼	35	63½	32¾	45¾	103	79¾	14¾	70¾	90¼	14¾	54	35½	46¾
ckington, B. and B.	131¼	142¼	142	110	139¾	92¼	150	126¼	121¾	177¾	16¾	121¾	53	71½	60¼
lslack	159	39½	39¾	138¼	42	120½	177¾	154½	70	4	165	60	128¾	110¼	121½
iskerotn	64¾	94	93¾	4¾	91½	13	83½	60¼	73½	129½	88½	73½	52¼	33¾	45
orge Mills	87½	98½	98¼	66¼	96	48½	106¼	82½	78	134	27	78	9¼	27¾	16½
ulridge	164¼	44¾	45	143½	47¼	125¾	183	159¾	75¼	9¼	170¼	65¼	134	115½	126¾
risby	23	96½	96¼	46½	94	28¾	41¾	31½	76	132	91½	76	55¼	36¼	48
rocester	162¾	173¾	173½	141½	171¼	123¾	181½	157¾	153¼	209¼	48¼	153¼	84½	103	91¾
lenfield	45¼	103¼	103	55¾	100¾	38	64	29	82¾	138¾	76¼	82¾	40	32½	32¾
loucester	150	161	160¾	128¾	158½	111	168¾	145	140½	196½	35½	140½	71¾	90¼	79
loucester Docks ...	151¾	162¾	162½	130½	160¼	112¾	170½	146¾	142¼	198¼	37¼	142¼	73½	92	80¾
resley	60¼	81¼	81	49	78¾	31¼	79	45¼	60¾	116¾	54¼	60¾	18	10½	10¾

ote.—In this Table, the distance between Woodhouse Mill and Beighton Junction, from Junctions North of those points, is twice included.
e Midland Company are allowed two miles for break of gauge to all Stations on B. and B. Branch beyond Gloucester; it is included in Table.

MIDLAND RAILWAY—*Continued.*

STATIONS.	Abbott's Wood.	Altofts Junction.	Beighton Junc.	Birmingham, Lawley Street.	Birmingham, L. & N. W.	Bristol.	Burton.	Colne.	Colwick.	Doncaster.	Gloucester.	Hampton.	Leeds, Northern Junction.	Leeds and Dewsbury Junc.	Lincoln.
Hampton	47¼	102¼	72½	17½	17¾	111¼	27½	150¾	56½	92¼	71¾	...	114	113¾	87
Haselour	51½	83½	53¾	21¾	22	115½	8¾	132	37¾	73½	76	18¾	95¼	95	68¼
Heanor Junction ...	89½	82½	52¾	59¾	60	153½	29¼	131	17¾	72½	114	56¾	94¼	94	48¼
Helpstone	138	130½	100¾	108¼	108½	202	77¾	179	67	120½	162½	105¼	142¼	142	97½
Hexthorpe	123½	26½	26¼	93¾	94	187½	62¾	75	70¾	1½	148	90¾	38¼	38	101¼
High Peak Junction	85	57	27¼	55¼	55½	149	24¾	105½	32¼	47	109½	52¼	68¾	68½	62¾
Holmes	111¾	24¾	14½	82	82¼	175¾	51½	73¼	59	14¾	136¼	79	36½	36¼	89½
Hucknall	94¾	87¾	58	65	65¼	158¾	34½	136¼	11	77¾	119¼	62	99½	99¼	41½
Hykeham	116½	109½	79¾	86¾	87	180½	56½	158	27¼	99½	141	83¾	121¼	121	3¼
Idle	155½	20½	58¼	125¾	126	219½	95¼	28	102¾	48½	180	122¾	8¾	9	133¼
Ilkeston Junction ...	86¾	79¾	50	57	57¼	150¾	26½	128¼	15	69¾	111¼	54	91½	91¼	45½
Ilkeston Station......	89¼	82¼	52½	59½	59¾	153¼	29	130¾	17½	72¼	113¾	56½	94	93¾	48
Kegworth	83	76	46¼	53¼	53½	147	22¾	124½	12½	66	107½	50¼	87¾	87½	43
Keighley	163¼	28¼	66	133½	133¾	227¼	103	20¼	110½	56¼	187¾	130½	16½	16¾	141
Ketton	128	120½	90¾	98¼	98½	192	67¾	169	57	110½	152½	95¼	132¼	132	87½
Kildwick	167¾	32¾	70½	138	138¼	231¾	107½	15¾	115	60¾	192¼	135	21	21¼	145½
Kilnhurst	115	20	17¾	85¼	85½	179	54¾	68½	62¼	10	139½	82¼	31¾	31½	92¾
Kingsbury............	41¾	93¼	63½	12	12¼	105¾	18½	141¾	47½	83¼	66¼	9	105	104¾	78
King's Norton	22	113	83¼	[illegible]	6½	86	38¼	161½	67¼	103	46½	25¼	124¾	124½	97¾
Kirby..................	103¾	96¼	66½	74	74¼	167¾	43½	144¾	32¾	86¼	128¼	71	108[illegible]	107¾	63¼
Kirkby	99½	92½	62¾	69¾	70	163½	39¼	141	15¾	82½	124	66¾	104¼	104	46¼
Kirkstall	149¼	14¼	52	119½	119¾	213¼	89	34¼	96½	42¼	173¾	116½	2½	2¾	127
Kirkstall Forge	150	15	52¾	120¼	120½	214	89¾	33½	97¼	43	174½	117¼	3¼	3½	127¾
Langley Mill	90¼	83¼	53½	60½	60¾	154¼	30	131¾	18½	73¼	114¾	57½	95	94¾	49
Leeds and Dewsbury Junction...	146½	11½	49¼	116¾	117	210½	86¼	37	93¾	39½	171	113¾		...	124¼
Leeds, Hunslet Lane	144¼	9¼	47	114½	114¾	208¼	84	39¼	91½	37¼	168¾	111½	2½	2¼	122

NOTE.—In this Table, the distance between Woodhouse Mill and Beighton Junction, from Junctions North of those points, is twice included. The Midland Company are allowed two miles for break of gauge to all Stations on P. and B. Branch beyond Gloucester; it is included in this Table.

MIDLAND RAILWAY—*Continued.*

STATIONS.	Luffenham.	Methley, G. N. Junction.	Methley, Y. N. M. Junc.	Newark.	Normanton.	Nottingham, (Goods.)	Peterboro'.	Rugby.	Sheffield.	Skipton.	Stoke Works.	Swinton.	Tamworth.	Willington Junc.	Wichnor Junc.
mpton	92¾	103¾	103½	71½	101¼	53¾	111½	87¾	83¼	139¼	36¼	83¼	14½	33	21¾
elour	74	85	84¾	52¾	82½	35	92¾	69	64½	120½	40½	61½	4¼	14¼	3
anor Junction ...	54¾	84	83¾	32¾	81½	15	73½	50¼	63½	119½	78½	63½	42¼	23¾	35
pstone	12½	132	131¾	82	129½	64¼	6¼	67	111½	167½	127	111½	90¾	71¾	83½
xthorpe	106½	28	27¾	85¾	25½	68	125¼	102	17½	63½	112½	7½	76¼	57¾	69
gh Peak Junction	68	58½	58¼	47¼	56	29½	86¾	63½	38	94	74	38	37¾	19¼	30½
mes	94¾	26¼	26	74	23¾	56¼	113½	90¼	4¼	61¾	100¾	5¾	64½	46	57¼
cknall	60	89¼	89	26	86¾	8¼	78¾	55½	68¾	124¾	83¾	68¾	47½	29	40¼
keham	81¾	111	110¾	12¼	108½	30	100½	77¼	90½	146½	105½	90½	69¼	50¾	62
....	138½	19	19¼	117¾	21½	100	157¼	134	49½	16½	144½	39½	108¼	89¾	101
ston Junction ...	52	81¼	81	30	78¾	12¼	70¾	47½	60¾	116¾	75¾	60¾	39½	21	32¼
ston Station......	54½	83¾	83½	32½	81¼	14¾	73¼	50	63¼	119¼	78¼	63¼	42	23½	34¾
worth	42	77½	77¼	27½	75	9¾	60¾	37½	57	113	72	57	35¾	17¼	28½
ghley............	146¼	26¾	27	125½	29¼	107¾	165	141¾	57¼	8¾	152¼	47¼	116	97½	108¾
ton	2½	122	121¾	72	119½	54¼	16¼	57	101½	157½	117	101½	80¾	61¾	73½
wick	150¾	31¼	31½	130	33¾	112¼	169½	146¼	61¾	4¼	156¾	51¾	120½	102	113½
hurst	98	21½	21¼	77¼	19	59½	116¾	93½	9	57	114	1	67¾	49¼	60½
gsbury	83¾	94¾	94½	62½	92½	44¾	102½	78¾	74¼	130¼	30¾	74¼	5½	24	12¾
g's Norton	103½	114½	114¼	82¼	112	64½	122¼	98½	94	150	11	94	25¼	43¾	32½
by............	21¾	97¾	97½	47¾	95¼	30	40½	32¾	77¼	133¼	92¾	77¼	56½	37½	49¼
kby	64¾	94	93¾	30¾	91½	13	83½	60¼	73½	129½	88½	73½	52¼	33¾	45
kstall	132¼	12¾	13	111½	15¼	93¾	151	127¾	43¼	22¾	138¼	33¼	102	83½	94¾
kstall Forge......	133	13½	13¾	112¼	16	94½	151¾	128½	44	22	139	34	102¾	84¼	95½
gley Mill.........	55½	84¾	84½	33½	82¼	15¾	74¼	51	64¼	120¼	79¼	64¼	43	24½	35¾
ls and Dews- ry Junction ...	129½			108¾	12½	91	148¼	125	40½	25½	135½	30½	99¼	80¾	92
ls, Hunslet Lane	127¼	7¾	8	106½	10¼	88¾	146	122¾	38¼	27¾	133¼	28¼	97	78½	89¾

E.—In this Table, the distance between Woodhouse Mill and Beighton Junction, from Junctions North of those points, is twice included. Midland Company are allowed two miles for break of gauge to all Stations on B. and B. Branch beyond Gloucester; it is included in ble.

MIDLAND RAILWAY—*Continued.*

STATIONS.	Abbott's Wood.	Altofts Junction.	Beighton Junc.	Birmingham, Lawley Street.	Birmingham, L. & N. W.	Bristol.	Burton.	Colne.	Colwick.	Doncaster.	Gloucester.	Hampton.	Leeds, Northern Junction.	Leeds and Dewsbury Junc.	Lincoln.
Leeds, Northern Jnc.	146¾	11¾	49½	117	117¼	210¾	86½	36¾	94	39¾	171¼	114	...		124½
Leeds, Wellington ...	146½	11½	49¼	116¾	117	210½	86¼	37½	93¾	39½	171	113¾	¾	½	124¼
Leicester	91¼	93¼	63½	61½	61¾	155¼	31	141¾	29¾	83¼	115¾	58½	105	104¾	60¼
Lenton	87¾	80¾	51	58	58¼	151¾	27½	129¼	4	70¾	112¼	55	92½	92¼	34½
Linby................	95¾	88¾	59	66	66¼	159¾	35½	137¼	12	78¾	120¼	63	100½	100¼	42½
Lincoln	119¾	112¾	83	90	90¼	183¾	59½	161¼	30½	102¾	144¼	87	124½	124¼	...
Little Eaton	74½	67½	37¾	44¾	45	138½	14¼	116	21¾	57½	92¾	41¾	79¼	79	52¼
Locoford.............	96	39	9¼	66¼	66½	100	35¾	87½	43¼	29	120½	63¼	50¾	50½	73¾
Long Eaton Junction	80½	73½	43¾	50¾	51	144½	20¼	122	8¾	63½	105	47¾	85¼	85	39¼
Lowdham	94½	87½	57¾	64¾	65	158½	34¼	136	5¼	77½	119	61¾	99¼	99	25¼
Loughboro'	88	81	51¼	58¼	58½	152	27¾	129½	17½	71	112½	55¼	92¾	92½	48
Luffenham	125½	118	88¼	95¾	96	189½	65¼	166½	54½	108	150	92¾	129¾	129½	85
Mangotsfield	58¼	193¼	163½	88	86¾	5¾	118½	241¾	147½	183¼	31¾	105½	205	204¾	178
Mansfield	103½	96½	66¾	73¾	74	167½	43¼	145	19¾	86½	128	70¾	108¼	108	50¼
Manton	121½	114	84¼	91¾	92	185½	61¼	162½	50½	104	146	88¾	125¾	125½	81
Masboro'	111	24	13¾	81¼	81½	175	50¾	72½	58¼	14	135½	78¼	35¾	35½	88¾
Matlock Bath.........	87½	59½	29¾	57¾	58	151½	27¼	108	34¾	49½	112	54¾	71¼	71	65¼
Matlock Bridge	88½	60½	30¾	58¾	59	152½	28¼	109	35¾	50½	113	55¾	72¼	72	66¼
Melton	106¼	98¾	69	76½	76¾	170¼	46	147¼	35¼	88¾	130¾	73½	110½	110¼	65¾
Merrylees	81½	96	66¼	51¾	52	145½	21¼	144½	39½	86	106	48¾	107¾	107½	70
Methley	137¼	2¼	40	107½	107¾	201¼	77	46¼	84½	30¼	161¾	104½	9½	9¼	115
Methley, G. N. Junc.	136½	1½	39¼	106¾	107	200½	76¼	47	83¾	29½	161	103¾			114¼
Methley, Y. & N. M. Junction...	136¼	1¼	39	106½	106¾	200¼	76	47¼	83½	29¼	160¾	103½			114
Mexboro'	117	20	19¾	87¼	87½	181	56¾	68½	64¼	8	141½	84¼	31¾	31½	94¾
Moira.................	67¾	82¼	52½	38	38¼	131¾	7½	130¾	36½	72¼	92¼	35	94	93¾	67
Moseley	24½	110½	80¾	5¼	4	88½	35¾	159	64¾	100½	49	22¾	122¼	122	95¼

NOTE.—In this Table, the distance between Woodhouse Mill and Beighton Junction, from Junctions North of those points, is twice included. The Midland Company are allowed two miles for break of gauge to all Stations on B. and B. Branch, beyond Gloucester; it is included in this Table.

MIDLAND RAILWAY—*Continued.*

STATIONS.	Luffenham.	Methley, G. N. Junction.	Methley, Y. N. M. Junc.	Newark.	Normanton.	Nottingham, (Goods.)	Peterboro'.	Rugby.	Sheffield.	Skipton.	Stoke Works.	Swinton.	Tamworth.	Willington Junc.	Wichnor Junc.
Leeds, Northern Jnc.	129¾			109	12¾	91¼	148½	125¼	40¾	25¼	135¾	30¾	99½	81	92¼
Leeds, Wellington ...	129½	10	10¼	108¼	12½	91	148¼	125	40½	26	135½	30½	99¼	80¾	92
eicester	34¼	94¾	94½	44¾	92¼	27	53	20¼	74¼	130¼	80¼	74¼	44	34½	36¾
enton	53	82¼	82	19	79¾	1¼	71¾	48½	61¾	117¾	76¾	61¾	40½	22	33¼
inby	61	90¼	90	27	87¾	9¼	79¾	56½	69¾	125¾	84¾	69¾	48½	30	41¼
incoln	85	114¼	114	15½	111¾	33¼	103¾	80½	93¾	149¾	108¾	93¾	72½	54	65¼
ittle Eaton	57½	69	68¾	36¾	66½	19	76¼	53	48½	104½	63½	48½	27¼	8¾	20
ocoford	79	40½	40¼	58¼	38	40½	97¾	74½	20	76	85	20	48¾	30¼	41½
ong Eaton Junction	45¾	75	74¾	23¾	72½	6	64½	41¼	54½	110½	69½	54½	33¼	14¾	26
owdham	59¾	89	88¾	9¾	86½	8	78½	55¼	68½	124½	83½	68½	47¼	28¾	40
oughboro'	37	82½	82¼	32½	80	14¾	55¾	32½	62	118	77	62	40¾	22¼	33½
uffenham	...	119½	119¼	69½	117	51¾	18¾	54½	99	155	114½	99	78¼	59¼	71
Iangotsfield	183¾	194¾	194½	162½	192¼	144¾	202½	178¾	174¼	230¼	69¼	174¼	105½	124	112¾
Iansfield	68¾	98	97¾	34¾	95½	17	87½	64¼	77½	133½	92½	77½	56¼	37¾	49
Ianton	4	115½	115¼	65½	113	47¾	22¾	50½	95	151	110½	95	74¼	55¼	67
Iasboro'	94	25½	25¼	73¼	23	55½	112¾	89½	5	61	100	5	63¾	45¼	56½
Iatlock Bath.........	70½	61	60¾	49¾	58½	32	89¼	66	40½	96½	76½	40½	40¼	21¾	33
Iatlock Bridge	71½	62	61¾	50¾	59½	33	90¼	67	41½	97½	77½	41½	41¼	22¾	34
Ielton	19¼	100¼	100	50¼	97¾	32½	38	35¼	79¾	135¾	95¼	79¾	59	40	51¾
Ierrylees	44	97½	97¼	54½	95	36¾	62¾	29	77	133	70½	77	34¼	26¾	27
Iethley	120¼	¾	1	99½	3¼	81¾	139	115¾	31¼	34¾	126¼	21¼	90	71½	82¾
Iethley, G. N. Junc.	119½	...	¼	98¾	2½	81	138¼	115	30½	35½	125½	20½	89¼	71¾	82
Iethley, Y. & N. M. Junction....	119¼	¼	...	98½	2¼	80¾	138	114¾	30¼	35¾	125¼	20¼	89	71½	81¾
Iexboro'	100	21½	21¼	79¼	19	61½	118¾	95½	11	57	106	1	69¾	51¼	62½
Ioira	57¾	83¾	83½	51½	81¼	33¾	76½	42¾	63¼	119¼	56¾	63¼	20½	13	13¼
Ioseley	101	112	111¾	79¾	109½	62	119¾	96	91½	147½	13½	91½	22¾	41¼	30

OTE.—In this Table, the distance between Woodhouse Mill and Beighton Junction, from Junctions North of those points, is twice included. he Midland Company are allowed two miles for break of gauge to all Stations on B. and B. Branch beyond Gloucester; it is included in Table.

MIDLAND RAILWAY—*Continued.*

STATIONS.	Abbott's Wood.	Altofts Junction.	Beighton Junc.	Birmingham, Lawley Street.	Birmingham, L. & N. W.	Bristol.	Burton.	Colne.	Colwick.	Doncaster.	Gloucester.	Hampton.	Leeds, Northern Junction.	Leeds and Dewsbury Junc.	Lincoln.
Newark	104¼	97¼	67½	74½	74¾	168¼	44	145¾	15	87¼	128¾	71½	109	108¾	15½
Newlay	150¾	15¾	53½	121	121¼	214¾	90½	32¾	98	43¾	175¼	118	4	4¼	128½
Normanton	134	1	36¾	104¼	104½	198	73¾	49½	81¼	27	158½	101¼	12¾	12½	111¾
Nottingham (Goods)	86½	79½	49¾	56¾	57	150½	26¼	128	2¾	69½	111	53¾	91¼	91	33¼
Oakenshaw	131¼	3¾	34	101½	101¾	195¼	71	52¼	78½	24¼	155¾	98½	15½	15¼	109
Oakham	118	110½	80¾	88¼	88½	182	57¾	159	47	100½	142½	85¼	122¼	122	77½
Oakley	53½	81½	51¾	23¾	24	117½	6¾	130	35¾	71½	78	20¾	93¼	93	66¼
Peterboro'	144¼	136¾	107	114½	114¾	208¼	84	185¼	73¼	126¾	168¾	111½	148½	148¼	103¾
Pinxton	96¾	89¼	59½	66½	66¾	160¼	86	137¾	24½	79¼	120¾	63½	101	100¾	55
Portland	98¼	90¾	61	68	68¼	161¾	37½	139¼	26	80¾	122¼	65	102½	102¼	56½
Pye Bridge	94¼	87¼	57½	64½	64¾	158¼	34	135¾	22½	77¼	118¾	61½	99	98¾	53
Radford	88½	81½	51¾	58¾	59	152½	28¼	130	4¾	71½	113	55¾	93¼	93	35¼
Ratby	85½	100	70¼	55¾	56	149½	25¼	148½	39	90	110	52¾	111¾	111½	69½
Rearsby	99¼	91¾	62	69½	69¾	163¼	39	140¼	28¼	81¾	123¾	66½	103½	103¼	58¾
Rolleston Junction...	100¼	93¼	63½	70½	70¾	164¼	40	141¾	11	83¼	124¾	67½	105	104¾	19½
Rotherham............	112¼	25¼	15	82½	82¾	176¼	52	73¾	58½	15¼	136¾	79½	37	36¾	90
Rothwell Haigh......	141¼	6¼	44	111½	111¾	205¼	81	42¼	88½	34¼	165¾	108½	5½	5¼	119
Rowsley...............	93	65	35¼	63¼	63½	157	32¾	113½	40¼	55	117½	60¼	76¾	76½	70¾
Royston	127¼	7¾	30	97½	97¾	191¼	67	56¼	74½	20¼	151¾	94½	19½	19¼	105
Rugby	111½	113½	83¾	81¾	82	175½	51¼	162	50	108½	136	78¾	125¼	125	80½
Sandiacre	83	76	46¼	53¼	53½	147	22¾	124½	11¼	66	107½	50¼	87¾	87½	41¾
Sawley	78	71	41¼	48¼	48½	142	17¾	119½	11¼	61	102½	45¼	82¾	82½	41¾
Saxby..................	110	102½	72¾	80¼	80½	174	49¾	151	39	92½	134½	77¼	114¼	114	69½
Sheffield..............	116	29	18¾	85¼	85½	180	55¾	77½	63¼	19	140½	83¼	40¾	40½	93¾
Sheffield, M. S and L. Junction ...	116¾	29¾	19½	86	86¼	180¾	56½	78¼	64	19¾	141¼	84	41½	41¼	94½
Shipley	156¾	21¾	59½	127	127¼	220¾	96½	26¾	104	49¾	181¼	124	10	10¼	134½

NOTE.—In this Table, the distance between Woodhouse Mill and Beighton Junction, from Junctions North of those points, is twice included. The Midland Company are allowed two miles for break of gauge to all Stations on B. and B. Branch beyond Gloucester; it is included in this Table.

MIDLAND RAILWAY—*Continued.*

STATIONS.	Luffenham.	Methley, G. N. Junction.	Methley, Y. N. M. Junc.	Newark.	Normanton.	Nottingham, (Goods.)	Peterboro'.	Rugby.	Sheffield.	Skipton.	Stoke Works.	Swinton.	Tamworth.	Willington Junc.	Wichnor Junc.
Newark	69½	98¾	98½	...	96¼	17¾	88¼	65	78¼	134¼	93¼	78¼	57	38½	49¾
Newlay	133¾	14¼	14½	113	16¾	95¼	152½	129¼	44¾	21¼	139¾	34¾	103½	85	96¼
Normanton	117	2½	2¼	96¼	...	78½	135¾	112½	28	38	123	18	86¾	68¼	79½
Nottingham (Goods)	51¾	81	80¾	17¾	78½	...	70½	47¼	60½	116½	75½	60½	39¼	20¾	32
Oakenshaw	114¼	5¼	5	93½	2¾	75¾	133	109¾	25¼	40¾	120¼	15¼	84	65½	76¾
Oakham	7½	112	111¾	62	109½	44¼	26¼	47	91½	147½	107	91½	70¾	51¾	63½
Oakley	72	83	82¾	50¾	80½	33	90¾	67	62½	118½	42½	62½	6¼	12¼	1
Peterboro'	18¾	138¼	138	88¼	135¾	70½	...	73¼	117¾	173¾	133¼	117¾	97	78	89¾
Pinxton	61½	90¾	90½	39½	88¼	21¾	80¼	57	70¼	126¼	85¼	70¼	49	30½	41¾
Portland	63	92¼	92	41	89¾	23¼	81¾	58½	71¾	127¾	86¾	71¾	50½	32	43¼
Pye Bridge	59½	88¾	88½	37½	86¼	19¾	78¼	55	68¼	124¼	83¼	68¼	47	28½	39¾
Radford	53¾	83	82¾	19¾	80½	2	72½	49¼	62½	118½	77½	62½	41¼	22¾	34
Ratby	43½	101½	101¼	54	99	36¼	62¼	27¼	81	137	74½	81	38¼	30¾	31
Rearsby	26¼	93¼	93	43¼	90¾	25½	45	28¼	72¾	128¾	88¼	72¾	52	33	44¾
Rolleston Junction	65½	94¾	94½	4	92¼	13¾	84¼	61	74¼	130¼	89¼	74¼	53	34½	45¾
Rotherham	95¼	26¾	26½	74½	23¼	55¾	114	90¾	5¼	62¼	101¼	6½	65	46½	57¾
Rothwell Haigh	124¼	4¾	5	103½	7¼	85¾	143	119¾	35¼	30¾	130¼	25¼	94	75½	86¾
Rowsley	76	66½	66¼	55¼	64	37½	94¾	71½	46	102	82	46	45¾	27¼	38½
Royston	110¼	9¼	9	89½	6¾	71¾	129	105¾	21¼	44¾	116¼	11¼	80	61½	72¾
Rugby	54½	115	114¾	65	112½	47¼	73¼	...	94½	150½	100½	94½	64¼	54¾	57
Sandiacre	48¼	77½	77¼	26¼	75	8½	67	43¾	57	113	72	57	35¾	17¼	28½
Sawley	47	72½	72¼	26¼	70	8½	65¾	42½	52	108	67	52	30¾	12¼	23½
Saxby	15½	104	103¾	54	101½	36¼	34¼	39	83½	139½	99	83½	62¾	43¾	55½
Sheffield	99	30½	30¼	78¼	28	60½	117¾	94½	...	66	105	10	68¾	50¼	61½
Sheffield, M.S. and L. Junction	99¾	31¼	31	79	28¾	61¼	118½	95¼	¾	66¾	105¾	10¾	69½	51	62¼
Shipley	139¾	20¼	20½	119	22¾	101¼	158½	135¼	50¾	15¼	145¾	40¾	109½	91	102¼

NOTE.—In this Table, the distance between Woodhouse Mill and Beighton Junction, from Junctions North of those points, is twice included. The Midland Company are allowed two miles for break of gauge to all Stations on B. and B. Branch beyond Gloucester; it is included in this Table.

MIDLAND RAILWAY—*Continued.*

STATIONS.	Abbott's Wood.	Altofts Junction.	Beighton Junc.	Birmingham, Lawley Street.	Birmingham, L. & N. W.	Bristol.	Burton.	Colne.	Colwick.	Doncaster.	Gloucester.	Hampton.	Leeds, Northern Junction.	Leeds and Dewsbury Junc.	Lincoln.
Shipley Gate	88¾	81¾	52	59	59¼	152¾	28½	130¼	17	71¾	113¼	56	93½	93¼	47½
Sileby..................	92¾	85¾	56	63	63¼	156¾	32½	134¼	22¼	75¾	117¼	60	97½	97¼	52¾
Skipton	172	37	74¾	142¼	142½	236	111¾	11½	119¼	65	196½	139¼	25¼	25½	149¾
Southwell...............	102¾	95¾	66	73	73¼	166¾	42½	144¼	13½	85¾	127¼	70	107½	107¼	22
Spetchley..............	2½	132½	102¾	27¼	26	66½	57¾	181	86¾	122½	27	44¾	144¼	144	117¼
Spondon...............	73½	66½	36¾	43¾	44	137½	13¼	115	15¾	56½	98	40¾	78¼	78	46¼
Sprotsboro'............	122	25	24¾	92¼	92½	186	61¼	73½	69¼	3	146½	89¼	36¾	36½	99¾
Stamford...............	131½	124	94¼	101¾	102	195½	71¼	172½	60½	114	156	98¾	135¾	135½	91
Stanton Gate	84¼	77¼	47½	54½	54¾	148¼	24	125¾	12½	67¼	108¾	51½	89	88¾	43
Staveley................	98¾	36¼	6½	69	69¼	162¾	38½	84¾	46	26¼	123¼	66	48	47¾	76½
Steeton	166	31	68¾	136¼	136½	230	105¾	17½	113¼	59	190½	133¼	19¼	19½	143¾
Stone House	35½	170½	140¾	65¼	64	28½	95¾	219	124¾	160½	9	82¾	182¼	182	155¼
Stoke Works	11	124	94¼	18¾	17½	75	49¼	172½	78¼	114	35½	36¼	135¾	135½	108¾
Stoneyford	91¾	84¾	55	62	62¼	155¾	31½	133¼	20	74¾	116¼	59	96½	96¼	50½
Stretton	88½	46½	16¾	58¾	59	152½	28¼	95	35¾	36½	113	55¾	58¼	58	66¼
Sutton..................	101	94	64¼	71¼	71½	165	40¾	142½	17¼	84	125½	68¼	105¾	105½	47¾
Swadlincote	66	80½	50¾	36¼	36½	130	5¾	129	34¾	70½	90½	33¼	92¼	92	65¼
Swannington..........	73¾	88¼	58½	44	44¼	137¾	13½	136¾	42½	78¼	98¼	41	100	99¾	73
Swinderby	111½	104½	74¾	81¾	82	175½	51¼	153	22¼	94½	136	78¾	116¼	116	8¼
Swinton	116	19	18¾	86¼	86½	180	55¾	67½	63¼	9	140½	83¼	30¾	30½	93¾
Syston..................	96	88½	58¾	66¼	66½	160	35¾	137	25	78½	120½	63¼	100¼	100	55½
Tamworth	47¼	87¾	58	17½	17¾	111¼	13	136¼	42	77¾	71¾	14½	99½	99¼	72½
Tewkesbury	13	148	118¼	42¾	41½	56	73¼	196¼	102¼	138	16½	60¼	159¾	159½	132¾
Thornton	177¼	42¼	80	147½	147¾	241¼	117	6¼	124½	70¼	201¾	144½	30½	30¾	155
Thorpe................	114½	107½	77¾	84¾	85	178½	54¼	156	25¼	97½	139	81¾	119¼	119	5¼
Thurgarton...........	96¾	89¾	60	67	67¼	160¾	36½	138¼	7½	79¾	121¼	64	101½	101¼	23

NOTE.—In this Table, the distance between Woodhouse Mill and Beighton Junction, from Junctions North of those points, is twice included. The Midland Company are allowed two miles for break of gauge to all Stations on B. and B. Branch beyond Gloucester; it is included in this Table.

MIDLAND RAILWAY —*Continued.*

STATIONS.	Luffenham.	Methley, G. N. Junction.	Methley, Y. N. M. Junc.	Newark.	Normanton.	Nottingham, (Goods.)	Peterboro'.	Rugby.	Sheffield.	Skipton.	Stoke Works.	Swinton.	Tamworth.	Wellington Junc.	Wichner Junc.
Shipley Gate	54	83¼	83	32	80¾	14¼	72¾	49½	62¾	118¾	77¾	62¾	41½	23	34¼
Sileby....................	32¼	87¼	87	37¼	84¾	19½	51	27¾	66¾	122¾	81¾	66¾	45½	27	38¼
Skipton	155	35½	35¾	134¼	38	116½	173¾	150½	66	...	161	56	124¾	106¼	117½
Southwell	68	97¼	97	6½	94¾	16¼	86¾	63½	76¾	132¾	91¾	76¾	55½	37	48¼
Spetchley	123	134	133¾	101¾	131½	84	141¾	118	113½	169½	8½	113½	44¾	63¼	52
Spondon	51½	68	67¾	30¾	65½	13	70¼	47	47½	103½	62½	47½	26¼	7¾	19
Sprotsboro'	105	26½	26¼	84¼	24	66½	123¾	100½	16	62	111	6	74¾	56¼	67½
Stamford...............	6	125½	125¼	75½	123	57¾	12¾	60½	105	161	120½	105	84¼	65¼	77
Stanton Gate	49½	78¾	78½	27½	76¼	9¾	68¼	45	58¼	114¼	73¼	58¼	37	18½	29¾
Staveley	81¾	37¾	37½	61	35¼	43¼	100½	77¼	17¼	73¼	87¾	17¼	51½	33	44¼
Steeton	149	29½	29¾	128¼	32	110½	167¾	144½	60	6	155	50	118¾	100¼	111½
Stone House	161	172	171¾	139¾	169½	122	179¾	156	151½	207½	46½	151½	82¾	101¼	90
Stoke Works	114½	125½	125¼	93¼	123	75½	133¼	109½	105	161	...	105	36¼	54¾	43½
Stoneyford	57	86¼	86	35	83¾	17¼	75¾	52½	65¾	121¾	80¾	65¾	44½	26	37¼
Stretton	71½	48	47¾	50¾	45½	33	90¼	67	27½	83½	77½	27½	41¼	22¾	34
Sutton	66¼	95½	95¼	32¼	93	14½	85	61¾	75	131	90	75	53¾	35¼	46½
Swadlincote	64½	82	81¾	49¾	79½	32	83¼	49½	61½	117½	55	61½	18¾	11¼	11½
Swannington	51¾	89¾	89½	57½	87¼	39¾	70½	36¾	69¼	125¼	62¾	69¼	26½	19	19¼
Swinderby	76¾	106	105¾	7¼	103½	25	95½	72¼	85½	141½	100½	85½	64¼	45¾	57
Swinton	99	20½	20¼	78¼	18	60½	117¾	94½	10	56	105	...	68¾	50¼	61½
Syston	29½	90	89¾	40	87½	22¼	48¼	25	69½	125½	85	69½	48¾	29¾	41½
Tamworth	78¼	89¼	89	57	86¾	39¼	97	73¼	68¾	124¾	36¼	68¾	...	18½	7¼
Tewkesbury	138½	149½	149¼	117¼	147	99½	157¼	133½	129	185	24	129	60¼	78¾	67½
Thornton	160¼	40¾	41	139½	43¼	121¾	179	155¾	71¼	5¼	166¼	61¼	130	111½	122¾
Thorpe	79¾	109	108¾	10¼	106½	28	98½	75¼	88½	144½	103½	88½	67¼	48¾	60
Thurgarton............	62	91¼	91	7½	88¾	10¼	80¾	57½	70¾	126¾	85¾	70¾	49½	31	42¼

NOTE.—In this Table, the distance between Woodhouse Mill and Beighton Junction, from Junctions North of those points, is twice included. The Midland Company are allowed two miles for break of gauge to all Stations on B. and B. Branch beyond Gloucester; it is included in his Table.

MIDLAND RAILWAY—*Continued.*

STATIONS.	Abbott's Wood.	Altofts Junction.	Beighton Junc.	Birmingham, Lawley Street.	Birmingham, L. & N. W.	Bristol.	Burton.	Colne.	Colwick.	Doncaster.	Gloucester.	Hampton.	Leeds, Northern Junction.	Leeds and Dewsbury Junc.
Toton	81¼	74¼	44½	51½	51¾	145¼	21	122¾	9½	64¼	105¾	48½	86	85¾
Trent Junction	80¼	73¼	43½	50½	50¾	144¼	20	121¾	9¾	63¼	104¾	47½	85	84¾
Uffington	134¼	126¾	97	104½	104¾	198¼	74	175¼	63¼	116¾	158¾	101½	138½	138¼
Ullesthorpe	103½	105½	75¾	73¾	74	167½	43¼	154	42	95½	128	70¾	117¼	117
Wadboro'	1	136	106¼	30¾	20½	63	61¼	184½	90¼	126	23½	48¼	147¾	147½
Walton Junction ...	141¼	133¾	104	111½	111¾	205¼	81	182¼	70¼	123¾	165¾	108½	145½	145¼
Water Orton	36½	98½	68¾	6¾	7	100½	23¾	147	52¾	88½	61	10¾	110¼	110
Wath	118	17	20¾	88¼	88½	182	57¾	65½	65¼	11	142½	85¼	28¾	28½
Watstandwell.........	84	56	26¼	54¼	54½	148	23¾	104½	31¼	46	108½	51¼	67¾	67½
West Bridge	90	104½	74¾	60¼	60½	154	29¾	153	43½	94½	114½	57¼	116¼	116
Westerleigh Junc.	56¼	191¼	161½	86	82¾	7¾	116½	239¾	145½	181¼	29¾	103½	203	202¾
Whissendine	112½	105	75¼	82¾	83	176½	52¼	153½	41½	95	137	79¾	116¾	116½
Whitacre	40	95	65¼	10¼	10½	104	20¼	143½	49¼	85	64½	7¼	106¾	106½
Wichnor Junction...	54½	80½	50¾	24¾	25	118½	5¾	129	34¾	70½	79	21¾	92¼	92
Wickwar	48¾	183¾	154	78½	77¼	15¼	109	232¼	138	173¾	22¼	96	195½	195¼
Wigston	95	97	67¼	65¼	65½	159	34¾	145½	33½	87	119½	62¼	108¾	108½
Willington Junction.	65¾	69¼	39½	36	36¼	129¾	5½	117¾	23½	59¼	90¼	33	81	80¾
Willington Station...	64¾	70¼	40½	35	35¼	128¾	4½	118¾	24½	60¼	89¼	32	82	81¾
Wilnecote	45½	89½	59¾	15¾	16	109½	14¾	138	43¾	79½	70	12¾	101¼	101
Wingerworth	94	41	11¼	64¼	64½	158	33¾	89½	41¼	31	118½	61¼	52¾	52½
Wingfield	85	50	20¼	55¼	55½	149	24¾	98½	32¼	40	109½	52¼	61¾	61½
Wooden Box.........	69	83½	53¾	39¼	39½	133	8¾	132	37¾	73½	93½	36¼	95¼	95
Woodhouse Mill ...	106¼	28¾	9	76½	76¾	170¼	46	77¼	53½	18¾	130¾	73½	40½	40¼
Woodlesford	139	4	41¾	109¼	109½	203	78¾	44½	86¼	32	163½	106¼	7¾	7½
Yate	53½	188½	158¾	83¼	82	10½	113¾	237	142¾	178½	27	100¾	200¼	200

NOTE.—In this Table, the distance between Woodhouse Mill and Beighton Junction, from Junctions North of those points, is twice in
The Midland Company are allowed two miles for break of gauge to all Stations on B. and B. Branch beyond Gloucester; it is incl
this Table.

MIDLAND RAILWAY—*Continued.*

STATIONS.	Luffenham.	Methley, G. N. Junction.	Methley, Y. N. M. Junc.	Newark.	Normanton.	Nottingham, (Goods.)	Peterboro'.	Rugby.	Sheffield.	Skipton.	Stoke Works.	Swinton.	Tamworth.	Willington Junc.	Wichnor Junc.
Toton	46½	75¾	75½	24½	73¼	6¾	65¼	42	55¼	111¼	70¼	55¼	34	15½	26¾
Trent Junction	44¾	74¾	74½	24¾	72¼	7	63½	40¼	54¼	110¼	69¼	54¼	33	14½	25¾
Uffington	8¾	128¼	128	78¼	125¾	60½	10	63¼	107¾	163¾	123¼	107¾	87	68	79¾
Ullesthorpe	46½	107	106¾	57	104½	39¼	65¼	8	86½	142½	92½	86½	56¼	46¾	49
Wadboro'	126½	137½	137¼	105¼	135	87½	145¼	121½	117	173	12	117	48¼	66¾	55½
Walton Junction	15¾	135¼	135	85¼	132¾	67½	3	70¼	114¾	170¾	130¼	114¾	94	75	86¾
Water Orton	89	100	99¾	67¾	97½	50	107¾	84	79½	135½	25½	79½	10¾	29¼	18
Wath	101	18½	18¼	80¼	16	62½	119¾	96½	12	54	107	2	70¾	52¼	63½
Watstandwell	67	57½	57¼	46¼	55	28½	85¾	62½	87	93	73	37	36¾	18¼	29½
West Bridge	48	106	105¾	58½	103½	40¾	66¾	31¾	85½	141½	79	85½	42¾	35¼	35½
Westerleigh Junction	181¾	192¾	192½	160½	190¼	142¾	200½	176¾	172¼	228¼	67¼	172¼	103½	122	110¾
Whissendine	13	106½	106¼	56½	104	38¾	31¾	41½	86	142	101½	86	65¼	46¼	58
Whitacre	85½	96½	96¼	64¼	94	46½	104¼	80½	76	132	29	76	7¼	25¾	14½
Wichnor Junction	71	82	81¾	49¾	79½	32	89¾	57	61½	117½	43½	61½	7¼	11½	...
Wickwar	174½	185¼	185	153	182¾	135¼	193	169¼	164¾	220¾	59¾	164¾	96	114½	103¼
Wigston	38	98½	98¼	48½	96	30¾	56¾	16½	78	134	84	78	47¾	38¼	40½
Willington Junction	59¼	70¾	70½	38½	68¼	20¾	78	54¾	50¼	106¼	54¾	50¼	18½	...	11½
Willington Station	60¼	71¾	71½	39½	69¼	21¾	79	55¾	51¼	107¼	53¾	51¼	17½	1	10¼
Wilnecote	80	91	90¾	58¾	88½	41	98¾	75	70½	126½	34¼	70½	1¾	20¼	9
Wingerworth	77	42½	42¼	56¼	40	38½	95¾	72½	22	78	83	22	46¾	28¼	39½
Wingfield	68	51½	51¼	47¼	49	29½	86¾	63½	31	87	74	31	37¾	19¼	30½
Wooden Box	61	85	84¾	52¾	82½	35	79¾	46	64½	120½	58	64½	21¾	14¼	14½
Woodhouse Mill	89¼	30¼	30	68½	27¾	50¾	108	84¾	9¾	65¾	95¼	9¾	59	40½	51¾
Woodlesford	122	2½	2¾	101¼	5	83½	140¾	117½	33	33	128	23	91¾	73¼	84½
Yate	179	190	189¾	157¾	187½	140	197¾	174	169½	225½	64½	169½	100¾	119¼	108

NOTE.—In this Table, the distance between Woodhouse Mill and Beighton Junction, from Junctions North of those points, is twice included. The Midland Company are allowed two miles for break of gauge to all Stations on B. and B. Branch beyond Gloucester; it is included in this Table.

M'Corquodale & Co., Printers.

MONKLAND RAILWAY.

STATIONS.	Campsie Junc.	Causeway End Junction.	Garngabber Junction.	Gartgill, or Gartsherrie Jun.
Airdrie Hill	10	14	10	4½
Airdrie Station	9½	15½	9	3
Aitken and Robertson's Pit.	10	15	9½	4
Arden Branch Junction ...	11½	12½	10½	5½
Arden Pit, No. 4	12	12	11½	6
Arnloss	17	7	16½	12
Avenuehead	3½	20½	3	3
Avonbridge Saw Mill	18½	5½	18	13½
Avonbridge Station	19½	4	19	14½
Avonhead, Mr. Jack.........	13	11	12	7
Balquhatson Colliery.........	16½	7½	16	10½
Ballochney, End of Branch.	11	14½	10½	5½
Binniehill	16	8	15	10
Bo'ness	29	4¾	28¼	23
Bowhouse	22½	1½	22	16½
Bridgend	2½	21½	2	4
Brodie's Tile Works.........	10½	14½	10	4½
Calder Iron Works	8½	18½	8	3
Campsie Junction	...	23½	1	6
Carlisle Road..................	9½	14	9	4
Causeway End Junction ...	23½	...	23	18½
Chapelside.....................	9	15½	8½	3
Clarkston Branch Junction..	9½	14½	9	4
Coatbridge.....................	7½	17½	7	1½
Commonhead..................	9	15	8	3
Commonhead Junction, Sneddon Incline	9	15	8½	3

MONKLAND RAILWAY—*Continued.*

STATIONS.	Campsie Junc.	Causeway End Junction.	Garngabber Junction.	Gartgill, or Gartsherrie Jun.							
Commonhead Junction, Sneddon Pit............	9	15	8½	3							
Cotton Mill Lye.............	9½	14½	9	4							
Darngavil Colliery...........	11½	13	10½	5½							
Drumclair Colliery	17	7	16½	12							
Drumgray	11½	15	11	5							
Dundyvan Iron Works......	8	18	7½	1½							
Dykehead, Branch Junction	10	14	9½	5							
Dykehead, Branch Junc. (end of)	11½	15	11	5							
Garngabber Junction	1	23	...	5½							
Garngabber Junc. (at Tank)	1	23	½	6							
Garnqueen.....................	5	19	4½	1½							
Gartferry	3	21	2	3½							
Gartgill, (Caledonian Rail.)...	6½	17½	5½	...							
Gartsherrie Iron Works ...	8	17	7	1							
Gavil, Branch Junction......	11½	13	10½	5 ·							
Gavin Addies Pit	9½	14½	9	3½							
Glenboig Brick and Tile Works	5	19	4½	1½							
Glentore	11½	15	11	5½							
Howe's Basin.................	8	17	7	1½							
Jawcrnig	18	7½	17½	12							
Kinneil Iron Works	28	5	27½	22							
Kipp's Byre Colliery	8	16	7	2							
Kipp's Colliery	8	16	7	2							
Kirkintilloch	2½	24½	2	7							
Langloan Iron Works	7½	17½	7	1½							
Leckethill	4	20	3½	2½							

MONKLAND RAILWAY—*Continued.*

STATIONS.	Campsie Junc.	Causeway End Junction.	Garngabber Junction.	Gartgill, or Gartsherrie Jun.							
Lodge..........................	15½	8½	14½	9½							
Moffat Colliery	10½	15½	10	4½							
New Craig Colliery	18	7½	17½	12							
Palace Craig	9½	19	8½	2							
Rochsoles, Branch (end of)..	10	17	9	5½							
Rochsoles Colliery	11	14½	10½	5							
Rosehall Colliery	8½	18½	8	2							
Shankry Muir Tile Works...	4	20	3	3							
Slamannan Station	16½	7½	15½	10							
Stanrigg Colllery, (Bal-lochney Branch) ...... }	10½	14	10	4½							
Stanrigg Colliery, Quarry Pit .... }	11	13	10½	5							
Strathavon, Branch (end of)	18	7½	17½	12							
Summerlee Iron Works......	8	17	7½	1							
Whifflet, Caledonian Railway	8½	18	7½	2							
Whitehill Colliery............	9	16½	8½	3							
Whiterigg Colliery	11	13	10	4½							
Whiterigg Colliery, Low-est Pit .... }	10½	13	10	4½							
Woodlee Siding...............	½	23½	1	6							

NEWCASTLE & CARLISLE RAILWAY.

STATIONS.	Carlisle, L. & C. & Cal. Junc.	Carlisle, M. & C. Junction.	Newcastle.
Acombe Colliery	38½	39	20¾
Allerwash	33½	34	25¾
Alston	35	35½	50
Barcombe Colliery, Quarry, and Kilns	27	27½	32½
Bardon Mill	27	27½	32½
Blaydon	55½	55¾	4
Blenkensopp Colliery	19½	19¾	40
Broadwath Coal Depot	4½	5	54½
Carlisle Canal Goods Shed	1½	1	61
Carlisle Canal Shipping Wharf	1½	1¼	61
Carlisle, Dalston Road, Coal Depot	1	¾	60½
Carlisle, L. and C. and Caledonian Junction	...	¼	59½
Carlisle, London Road	...	½	59½
Carlisle, Maryport and Carlisle Junction	¼	...	59¾
Corbridge	41¾	42	17½
Corby Coal Depot	3½	3¾	56
Cowen and Co.'s Works	55	55½	4½
Dilston Coal Depot	41¼	41½	18
Elswick Works	58	58¼	1½
Featherstone	25¼	25½	40
Fourstones	34½	35	24¾
Greenhead	19¼	19½	40
Haltwistle	22¼	22½	37
Haydon Bridge	31	31½	28¼
Hedley Bank Colliery	46½	46¾	13
Hexham	38½	39	20¾

NEWCASTLE AND CARLISLE RAILWAY—*Continued.*

STATIONS.	Carlisle, L. & C. Cal. Junc.	Carlisle, M. & C. Junc.	Newcastle.
Howmill	6½	7	52¾
Humble's Works	48½	48¾	11
Lambly	26½	27	41½
Laycock's Work's	54½	54¾	5
Lowrow	13¼	13½	46
Mickley Bank Colliery	46½	46¾	13
Mickley Colliery	47¾	48	11½
Milton	10¼	10½	49
Milton Coal Depot	10½	11	48½
Newcastle	59½	59¾	...
Prudhoe	49	49¼	10½
Prudhoe Coal & Lime Depot	48½	49	10¾
Riding Mill	44	44½	15¼
Rosehill	17	17½	42½
Ryton	53¼	53½	6
Scotby	1¾	2	57½
Scotswood	56½	56¾	3
Slagyford	30½	31	45½
South Tyne Colliery	22½	23	36½
Stella Lime Depot	54½	55	4¾
Stocksfield	46½	46¾	13
Townley Coke Junction	55½	56	4
Townley Colliery	54¾	55	4½
Wetherall	3½	4	55¾
Wylam	51	51½	8¼

NEWMARKET RAILWAY.

STATIONS.	Cambridge.											
Cambridge......................	...											
Cherry Hinton	2											
Dullingham	11											
Fulbourn	4½											
Newmarket	15											
Six Mile Bottom	8											

NORFOLK RAILWAY.

STATIONS.	Brandon.	Dereham.	Reedham.	Trowse Junction.							
Attleborough	21¾	17	28¼	14¾							
Brandon	...	38¾	50	36½							
Brundall	43½	27¼	6½	7¼							
Buckenham	45½	29¼	4½	9¼							
Cantley	47¾	31½	2¼	11¼							
Dereham	38¾	...	33¾	20¾							
Eccles Road	18	20¾	32	18½							
Elmham	43¼	4½	38¼	25¼							
Fakenham	51	12¼	46	33							
Hardingham	33	5¾	28	14¾							
Harling Road	15	23¾	35	21½							
Hethersett	31½	15¼	18½	5							
Kimberley	31¼	7½	26¼	13¼							
Norwich	37¾	21½	12¼	1¼							
Reedham	50	33¾	...	13¼							
Ryburgh	48½	9¾	43½	30¼							
Spooner Row	25	13¾	25	11½							
Thetford	7¼	31½	42¾	29½							
Thuxton	34¼	4½	29¼	16¼							
Trowse	36¾	20½	13¼	¼							
Trowse Junction	36½	20¾	13¼	...							
Wymondham	27½	11¼	22½	9¼							
Yarmouth	58¼	42	8¼	21¼							
Yaxham	37	1¾	32	18¾							

NORTH BRITISH RAILWAY.

STATIONS.	Berwick.	Edinburgh.	Sprouston.
Arniston	63½	11½	42
Auchincrow	13	48	95½
Ayton	7¼	50¼	98
Beltonford	31	27	74½
Belses	97	45½	16¾
Berwick	...	57½	105¼
Bowland Bridge	81½	30	23¾
Bowshank	80¾	28¾	24¾
Burnmouth	5½	52	99¾
Butterdean	16¾	41¼	88¾
Cairney	57¼	5¼	48¼
Chirnside	15½	50½	98¼
Coaty Burn	46	15	62½
Cockburnspath	21	36½	84¼
Crimstone	18½	53½	101
Dalhousie	60½	9	44¾
Dalkeith	59½	8	45¾
Dalkeith Junction	59¾	7¾	45¾
Darnick	88	36	17½
Dirleton	42	20	67¾
Drem	39¾	17¾	65½
Dunbar	28¼	29¼	77
Dunse	20	55	102¾
East Barns	26½	31½	79
East Bryans	61¼	9¼	44¼
East Fortune	36½	21	68¾

NOTE.— All the distances are given upon the assumption that the route of the North British Line alone is used.

M'Corquodale and Co., Printers.

NORTH BRITISH RAILWAY—*Continued.*

STATIONS.	Berwick.	Edinburgh.	Sprouston.
Edinburgh	57½	...	53¾
Edron	18½	53½	101¼
Falahill	69¾	17¾	35¾
Fisherrow	57½	6	50¾
Fushiebridge	64½	13	40¾
Fountainhall	74¼	22¾	31
Galashiels	85	33½	20¼
Glenesk	60¾	8¾	44¾
Gorebridge	63½	12	41¾
Grantshouse	16¼	41¼	89
Greenend	95¾	43¾	16¼
Haddington	49	18	65¾
Hardengreen	60	8½	45¼
Hardengreen Siding	60½	8½	45
Hassendean	100½	49	20¼
Hawick	104½	53	24¼
Heiton	102	50	3½
Heriot	70¾	19¼	34½
Houndwood	13¼	44¾	92¼
Innerwick	23¾	33¾	81
Inveresk	51	6½	54¼
Kelloe	16¾	51¾	99¼
Kelso	104	52½	1¼
Laverock Law	46½	15½	63
Leith	57½	6	53¾
Leith Branch Junction	55½	2½	51

NOTE.—All the distances are given upon the assumption that the route of the North British Line alone is used.

NORTH BRITISH RAILWAY—*Continued.*

STATIONS.	Berwick.	Edinburgh.	Sprouston.								
Linton	34	23½	71¼								
Longniddry	44¼	13¼	61								
Longniddry, Henderson's Siding	45	13	60½								
Marshall Meadows	3	55	102½								
Maxton	95	43½	10¼								
Meadow Bank—Manure Loading-Bank	56¾	1¼	52¼								
Meadow Mill	47¾	10¼	57¾								
Melrose	88¾	37¼	16½								
Millerhill	58	6	47½								
Murderdean	61¾	9¾	43¾								
Musselburgh	57½	6	50¾								
Newstead	90	38½	15¼								
Newtown (St. Boswell's)	92	40½	13¼								
Niddrie	56	4½	49¼								
North Berwick	44½	22½	70¼								
Oxwell Mains	26¾	31¼	78¾								
Pease Bridge	20	38	85½								
Portobello	54½	3	50¾								
Prestongrange	49½	8½	56								
Renton	16	42	89½								
Reston	11¼	46¼	94								
Riggenhead	46¾	11¼	58¾								
Rose Lane	57	1	52½								
Roxburgh	101	49½	4¼								
Saint Boswell's (Newtown)	92	40½	13¼								
Saint Germains	46½	11½	59								

NOTE.—All the distances are given upon the assumption that the route of the North British Line alone is used.

NORTH BRITISH RAILWAY—*Continued.*

STATIONS.	Berwick.	Edinburgh.	Sprouston.								
Saint Leonard's	59½	8	52¾								
Saint Margaret's	56½	1	52¾								
Spittal	43½	14½	62								
Sprouston	105¼	53¾	...								
Standhill......................	98¾	46¾	19¼								
Stow	78½	27	26¾								
Tranent	48	9½	57¼								
Tynehead	67½	16	37¾								
Vogrie............................	64¼	12¼	41¼								
West Bryans	62¼	10¼	43¼								

NOTE.—All the distances are given upon the assumption that the route of the North British Line alone is used.

NORTH & SOUTH WESTERN JUNCTION RAILWAY.

STATIONS.	Kew Junction.	Willesden Junc.									
Kew Junction	...	4									
Willesden Junction	4	...									

NORTH STAFFORDSHIRE RAILWAY.

STATIONS.	Burton.	Colwich.	Crewe.	Macclesfield.	Norton Bridge.	Sandbach.	Willington.				
Alsager	38½	27	6½	16	19¼	6¾	39				
Alton	20¾	43½	37½	24½	35½	36¾	21¼				
Ashbourne	24¾	46¾	43	34¾	38¾		25				
Barlaston	34½	14	19½	24½	6	18¾	35				
Blyth Bridge	24¼	24¼	20½	25½	16¼	19¾	24¾				
Bosley	39	35½	19½	6½	27½	18½	39¼				
Bromshall	16¼	32¼	28¾	33¾	24½	28	16½				
Burslem	33	21½	12	17	13½	11	33¼				
Burton	...	48¾	45	45¾	40¾	44¼	8				
Cheddleton	29¼	45	30	16	37	28¼	29¾				
Churnet Valley Junction	13	35¾	32	32½	27¾	31	13½				
Clifton	23¾	45¾	42	33¾	37¾		24				
Colwich	48¾	...	33½	38½	15	32¾	49				
Congleton	41¾	30¼	14¼	8¼	22¼	13½	42				
Cresswell	22½	26¼	22½	27½	18¼	21½	23				
Crewe	45	33½	...	22¾	25¾	13¾	45½				
Egginton	6¼	46¾	43¼	43¾	39	42¼	2¼				
Etruria	31¼	19¾	13½	18¾	12	12¾	31¾				
Froghall	25	48	34¼	20¼	40	32½	25½				
Harecastle	36¼	24¾	8¾	13¾	16¾	8	36½				
Horton Rudyard	32¾	40½	24½	11½	32¾	23¾	34¼				
Lawton Junction	37	26¼	7¼	15¼	18¼	6½	38				
Leek	31¾	42½	26½	13½	34¾	25¾	32½				
Leigh	19¼	29¼	25½	30½	21¼	24¾	19¾				
Longton	27¾	21	17¼	22¾	13	16½	28				
Macclesfield	45¾	38½	22¾	...	30¾	21¾	46				

NORTH STAFFORDSHIRE RAILWAY—*Continued.*

STATIONS.	Burton.	Colwich.	Crewe.	Macclesfield.	Norton Bridge.	Sandbach.	Willington.				
Malkins Bank	36¼	28¾	9¾	17¾	20¾	4	40½				
Marston Junction	4	44½	41	41½	36¾	38½	4½				
Mowcop	38½	26¾	11½	11½	19¼	10¼	39				
Newcastle	32	20½	17	22	12¾	16	32½				
Norbury	20¾	42¾	39	30¾	34¾		21				
North Rode	40¾	33¾	17¾	4¾	25¾	17	41				
Norton Bridge	40¾	15	25¾	30¾	...	24¾	41¼				
Oakamoor	22½	45	37	23	37¼	35	22¾				
Radway Green	40½	28¾	4¾	17¾	20¾	9	40¾				
Rocester	18	40	36¼	28	32	35½	18½				
Rushton	36¾	37½	21½	8½	29½	20¾	37¼				
Sandbach	44¼	32¾	13¾	21¾	24¾	...	44½				
Sandon	41½	7	26½	31½	8	25¾	43				
Scropton	7	41¾	38	38½	33¾	37¼	7¼				
Stoke-on-Trent	30	18½	15	20	10¾	14	30½				
Stone	37	11½	22	27	3½	21¼	37½				
Sudbury	8¾	39¾	36¼	36½	32	35¼	9¼				
Trentham	33	15½	18	23	7¾	17	33½				
Tutbury	5½	43¼	39½	40	35¼	38¾	6				
Uttoxeter, East	13½	35¾	32	32	27¾	31¼	14				
Uttoxeter, West	13½	35¼	31½	32½	27¼	30¾	14				
Weston	44	4½	29	34	10½	28¼	44½				
Wheelock	42¾	31¼	12¼	20¼	23¼	1½	43				
Willington	8½	49	45½	46	41¼	44½	...				

NORTH UNION RAILWAY.

STATIONS.	Farrington.	Parkside.	Preston.	Wigan.
Charnock Richard Collieries				
Darlington's, John	5¾	14	8¼	7¼
Smith's, John	5¾	13¾	8½	7¼
Coppull	7	12¾	9¾	6
Coppull Collieries—				
Darlington's, John	6½	13	9¼	6½
Hargrave's, John.........	6¾	13	9¼	6¼
Stopford's, Thomas	7¾	12	10¼	5¼
Euxton	3¾	16¼	6¼	9¼
Farrington.....................	...	19¾	2¾	12¾
Golborne	17¾	2¼	20¼	5
Golborne Colliery—				
Evans, Richard	17	2¾	19½	4¼
Ince Collieries—				
Blundell's, J., and Sons..	14½	5¼	17¼	1¾
Byrom, Taylor, and Byrom's	15¼	4½	17¾	2½
Ince Hall..................	14½	6	17¼	1¾
Ince Hall..................	14¾	6¼	17½	2
Ince Hall..................	15	6½	17¾	2¼
Halleburton's, A. F. ...	15¼	6¾	17¾	2½
Hall, Kirkless	16	7½	18½	3¼
Hall, Kirkless	16¼	7½	18¾	3½
Moss Hall	14¾	6¼	17½	2
Pearson's, Thomas	13¾	5¾	16½	1
Pearson's, Thomas	14½	5¾	17	1¾
Thicknesse, R.A.........	16½	8	19.	3¾

NORTH UNION RAILWAY—*Continued.*

STATIONS.	Farrington.	Parkside.	Preston.	Wigan.
Leyland	1¾	18¼	4¼	11¼
Parkside	19¾	...	22¼	7
Preston	2¾	22¼	...	15½
Standish	9¾	10¼	12¼	3¼
Standish Collieries—				
Fisher's, Richard	9	10½	11¾	4
Fouracre's, Mrs.	10¼	9½	12¾	2¾
Wigan	12¾	7	15½	...
Wigan Collieries—				
Blundell, J., & Son	12½	7¼	15	½
Kaye's, James	13¼	6¼	16	½
Liverpool & Bury Junc.	13	6¾	15½	¼
Ryland's Josh	11½	8¼	14¼	1½
Wood's, Henry	11½	8	14¼	1½

M'Corquodale & Co., Printers.

NORTH WESTERN RAILWAY.

STATIONS.	Lancaster, Castle Street.	Lancaster, Green area.	Skipton.								
Bell Busk	34	33	6								
Bentham, High	15	14	25								
Bentham, Low	14	13	26								
Caton...........................	5	4	35								
Clapham	19	18	21								
Claughton	8	7	32								
Gargrave	37	36	3								
Halton	4	3	36								
Hellifield	30	29	10								
Hornby.........................	9	8	31								
Ingleton	23	22	25								
Kirby Lonsdale, at Hornby											
Lancaster, Castle Street	...	1	40								
Lancaster, Greenarea	1	...	39								
Laneside........................	20	19	20								
Long Preston..	29	28	11								
Morecombe	5	4	43								
Settle...........................	25	24	15								
Skipton	40	39	...								
Wennington	11	10	29								
Wray............................	10	9	30								

OXFORD, WORCESTER, & WOLVERHAMPTON RAILWAY.

STATIONS.	Abbott's Wood Junction.	Dudley.	Duke's Lock Jun.	Norton Junction.	Oxford.	Priestfield Junc.	Show Hill.	Stoke Junction.	Stour Valley Junction.	Worcester.
Abbott's Wood Junction ...	...	31½	51¾		54¾		38¾	13¾		4
Addlestrop	30½	60½	21	29¾	24	65	68	42¾	61¾	33
Aldington Siding	12¾	42¾	39	12	42	47	50	25	44	15
Ascott	37½	67½	14¼	36¾	17¼	71¾	74¾	49¾	68¾	40
Bilston	35	3½	85	34	88	1	4	29½	2	31
Blockley Coal Siding.........	23	53	28¾	22¼	31¾	57¼	60¼	35¼	54¼	25½
Bloomfield (Goods)	33¼	1¾	83¼	32½	86¼	2¾	5¾	27¾	½	29¼
Brettel Lane	27½	4	77¾	26¾	80¾	8¼	11¼	22	6¼	23½
Campden	21	51	30½	20¼	33½	55½	58½	33¼	52¼	23½
Caponfield	34½	3	84½	33¾	87½	1½	4½	29	1¾	30½
Charlbury	41¼	71¼	10½	40½	13½	75½	78½	53½	72½	43½
Churchill	22	9½	72¼	21¼	75¼	13¾	16¾	16½	10¾	18
Droitwich	9½	22	59¾	8¾	62¾	26¼	29¼	4¼	23¼	5¾
Dudley	31½	...	81¾	30¾	84¾	4¼	7¼	26	1¼	27½
Duke's Lock Junction	51¾	81¾	...	51	3	86	89	63¾	83	54
Evesham	11½	41¼	40¼	10¾	43¼	45¾	48¾	23½	42¾	13¾
Fearnall Heath	6½	25	56¾	5¾	59¾	29¼	32½	7¼	26¼	2¾
Fladbury	8¼	38¼	43½	7½	46½	42½	45½	20½	39½	10½
Handborough	47½	77¼	4¼	46¾	7¼	81¾	84¾	59½	78¾	49¾
Hartlebury.........................	15¼	16¼	65½	14½	68½	20½	23½	9¾	17½	11¼
Honeybourne.........................	16¼	46¼	35½	15½	38½	50½	53½	28½	47½	18¾
Kidderminster	19	12½	69	18	72	17	20	13½	14	15
Moreton	26¼	56¼	25½	25½	28½	60½	63½	38½	57½	28¾
Netherton	30½	1	80½	29½	83½	5½	8½	25	2½	26½
Norton Junction		30¾	51	...	54		38	13		3¼
Oxford	54¾	84¾	3	54	...	89	92	66¾	86	57

OXFORD, WORCESTER, & WOLVERHAMPTON RAILWAY—*Continued.*

STATIONS.	Abbott's Wood Junction.	Dudley.	Duke's Lock Jun.	Norton Junction.	Oxford.	Priestfield Junc.	Show Hill.	Stoke Junction.	Stour Valley Junction.	Worcester.
Parkhead, or Blowers Green (Goods)	30	1½	80	29¼	83	6	9	24½	2¾	26
Pershore	5½	35½	46¼	4¾	49¼	39¾	42¾	17¾	36¾	7¾
Priestfield Junction		4¼	86		89	...	3	30½		32
Round Oak	28¾	2¾	79	28	82	7	10	23¼	4	24¾
Shipton	36¼	66¼	15½	35½	18½	70½	73½	48½	67½	38½
Show Hill	38¾	7¼	89	38	92	3	...	33½	6	35
Stoke Prior Junction.........	13¾	26	63¾	13	66¾	30½	33½	...	27¼	9¾
" " Station.........	13½	26	63¾	12¾	66¾	30¼	33¼	¼	27	9½
Stourbridge	26	5½	76	25¼	79	10	13	20½	6¾	22
Stour Valley Junction		1¼	83		86		6	27¼	...	28¾
Tipton	32½	1	82¾	31¾	85¾	3¼	6¼	27¼	¼	28¾
Wolverhampton (Goods) ...	36¾	5¼	87	36	90	1	2	31¼	4	32¾
" (Passenger)	37¼	5¾	67½	36½	90½	1½	1½	31¾	4½	33¼
Worcester	4	27½	54	3¼	57	32	35	9¾	28¾	...

SAINT ANDREW'S JUNCTION RAILWAY.

STATIONS.	St. Andrew's Jun.									
Guard Bridge, or Leggir ...	3									
Meldrum's Sidings............	4									
St. Andrew's	5									
St. Andrew's Junction	...									

SAINT HELENS RAILWAY.

STATIONS.	St. Helens.	St. Helens Junc.	Warrington
Appleton	6¼	5¼	7
Ditton	8¾	7¾	7¼
Farnworth	5	4	8
Fiddlers Ferry	10¾	9¾	2¼
Garston	14¼	13¼	12¾
Halewood	10	9	8½
Runcorn Gap	7¼	6¼	5¾
St. Helens	...	2	13
St. Helens Junction	2	...	12
Sankey Bridges	12¼	11¼	3¼
Speke	12¼	11¼	10¾
Warrington	13	12	...

SCOTTISH CENTRAL RAILWAY.

STATIONS.	Greenhill.	Hilton Junction, for E. P. D.	Larbert Junction.	Perth.	Stirling Junc.
Alloa	11	42	7½	44	11½
Alloa Junction	6	37	2½	39	6½
Auchterarder	31½	11½	28	13½	19
Bannockburn	9½	33½	6	35½	3
Bannockburn Coal Siding	8½	34½	5	36½	4
Bannockburn Quarry Siding	8	35	4½	37	4½
Blackford	27	16	23½	18	14½
Bridge of Allan	15	28	11½	30	2½
Dunblane	17	26	13½	28	4½
Dunning	35½	7½	32	9½	23
Forgandenny	41	2	37½	4	28½
Forteviot	38	5	34½	7	25½
Greenhill	...	43	3½	45	12½
Greenloaning	23	20	19½	22	10½
Hilton Junction	43	...	39½	2	30½
Kinbuck	19½	23½	16	25½	7
Larbert	4	39	½	41	8½
Larbert Junction	3½	39½	...	41½	9
Larbert Siding	4¾	38¼	1¼	40¼	7¼
Perth	45	2	41½	...	32½
Stirling	12	31	8½	33	½
Stirling Junction	12½	30½	9	32½	...

SCOTTISH MIDLAND RAILWAY.

STATIONS.	Forfar.	Meigle Junc.	Newtyle Junc. with Dundee Ry.	Perth.
Ardler	14¼	3	4¾	18¼
Balathie	23	11¾	13½	9½
Belmont Coal Siding	12	¾	2¼	19¾
Cargill	21¼	10	11¾	11¼
Coupar Angus	16¾	5½	7¼	15¾
Drumgley Coal Siding	4	7¼	9	28½
Dunkeld Road	27½	16	17¾	5¼
Eassie	8¼	3	4¾	24¼
Forfar	...	11½	13¼	32½
Glammis	5¾	5½	7¼	26¾
Luncarty	28½	17¼	19	4
Meigle	11½	...	1¾	21¼
Newtyle Junction	13¼	1¾	...	23
Perth	32½	21¼	23	...
Stanley	26	14¾	16½	6½
Woodside	19	7¾	9½	13½

Note.—NEWTYLE BRANCH.—The Scottish Midland Junction Branch Line from Meigle Junction joins the Newtyle and Dundee Line at Newtyle; the length of this Branch is 1¾ miles, and all traffic to and from Dundee to Stations on the Scottish Midland passes over this Branch, and the Mileage will have to be credited accordingly.

SHEPRETH AND HITCHIN RAILWAY.

STATIONS.	Hitchin.	Shepreth.									
Ashwell	9	9									
Baldock	4½	13½									
Hitchin	...	18									
Meldreth	16	2									
Royston	13	5									
Shepreth	18	...									

SHREWSBURY AND BIRMINGHAM RAILWAY.

STATIONS.	Shrewsbury.	Wellington.	Wolverhampton.
Admaston	9¼	1	20
Albrighton	22	11¾	7½
Bennett's Siding	13	2¾	16½
Botfields	14¼	4	15¼
Codsall	25	14¾	4½
Hollingswood	13¾	2½	13¾
Ketley Siding	11½	1¼	17¾
Lilleshall	14¼	4¼	15¼
Lilleshall Branch	14¼	4¼	15¼
Oakengates	13¼	3	16¼
Shiffnall	17¼	7	12¼
Shrewsbury	...	10¼	29½
Slaney's Siding	18¾	8½	10¾
Stafford Road	28½	18¼	1
Upton Magna	3¾	6½	25¾
Walcot	6¼	3¾	23¼
Wellington	10¼	...	19¼
Wolverhampton	29½	19¼	...

SHREWSBURY AND CHESTER RAILWAY.

STATIONS.	Chester.	Saltney Wharf, or Holyhead Junc.	Shrewsbury.
Balderton	4¼	2¼	38¼
Baschurch	35	32¾	7½
Baschurch Ballast	34¼	32¼	8¼
Black Park	21	19	22¼
Brymbo Coal Wharf	14¼	12¼	35
Brymbo New Pit	14½	12½	35¼
Brymbo Ovens	13¾	11¾	34¾
Brymbo Works	13¾	11½	34½
Bryn Mally	13	11	33¾
Cefn	18¾	16¾	23¾
Cefn Wharf	18½	16¼	24
Chester	...	3¼	42½
*Chirk	21½	19¼	21
Ffron	14¾	12½	35½
Ffrwd	13¾	11¾	34½
Gobowan	24½	22¼	18
Gresford	9¼	7	33¼
Llangollen Road	20	18	22½
Leaton	38¼	36¼	4¼
Marford Ballast	8	6	34½
Minera	17	15	38
Nant Pits Wr. Co. 8	13	11	34
Old Woods Wharf	37	35	5½
Oswestry	26¾	24¾	20½
Pen-y-Coed	13¾	11¾	34¾
Plas Madoc Branch	18¼	16¼	25¾

SHREWSBURY AND CHESTER RAILWAY—*Continued.*

STATIONS.	Chester.	Saltney Wharf, or Holyhead Junc.	Shrewsbury.								
Presgwyn	22½	20½	20								
Ponkey Junction	16	14	26½								
Pulford	6	4	36½								
„ Quarry	16½	14½	37¼								
„ Quarry, Broughton	12¾	10¾	33½								
„ Quarry, Gwersyllt	12¼	10¼	33								
Rednall	29¼	27¼	13¼								
Rednall Wharf	29	27	14								
Rossett	7½	5½	35								
Ruabon	17	15	25½								
Saltney	2¼	1	40¼								
Saltney Wharf	3¼	...	40¼								
Shrewsbury	42½	40¼	...								
Shrewsbury Goods Yard	42¼	40¼	¾								
Slate Wharf	16	14	36¾								
South Sea Forge	14¼	12¼	35								
South Sea Pit, 1	13¼	11¼	34								
South Sea Pit, 2	13¾	11½	34½								
Vron Lime Rocks	20¼	18¼	23¾								
Wern Lane	10½	8¼	32								
Westminster Pits (Ffrwd, Br. 1)	12½	10½	33¼								
Westminster Pits (S. Sea, Br. 2)	13	11	34								
Wheatsheaf	11¾	9¾	32½								
Whittington	26¼	24¼	16¼								
Whittington Ballast	25¼	23¼	17¼								
Wrexham	12¼	10¼	30¼								

SHREWSBURY AND HEREFORD RAILWAY.

STATIONS.	Hereford.	Shrewsbury.								
Berrington.....................										
Bromfield		25								
Church Stretton		12½								
Condover		4¼								
Craven Arms.................		19¾								
Dinmore.....................										
Dorrington.....................		6¼								
Hereford	...									
Leebotwood		9¼								
Leominster.....................										
Ludlow		27¼								
Marsh Brook.................		15¼								
Moreton.....................										
Onibury.......................		22¾								
Shrewsbury		...								
Wooferton.....................										

SHROPSHIRE UNION RAILWAY.

STATIONS.	Shrewsbury.	Stafford.	Wellington.
Donnington	14¼	14¾	4
Gnosall	23	6	12¾
Hadley	11½	17½	1¼
Haughton	25¼	3¾	15
Newport	17¾	11¼	7½
Shrewsbury	...	29	10¼
Stafford	29	...	18¾
Trench	12	17	1¾
Upton Magna	3¾	25¼	6½
Walcot	6¼	22¾	4
Wellington	10¼	18¾	...

SOUTH STAFFORDSHIRE RAILWAY.

STATIONS.	Bescot Junction.	Birmingham.	Burton.	Dudley.	Dudley Port, Junc. with Stour Valley.	Trent Val. Junc.	Wichnor Junc.				
Alrewas	17½	26	7¼	22¼	22¼	3¾	1¼				
Barton and Walton	20¾	29¼	4	25½	25½	7	2				
Bescot Junction	...	8½	24¾	5½	5½	13¾	18¾				
Bescot Junction Station	¼	8¾	24½	5¼	5¼	13½	18½				
Birmingham	8½	...	33¼	14	14	22¼	27¼				
Brownhills	7	15½	17¾	11¾	11¾	6¾	11¾				
Brownhills, Branch to Colliery	8	16½	16¾	12¾	12¾	5¾	10¾				
Burton	24¾	33¼	...	29½	29½	11	6				
Dudley	5½	14	29½	...	1½	18½	23½				
Dudley Port	4½	13	28½	1¼	1¼	17½	22½				
Dudley Port, Junction with Stour Valley	5½	14	29½	1½	...	18½	23½				
Great Bridge	3½	12	27½	2	2	16½	21½				
Hammerwich	9	17½	15¾	13¾	13¾	4¾	9¾				
Lichfield	12½	21	12¼	17¼	17¼	1¼	6¼				
Newton Road	1½	7	26¼	7	7	15¼	20¼				
Pelsall	5	13½	19¾	9¾	9¾	8¾	13¾				
Pelsall, Branch to Basin and Colliery	5¾	14¼	19	10½	10½	8	13				
Perry Bar	5	3½	29¾	10½	10½	18¾	23¾				
Trent Valley Junction	13¾	22¼	11	18½	18½	...	5				
Walsall	1¾	10¼	23	6½	6½	12	17				
Wednesbury	2¼	10¾	26¼	3¼	3¼	15¼	20¼				
Wichnor Junction	18¾	27¼	6	23½	23½	5	...				

SOUTH YORKSHIRE RAILWAY.

STATIONS.	Barnsley, L. & Y. Junction.	Doncaster, G. N. Junction.	Swinton, Mid. Junction.
Ardsley	2	15	9½
Barnsley	...	17	11½
Conisbro'	11¾	5¼	3
Doncaster	17	...	8½
Elsecar	8¼	14	8¼
Hexthorpe	15½	1½	6¾
Mexbro'	9¾	7¼	1
Rotherham	16½	14	7¼
Sheffield	22¾	20	13½
Sprotbro'	14	3	5¼
Swinton	11½	8¼	...
Swinton Canal	9½	8½	1¼
Wath	7	10	4½
Wombwell	4¼	12¾	7¼
Worsbro'	5¾	16¼	10¾

STIRLING AND DUNFERMLINE RAILWAY.

STATIONS.	Dunfermline.	Junction with Scot. Central.	Stirling.
Alloa	14	6	7
Alloa Ferry	14½	6½	7½
Bogside	8	12	13
Cambus	16	4	5
Causewayhead	20		1
Charleston	1	19	20
Clackmannan	11¾	8¼	9¼
Dunfermline	...	20	21
East Grange	6	14	15
Elgin Junction	¾	19¼	20¼
Glen Foot	16½	8½	9½
Kennet	10½	9½	10½
Kincardine	10½	9½	10½
Oakley	4½	15½	16½
Scottish Central Junction	20	...	1
Stirling	21	1	...
Tillicoultry	17½	9½	10½
Wellwood	¾	19¼	20¼

M'Corquodale & Co., Printers.

STOCKTON & DARLINGTON RAILWAY.

STATIONS.	Darlington.	Eaglescliffe Junc.	Simpasture.								
Adelaide Colliery, Branch Junction	9¼	18	3½								
Aycliffe Lane	4½	13¼	1½								
Beechburn Colliery, Branch Junction	15¾	24½	10								
Bishop Auckland Station	10¾	19½	5								
Bishopley	24¾	33½	19¼								
Black Boy Colliery, Branch Junction	9¾	18¾	4								
Butterknowle Colliery	16	24¾	10¼								
Cargo Fleet	16½	7¾	22¼								
Carr House Depots	32½	41¼	26¾								
Cockfield	14¾	23½	9								
Cold Rowley	29½	38¼	23¾								
Consett Junction	31¾	40¾	26								
Copy Crooks Colliery, Branch Junction	8	16¾	2¼								
Crag Wood	14½	23¼	8¾								
Crook Depots	16½	25¼	10¾								
Crook Hall Junction	32½	41¼	26¾								
Crook Station	16½	25¼	10¾								
Darlington Station	...	9	5¾								
Eaglescliffe Junction	9	...	14½								
Eston Mines Junction	18	9¼	23¾								
Etherley, George, Colliery, Branch Junction	12½	21¼	6¾								
Etherley Station	13	22	7½								
Evenwood Colliery	13¾	22½	8								
Fighting Cocks Station	3¾	5¼	9½								
Frosterley	21¾	33½	19¼								
Hagger Leazes Lane	16	24¾	10¼								

STOCKTON & DARLINGTON RAILWAY—*Continued.*

STATIONS.	Darlington.	Eaglescliffe Junc.	Simpasture.
Harperley	18½	27½	13
Headley Hope	19½	28½	14
High Stoop	21½	30¼	15¾
Howden	15	23¾	9¼
Hownes Gill	30½	39¼	24¾
Lackenby	19	10¼	24¾
Lands Colliery	14½	23½	9
Lazenby	19¾	11	25½
Low Waskerley	27¼	36	21½
Marshall Green Colliery	15	23¾	9¼
Middlesbro' Coaching Station	15¼	6¼	20¾
Middlesbro' Dock	15¾	6¾	21¼
Middlesbro' Goods Station	15½	6¾	21¼
Middleton			
Newport	14	5¼	19¾
North Beechburn Colliery Junction	14½	23¼	8¾
Norwood Colliery, Branch Junction	13¾	22½	8
Parkhead	30	39	24½
Pease's, West, Edward, Colliery	19½	28½	14
Pease's, West, Emma, Colliery	17¼	26	11½
Pontop Junction	32¾	41⅓	27
Redcar	23	14¼	28¾
Saint Helens, Auckland	11¼	20	5½
Saint Helens, Colliery Junc.	10¼	19¼	4½
Shildon Coaching Station	7¾	16½	2
Shildon Goods Station	8¼	17	2½

STOCKTON & DARLINGTON RAILWAY—*Continued.*

STATIONS.	Darlington.	Eaglescliffe Junc.	Simpasture.								
Simpasture Junction.........	5¾	14½	...								
South Church	10	18¾	4¼								
South Durham Colliery, Branch Junction	9¼	18	3½								
Spring Gardens...............	12¼	21	6½								
Stanhope Depots	32¼	41¼	26¾								
Stanhope Lime Kilns	32½	41¼	26¾								
Stockton Depots	11¾	2¾	17¼								
Stockton Station	12	3¼	17¾								
Sunnyside Bank Foot........	17	25¾	11¼								
Sunnyside Depots	19	27¾	13¼								
Thistleflat Colliery, Branch Junction	16	25	10½								
Towlaw Junction	20¼	29	14¾								
Urlay Nook	7¾	1¼	13½								
Waskerley	26½	35¼	20¾								
West Auckland Colliery ...	11¼	20	5½								
Whitfield Colliery, Branch Junction	16	25	10½								
Witton	15½	24¼	9¾								
Witton Park Colliery, Branch Junction	13¼	22	7½								
Witton Park Iron Works...	13	22	7½								
Wolsingham	21½	30½	16								
Woodhouse Close, Colliery Junction	10¼	19	4½								
Woodifield Colliery, Branch Junction	16¼	25	10½								
Yarm Coaching Station......	8½	¾	14								
Yarm Goods Station.........	9	1¼	14¾								
York Junction	½	8½	6¼								

THIRSK AND MALTON RAILWAY.

STATIONS.	Malton.	Pillmoor Station, Boro'bridge Jun.									
motherby....................	4¼	19¾									
mpleforth....................	15½	8½									
arton-le-Street	6	18									
oxwold........................	18	6									
illing........................	13	11									
ovingham....................	9½	14½									
alton........................	...	24									
illmoor......................	24	...									
ingsby......................	7½	16½									

WEST HARTLEPOOL HARBOUR & RAILWAY.

STATIONS.	Ferry Hill, Y. N. & B. Junc.	Simpasture, S. & D. Junc.	Stockton, L. Northern Junc.	Todhills, W. Durham Junction.
Billingham	13	12¼	4	19¼
Bishopton Lane	7	5¼	7¼	13¼
Black Boy Colliery	9¾	17¾	19	15½
Byers Green	6	18	19¼	
Carlton	9¼	8½	4	15½
Chilton Branch Terminus	6½	14½	15¾	12¼
Coxhoe	3¼	15	16½	7¼
Elstob Lane	7½	4½	8	13¾
Ferry Hill	...	12	13¼	6
Greatham	16½	15¾	7½	22¾
Haverton Hill	15	14¼	6	21¼
Leasingthorne Colliery	7¾	15¾	17	13½
Merrington Lane	3¾	15½	16¾	2½
Norton Junction	11	10¼	2	17¼
Port Clarence	16¼	15½	7¼	22½
Portrack Lane	13¼	12½	¼	19½
Portrack Spout	13½	12¾	½	19¾
Preston	10	2¼	10¼	16
Ricknall	10½	1¾	10¾	16½
Seaton	18¾	18	9¾	25
Sedgefield	3	9	10¼	9¼
Simpasture	12	...	12¼	18
South Kelloe Colliery	3¾	15½	17	7¾
Spennymoor	4¼	16	17¼	2
Stillington	6¾	6	6½	13
Stockton	13	12¼	...	19¼

WEST HARTLEPOOL HARBOUR & RAILWAY—*Continued.*

STATIONS.	Ferry Hill, Y. N. & B. Junc.	Simpasture, S. & D. Junc.	Stockton, L. Northern Junc.	Todhills, W. Durham Junction.							
Thinford	1½	13½	14¾	5¾							
Todhills	6	18	19¼	...							
West Cornforth	1¼	13¼	14¼	5¼							
Westerton Colliery	9¾	17¾	19	15½							
West Hartlepool	21	20¼	12	27¼							
West Hetton Colliery	3¾	15½	17	7¾							
Whitworth	4½	16¼	17½	1½							
Whitton	8¼	7½	4¾	14½							
Willington Colliery	6	18	19¼								

WHITEHAVEN & FURNESS RAILWAY.

STATIONS.	Broughton.	Whitehaven.									
Bootle	14	21									
Broughton	...	35									
Drigg.,............................:	20½	14½									
Holborn Hill	5½	29½									
Nethertown	28	7									
Ravenglass.....................	18½	16½									
Seascale........................	22½	12½									
Sellafield.......................	24½	10½									
Silecroft........................	9	26									
St. Bees	31	4									
Whitehaven.....................	35	...									

WHITEHAVEN JUNCTION RAILWAY.

STATIONS.	Maryport.	Whitehaven.	Workington.								
Flimby	1¾	10¼	3¼								
Harrington	7¾	4¼	2¾								
Maryport	...	12	5								
Parton	10¼	1¾	5¼								
Whitehaven	12	...	7								
Workington	5	7	...								

YORK, NEWCASTLE, & BERWICK RAILWAY.

STATIONS.	Berwick, via Brockley Whins.	Berwick, via Washington.	Darlington, via Brockley Whins.	Darlington, via Washington.	East and West Yorkshire, via Brockley Whins.	East and West Yorkshire, via Washington.	Ferry Hill, via Brockley Whins.	Ferry Hill, via Washington.	Gateshead, via Brockley Whins.	Gateshead, via Washington.	Newcastle, via Brockley Whins.
Acklington	38½	...	71½	68¼	114	110¾	58½	55¼	32	...	28½
Ainderby	126	122½	16	...	31¾	...	29	...	55½	52	59
Alne	142¾	139½	33	...	9½	...	45¾	...	72½	69¼	76
Alnwick	35	...	80¾	77½	123¼	120	68	64½	41¼	...	37¾
Alnwick Branch Junction	32	...	77¾	74½	120¼	117	64¼	61½	38¼	...	34¾
Aycliffe	104½	101	5½	...	48	...	7½	...	34	30¾	37½
Beal	8¼	...	101½	98¼	144	141	88¾	85¼	62	...	58½
Bedale Branch Junction	123¼	120	13½	...	29	...	26¼	...	53	49½	56½
Bedale (for Distances see Leeming Lane)	...	...	...	...	...	...	...	...	...	...	...
Belford	15¼	...	94½	91¼	137	133¾	81¾	78¼	55	...	51½
Belmont	88¾	85½	21	...	63¾	...	8¼	...	18	15	21¾
Benton	62	...	48	44¾	90½	87¼	35	31¾	8½	...	5
Berwick	...	...	109¾	106½	152½	149	97	93¾	70½	...	67
Bilton	32	...	77¾	74½	120½	117	65	61¾	38¼	...	34¾
Boldon	78	...	32	...	74½	...	19	...	7½	...	11
Boro' Bridge	143¾	140½	33¾	...	20¼	...	46½	...	73¼	69¾	76¾
Boro' Bridge Branch Junc.	137¾	134½	28	...	14½	...	40¾	...	67½	64	71
Bradbury	99¾	96½	10	...	52¾	...	2¾	...	29¼	26	33
Brafferton	140¼	137	30½	...	16¾	...	43	...	69¾	66¼	73¼
Brockley Whins	76½	...	33¼	...	76	...	20½	...	6	...	9¾
Carham	19	...	126½	123	169	165¾	113¾	110¼	87	...	83½
Carr Houses	95½	92¼	41½	...	84	...	28¾	...	24¾	21½	28½
Castle Eden	103¾	100½	23	...	65¾	...	10¼	...	33¼	30	37
Castle Eden Colliery	105	101¾	24¼	...	67	...	11½	...	34½	31¼	38
Catterick Bridge	121½	118	11½	...	43½	...	24½	...	51	47½	54½
Chathill	21	...	89	85¾	131½	128¼	76	72¾	49½	...	46

1.—This Company is allowed by Act of Parliament three miles for the High Level Bridge, at Newcastle; ~~it is included in this Table.~~
2.—The distances in this Table are calculated *via* Brockley Whins, and *via* Washington; where the distances are only in one column, the Stations and Junctions are both North or South of those points, and are, consequently, not affected.

YORK, NEWCASTLE, & BERWICK RAILWAY—*Continued.*

STATIONS.	Newcastle, via Washington.	Pillmoor Junction, via Brockley Whins.	Pillmoor Junction, via Washington.	Sprouston, via Brockley Whins.	Sprouston, via Washington.	Thirsk, via Brockley Whins.	Thirsk, via Washington.	York, via Brockley Whins.	York, via Washington.
·klington	...	99½	96¼	57¼	...	93½	90	115¾	112½
ıderby	55½	17	...	144¾	141½	11	...	33½	...
ıe	72¾	5	...	161¾	158½	11	...	11¼	...
ıwick	...	108¾	105½	54	...	102¾	99½	125	121¾
ıtwick Branch Junction	...	105¾	102½	51	...	99¾	96½	122	118¾
cliffe	34½	33½	...	128¼	120¼	27½	...	49¾	...
ıl	...	129½	126¼	27	...	123½	120¼	145¾	142½
lale Branch Junction	53	14½	...	142¼	139	8½	...	30¾	...
lalo (for Distances see Leeming Lane)	...	...	...	...	...	...	...	...	...
ford	...	122½	119¼	34¼	...	116½	113¼	138¾	135½
mont	18½	49¼	...	107½	104½	43	...	65½	...
ıton	...	76	72¾	80¾	...	70	66¾	92¼	89
·wick	...	138	134¾	21	...	132	128½	154	151
ton	...	105¾	102½	51	...	99¾	96½	122	118¾
don	...	60	...	96¾	...	54	...	76¼	...
·o' Bridge	73½	5¾	...	162½	159¼	11¾	...	22	...
o' Bridge Branch Junc.	67¾	...	...	156¾	153	6	...	16¼	...
dbury	29½	38	...	118¾	115¾	32	...	54½	...
fferton	70	2¼	...	159	155¾	8¼	...	18½	...
ckley Whins	...	61½	...	95½	...	55¼	...	77½	...
ham	...	154½	151¼	2¼	...	148½	145¼	170¾	167½
r Houses	25¼	69½	...	114¼	111	63¼	...	85¾	...
tle Eden	33½	51	...	122¾	119½	45	...	67½	...
tle Eden Colliery	34¾	52½	...	123¾	120¾	46¼	...	68¾	...
terick Bridge	51¼	29	...	140¼	137¼	23	...	45	...
thill	...	117	113¾	39¾	...	111	107¾	133½	130

This Company is allowed by Act of Parliament three miles for the High Level Bridge, at Newcastle; it is included in this Table.
The distances in this Table are calculated *via* Brockley Whins, and *via* Washington; where the distances are only in one column,
tions and Junctions are both North or South of those points, and are, consequently, not affected.

YORK, NEWCASTLE, & BERWICK RAILWAY—*Continued.*

STATIONS.	Berwick, via Brockley Whins.	Berwick, via Washington.	Darlington, via Brockley Whins.	Darlington, via Washington.	East and West Yorkshire, via Brockley Whins.	East and West Yorkshire, via Washington.	Ferry Hill, via Brockley Whins.	Ferry Hill, via Washington.	Gateshead, via Brockley Whins.	Gateshead, via Washington.	Newcastle, via Brockley Whins.
Chevington	41¼	...	68½	65¼	111	107¾	55¾	52¼	29	...	25½
Christon Bank	24	...	86	82¾	128½	125¼	73	69¾	46½	...	43
Cleadon Lane	78½	...	35	...	77¾	...	22¼	...	8	...	11¾
Consett	95	91¾	41¼	...	84	...	28½	...	24¾	21½	28¼
Cornhill	13½	...	121	117½	163¾	160½	108	105	81¼	...	78
Cowton	116¾	113½	7	...	35¾	...	19¾	...	46½	43	50
Coxhoe	97	93¾	16½	...	59¼	...	3¾	...	26¾	23½	30¼
Crag Mill	14¼	...	95½	92¼	138	134¾	82¾	79¼	56	...	52½
Cramlington	57	...	52¾	49½	95½	92	40	36¾	13½	...	10
Croft	112½	109¼	2¾	...	40	...	15½	...	42	38¾	45¾
Dalton	115	111¾	5¼	...	37¼	...	18	...	44¾	41¼	48¼
Darlington	109¾	106½	...	...	42¾	...	12¾	...	39½	36¼	43
Durham	90¾	87½	23¼	...	66	...	10½	...	20½	17	24
Durham Branch Junction	88½	85¼	21	...	63¾	...	8½	...	18	14¾	21¾
East and West Yorkshire	152½	149	42¾	...	...	...	55½	...	82	79	85½
Felling	71¼	...	37½	34¼	80	76¾	24¾	21½	1¾	...	5½
Fence Houses	85¼	81¾	24¾	...	67¼	...	11¾	...	14¾	11¼	18¼
Ferry Hill	97	93¾	12¾	...	55½	...	...	...	26½	23¼	30
Gateshead	70½	...	39½	36¼	82	79	26½	23¼	...	...	3½
Hartlepool	110¾	107½	30	...	72¾	...	17¼	...	40¼	37	43¾
Hartlepool Branch Junction	95	92	14½	...	57¼	...	1¾	...	24¾	21½	28¼
Haswell Junction	103¼	100	22¾	...	65½	...	10	...	33	29½	36½
Heaton	65	...	44¾	41½	87¼	84	32	28½	5¼	...	1¾
Howdon	68¾	...	48¼	44¾	91	87½	35½	32	9	...	5¼
Hylton	85½	82¼	29¾	...	72¼	...	17	...	15	11¾	18½
Kelso	23½	...	131	127½	173¾	170¼	118	114¾	91¾	...	88

1.—This Company is allowed by Act of Parliament three miles for the High Level Bridge, at Newcastle; it is included in this Table.
2.—The distances in this Table are calculated *via* Brockley Whins, and *via* Washington; where the distances are only in one column, the Stations and Junctions are both North or South of those points, and are, consequently, not affected.

YORK, NEWCASTLE, & BERWICK RAILWAY—*Continued.*

STATIONS.	Newcastle, via Washington.	Pillmoor Junction, via Brockley Whins.	Pillmoor Junction, via Washington.	Sprouston, via Brockley Whins.	Sprouston, via Washington.	Thirsk, via Brockley Whins.	Thirsk, via Washington.	York, via Brockley Whins.	York, via Washington.
Chevington ...	...	96¾	93¼	60	...	90½	87¼	113	109½
Christon Bank ...	...	114	110¾	42¾	...	108	104½	130¼	127
Cloadon Lane ...	...	63¼	...	97¼	...	57¼	...	79¼	...
Consett ...	25	69½	...	114	110¾	63¼	...	85¾	...
Cornhill ...	...	149	146	7¾	...	143	140	165½	162
Cowton ...	46¾	21	...	135¾	132¾	15	...	37¼	...
Coxhoe ...	27	44¾	...	116	113	38¾	...	61	...
Crag Mill ...	...	123½	120¼	33¼	...	117½	114¼	139¾	136½
Cramlington ...	...	81	77¾	76	...	75	71¾	97	93¾
Croft ...	42¼	25½	...	131½	128½	19¼	...	41¾	...
Dalton ...	45	22¾	...	134	131	16¾	...	39	...
Darlington ...	39½	28	...	128¾	125½	22	...	44¼	...
Durham ...	20½	51½	...	109¾	106½	45½	...	67¾	...
Durham Branch Junction ...	18½	49¼	...	107½	104½	43¼	...	65½	...
East and West Yorkshire ...	82¼	14½	...	171½	168	20½	...	1¾	...
Felling ...	...	65¾	62½	92	...	59½	56¼	82	78¾
Fence Houses ...	15	52¾	...	104	101	46¾	...	69	...
Ferry Hill ...	26¾	41	...	116	112¾	35	...	57	...
Gateshead ...	...	67½	64	89¼	...	61½	58	83¾	80½
Hartlepool ...	40½	58	...	129¾	126½	52	...	74½	...
Hartlepool Branch Junction	25	42¾	...	114	111	36¾	...	59	...
Haswell Junction ...	33	50¾	...	122¼	119	44¾	...	67	...
Heaton ...	...	72¾	69½	84	...	66¾	63½	89	85¾
Howdon ...	...	76½	73	87¼	...	70¼	67	92¾	89¼
Hylton ...	15¼	57¾	...	104¼	101¼	51¾	...	74	...
Kelso ...	...	159	155¾	2¼	...	153	149¾	175½	172

1.—This Company is allowed by Act of Parliament three miles for the High Level Bridge, at Newcastle; it is included in this Table.
2.—The distances in this Table are calculated *via* Brockley Whins, and *via* Washington; where the distances are only in one column, the Stations and Junctions are both North or South of those points, and are, consequently, not affected.

YORK, NEWCASTLE, & BERWICK RAILWAY—*Continued.*

STATIONS.	Berwick, via Brockley Whins.	Berwick, via Washington.	Darlington, via Brockley Whins.	Darlington, via Washington.	East and West Yorkshire, via Brockley Whins.	East and West Yorkshire, via Washington.	Ferry Hill, via Brockley Whins.	Ferry Hill, via Washington.	Gateshead, via Brockley Whins.	Gateshead, via Washington.	Newcastle, via Brockley Whins.
Killingworth	61	...	48¾	45½	91½	88	36	32¾	9½	...	6
Leamside	87½	84¼	22¼	...	65	...	9½	...	17	13¾	20¾
Leeming Lane	128¾	125½	19	...	34¾	...	31¾	...	58½	55	62
Longhirst	46¾	...	63	59¾	105¾	102½	50¼	47	23¾	...	20
Longhoughton	29½	...	80½	77¼	123	119¾	67½	64¼	41	...	37½
Lucker	17¾	...	92	89	134¾	131½	79¼	76	52¾	...	49
Manors	66¼	...	43½	40	86	82¾	30¾	27¼	4	...	½
Morpeth	50¼	...	59½	56¼	102	98¾	46¾	43½	20	...	16½
Moulton	117½	114	7½	...	39½	...	20½	...	47	43½	50½
Netherton	53	...	56¾	53½	99½	96	44	40¾	17½	...	14
Newcastle-upon-Tyne	67	...	43	39½	85½	82¼	30	26¾	3½	...	...
Newham	19¾	...	90	86¾	132¾	129¼	77	74	50½	...	47
Norham	7¾	...	115¼	112	158	154¾	102½	99¼	76	...	72½
Northallerton	124	120¾	14¼	...	28½	...	27	...	53¾	50¼	57
North Shields	70¼	...	50¼	47	93	89¾	37½	34	11	...	7½
Otterington	127½	124¼	17¾	...	25	...	30½	...	57	54	60½
Pelaw Main	73¼	...	36¼	33	79	75¾	23½	20¼	3	...	6½
Pensher	83	79¾	26¾	...	69½	...	14	...	12¾	9¼	16
Pensher Branch Junction	82¾	79½	27	...	69¾	...	14	...	12¼	9	16
Percy Main	69½	...	49	45¾	91¾	88¼	36¼	33	9¾	...	6
Pillmoor Junction	138	134¾	28	...	14½	...	41	...	67½	64	71
Plessey	55½	...	54½	51	97	93¾	41¾	38¼	15	...	11½
Raskelf	140¾	137½	30¾	...	11¾	...	43¾	...	70¼	67	73¾
Richmond	125	121½	15	...	47	...	28	...	54½	51	58
Richmond Branch Junction	115	111¾	5	...	37¼	...	18	...	44½	41¼	48
Scarboro' Junction	153¾	150½	44	...	1¼	...	56¾	...	83¼	80	86¾

1.—This Company is allowed by Act of Parliament three miles for the High Level Bridge, at Newcastle; it is included in this Table.

YORK, NEWCASTLE, & BERWICK RAILWAY—*Continued.*

STATIONS.	Newcastle, via Washington.	Pillmoor Junction, via Brockley Whins.	Pillmoor Junction, via Washington.	Sprouston, via Brockley Whins.	Sprouston, via Washington.	Thirsk, via Brockley Whins.	Thirsk, via Washington.	York, via Brockley Whins.	York, via Washington.
gworth	...	77	73¾	80	...	71	67¾	93	89¾
side	17½	50½	...	106½	103½	44¼	...	66¾	...
ing Lane	58½	20	...	147¾	144½	14	...	36½	...
hirst	...	91	88	65¾	...	85	82	107½	104¼
houghton	...	108½	105	48¼	...	102½	99	124¾	121½
er	...	120¼	117	36½	...	114	111	136½	133
ors	...	71½	68¼	85¼	...	65½	62¼	88	84½
peth	...	87¾	84½	69	...	81½	78¼	104	100½
lton	47¼	25	...	136¼	133¼	19	...	41¼	...
erton	...	85	81¾	72	...	79	75¾	101	98
castle-upon-Tyne	...	71	67¾	85¾	...	65	61¾	87	84
ham	...	118	114¾	38¾	...	112	108¾	134¼	131
nam	...	143½	140¼	13½	...	137½	134¼	159¾	156½
thallerton	54	13¾	...	143	140	7¾	...	30	...
h Shields	...	78½	75¼	89	...	72½	69¼	94¾	91½
rington	57¼	10½	...	146½	143½	4½	...	26¾	...
w Main	...	64¼	61	92¼	...	58¼	55	80¾	77½
her	13	55	...	102	99	48¾	...	71	...
her Branch Junction	12½	55	...	101¾	98¾	49	...	71½	...
y Main	...	77	73¾	87¾	...	71	68	93½	90
moor Junction	67¾	...	...	156¾	153½	6	...	16	...
sey	...	82½	79¼	74¼	...	76½	73	98¾	95½
kelf	70½	2¾	...	159½	156¼	8¾	...	13½	...
mond	54¾	32½	...	143¾	140¾	26½	...	48¾	...
mond Branch Junction	45	23	...	134	131	16¾	...	39	...
boro' Junction	83½	15¾	...	173	169½	21¾	...	½	...

This Company is allowed by Act of Parliament three miles for the High Level Bridge, at Newcastle; it is included in this Table.
The distances in this Table are calculated *via* Brockley Whins, and *via* Washington; where the distances are only in one column, tions and Junctions are both North and South of those points, and are consequently not affected.

YORK, NEWCASTLE, & BERWICK RAILWAY—*Continued.*

STATIONS.	Berwick, via Brockley Whins.	Berwick, via Washington.	Darlington, via Brockley Whins.	Darlington, via Washington.	East and West Yorkshire, via Brockley Whins.	East and West Yorkshire, via Washington.	Ferry Hill, via Brockley Whins.	Ferry Hill, via Washington.	Gateshead, via Brockley Whins.	Gateshead, via Washington.	Newcastle, via Brockley Whins.
Scorton	119½	116¼	9¾	...	41¾	...	22½	...	49	45¾	52¾
Scremerston	3¼	...	106½	103	149	145¾	93¾	90¼	67	...	63½
Scruton	127½	124	17½	...	33	...	30¼	...	57	53½	60½
Sessay	136	132¾	26	...	16½	...	39	...	65½	62¼	69
Sherburn	90¼	87	19½	...	62	...	6¾	...	19¾	16½	23½
Shincliffe	92½	89	17½	...	60	...	4½	...	22	18¾	25½
Shipton	148½	145	38¾	...	4	...	51½	...	78	74¾	81¾
South Shields	79½	...	36	...	79	...	23½	...	9	...	12½
South Shields (High Station)	79	...	35¾	...	78½	...	23	...	8½	...	12
Sprouston	21	...	128¾	125½	171½	168	116	112¾	89¼	...	85¾
Springwell (for Jarrow)	74½	...	35¼	...	78	...	22½	...	4	...	7½
Sunderland, Fawcett Street Station	88½	...	32¾	...	75½	...	20	...	18	...	21½
Ditto Monkwearmouth Station	81½	...	38¼	...	81	...	25½	...	11	...	14¾
Ditto and South Shields Junction	76¾	...	33¼	...	76	...	20½	...	6	...	9½
Thirsk	132	128½	22	...	20½	...	35	...	61½	58	65
Tollerton	144¼	141	34½	...	8	...	47¼	...	74	70¾	77½
Trimdon	100	96¾	19½	...	62	...	6½	...	29½	26¼	33
Tweedmouth	1	...	108¾	105¼	151¼	148	95¾	92½	69¼	...	65¾
Tynemouth	71¼	...	51¼	48	94	90¾	38½	35	12	...	8½
Tynemouth Junction	65	...	45	41¾	87½	84¼	32	28¾	5½	...	2
Usworth	77	...	29¾	...	72¼	...	16¾	...	6½	...	10
Velvet Hall	5¼	...	112¾	109¼	155½	152	100	96½	73¼	...	69¾
Walker	63½	...	45½	42¼	88¼	85	32¾	29½	6	...	2¾
Wallsend	66½	...	46¾	43¼	89¼	86	34	30½	7¼	...	3¾
Wark	16¾	...	124	120¾	166¾	163½	111½	108	84¾	...	81
Warkwork	35	...	74¼	71½	117½	104	62	58¾	35½	...	32

1.—This Company is allowed by Act of Parliament three miles for the High Level Bridge, at Newcastle; it is included in this Table.
2.—The distances in this Table are calculated *via* Brockley Whins, and *via* Washington; where the distances are only in one column, the Stations and Junctions are both North or South of those points, and are, consequently, not affected.

YORK, NEWCASTLE, & BERWICK RAILWAY—*Continued.*

STATIONS.	Newcastle, via Washington.	Pillmoor Junction, via Brockley Whins.	Pillmoor Junction, via Washington.	Sprouston, via Brockley Whins.	Sprouston, via Washington.	Thirsk, via Brockley Whins.	Thirsk, via Washington.	York, via Brockley Whins.	York, via Washington.		
Scorton	49½	27	...	138½	135½	21	...	43½	...		
Scremerston	...	134½	131¼	22¼	...	128½	125¼	150¾	147½		
Scruton	57	18¾	...	146¼	143	12½	...	35	...		
Sessay	66	2	...	155	152	4	...	18	...		
Sherburn	20	47¾	...	109	106	41¾	...	64	...		
Shincliffe	22¼	45½	...	111¼	108¼	39½	...	61¼	...		
Shipton	78¼	10½	...	167½	164	16¾	...	5¾	...		
South Shields	...	64¼	...	98¼	...	58¼	...	80½	...		
South Shields (High Station)	...	63¾	...	98	...	57¾	...	80	...		
Sprouston	...	156¾	153½	...	...	150¾	147½	173	169¾		
Springwell (for Jarrow)	...	63½	...	93½	...	57½	...	79¾	...		
Sunderland, Fawcett Street Station	...	61	...	107¼	...	54¾	...	77	...		
Ditto Monkwearmouth Station	...	66½	...	100½	...	60½	...	82¾	...		
Ditto and South Shields Junction	...	61½	...	95½	...	55½	...	77¾	...		
Thirsk	61¾	6	...	150¾	147½	...	...	22¼	...		
Tollerton	74	6½	...	163¼	160	12½	...	9¾	...		
Trimdon	29¾	47½	...	119	115¾	41½	...	63¾	...		
Tweedmouth	...	136¾	133½	20	...	130¾	127½	153	149¾		
Tynemouth	...	79½	76¼	90	...	73½	70¼	95¾	92½		
Tynemouth Junction	...	73	69¾	83¾	...	67	63¾	89¼	86		
Usworth	...	57¾	...	95¾	...	51¾	...	74	...		
Velvet Hall	...	141	137½	16	...	134¾	131½	157	153¾		
Walker	...	73¾	70½	84½	...	67¾	64½	90	86¾		
Wallsend	...	74¾	71½	85½	...	68¾	65½	91	87¾		
Wark	...	152¼	149	4½	...	146¼	143¼	168½	165¼		
Warkwork	...	103	99¾	54	...	97	93½	119	116		

1.—This Company is allowed by Act of Parliament three miles for the High Level Bridge, at Newcastle; it is included in this Table.
2.—The distances in this Table are calculated *via* Brockley Whins, and *via* Washington; where the distances are only in one column, the Stations and Junctions are both North or South of those points, and are, consequently, not affected.

YORK, NEWCASTLE, & BERWICK RAILWAY—*Continued.*

STATIONS.	Berwick, via Brockley Whins.	Berwick, via Washington.	Darlington, via Brockley Whins.	Darlington, via Washington.	East and West Yorkshire, via Brockley Whins.	East and West Yorkshire, via Washington.	Ferry Hill, via Brockley Whins.	Ferry Hill, via Washington.	Gateshead, via Brockley Whins.	Gateshead, via Washington.	Newcastle, via Brockley Whins.
Washington	81¾	78½	28	...	70¾	...	15	...	11½	8	15
Widdrington	43¾	...	66	63	108¾	105½	53½	50	26¾	...	23
Wingate	102½	99¼	21¾	...	64½	...	9	...	32	28¾	35½
York	154	151	44½	...	1¾	...	57	...	83¾	80½	87¼

1.—This Company is allowed by Act of Parliament three miles for the High Level Bridge, at Newcastle; it is included in this Table.
2.—The distances in this Table are calculated *via* Brockley Whins, and *via* Washington; where the distances are only in one column, the Stations and Junctions are both North or South of those points, and are, consequently, not affected.

YORK, NEWCASTLE, & BERWICK RAILWAY—*Continued.*

STATIONS.	Newcastle, via Washington.	Pillmoor Junction, via Brockley Whins.	Pillmoor Junction, via Washington.	Sprouston, via Brockley Whins.	Sprouston, via Washington.	Thirsk, via Brockley Whins.	Thirsk, via Washington.	York, via Brockley Whins.	York, via Washington.		
Washington..............	11¼	56	...	100¾	97¾	50	...	72½	...		
Widdrington	...	94½	91	62½	...	88½	85	110½	107½		
Wingate...................	32	50	...	121½	118	48½	...	66	...		
York	84	16	...	173	169½	22½	...	...	...		

1.—This Company is allowed by Act of Parliament three miles for the High Level Bridge, at Newcastle; it is included in this Table.
2.—The distances in this Table are calculated *via* Brockley Whins, and *via* Washington; where the distances are only in one column, e Stations and Junctions are both North or South of those points, and are, consequently, not affected.

YORK, NEWCASTLE, AND BERWICK RAILWAY—*Continued.*

COLLIERIES.

BRANDLING JUNCTION COLLIERIES.		DURHAM AND SUNDERLAND RAILWAY.	
STATIONS.	Brandling Drops, (South Shields).	STATIONS.	Sunderland Dock.
Andrew's House Colliery	14¼	Belmont Colliery	11
Betty Pit	13¾	Broomsides Colliery	11¾
Burnup Field Colliery	16½	Fallowfield Colliery	8½
Crook Bank Coke Ovens	15¾	Haswell Colliery	10
„ „ Colliery	15¾	„ Station	9
East Tanfield Colliery	16	Hetton Colliery	8¼
Felling Colliery	7½	„ Station	8½
Harton Colliery	2	Moorsley Colliery	9¼
Marley Hill Coke Ovens	14	Murton Junction	6¾
„ „ Colliery	14	„ Station	7
Norwood Colliery	10¾	Old Durham, New Winning	14
„ New Pit	10½	Pittington Station	11
Team Colliery	13	Ryhope do.	2¾
Tanfield Lea Colliery	16½	Seaton do.	5¼
„ Moor Colliery	17¾	Sherburn do.	13¼
		Shincliffe Colliery	14½
		„ Station	14½
		South Hetton Colliery	8¼
		Whitwell	14

YORK, NEWCASTLE, AND BERWICK RAILWAY—*Continued.*

COLLIERIES.

DURHAM AND SUNDERLAND BRANCH.		DURHAM AND SUNDERLAND, AND HARTLEPOOL BRANCHES.	
STATIONS.	Sunderland Moor.	STATIONS.	Sunderland Moor.
Hetton	8¼	Castle Eden	14¼
Murton	6¾	Castle Eden Colliery	15¼
Murton Junction	6¾	Hartlepool	21¼
Pittington	11	Haswell	9
Ryhope	2¾	Haswell Junction	14
Seaton	5¼	Murton Junction	6¾
Sherburn	13¼	Ryhope	2¾
Shincliffe	14½	Seaton	5¼
Sunderland Moor	...	South Hetton	8
		Sunderland Moor	...
		Thornley	12

YORK, NEWCASTLE, AND BERWICK RAILWAY.—*Continued.*
COLLIERIES.

HARTLEPOOL RAILWAY.		HARTLEPOOL RAILWAY.	
STATIONS.	Hartlepool Drops.	STATIONS.	Hartlepool Drops.
Cassop, Old Colliery	12¾	South Wingate	9¼
Castle Eden Colliery	5¾	Thornley Colliery	11
Castle Eden Colliery Stations	5½	Thornley Station	8¾
Castle Eden Station	6¾	Trimdon Colliery	10½
Coxhoe	13	Trimdon Grange Colliery	10¼
Haswell Colliery	12¾	Trimdon Station	10¼
Haswell Station	11¾	Thinford (Junction with Main Line near)	15½
Kelloe	14¼	West Cornforth Colliery	15
Ludworth Colliery	11¾	Wingate Colliery	8¼
Raisby Hill Lime Kilns	12	Wingate New Winning	8
Shotton Colliery	10	Wingate Station	8
South Hetton Colliery			

YORK, NEWCASTLE, AND BERWICK RAILWAY—*Continued.*

COLLIERIES.

PONTOP AND SOUTH SHIELDS RAILWAY.		PONTOP AND SOUTH SHIELDS RAILWAY.	
STATIONS.	South Shields.	STATIONS.	South Shields.
Air Pit	15¼	Medomsley Colliery	23¼
Anfield Coke Ovens	19	Medomsley Lime Depot	23
Anfield Plain Lime Depot	18¾	Kettlesworth Colliery	16
Beamish Colliery	15½	Oxclose Colliery	10
Birtley Iron Works	13	Pelton Fell Colliery	13¼
Burnhope Colliery	18½	Pelton Level Depot	14
Carr Houses	22	Pontop Coke Ovens	19
Charlaw Colliery	16¼	Pontop Colliery......................................	19
Consett Coal Depot........... ⎫ *Via Stockton and Darlington Railway.*	23¾	Quay for Loading Flints	14¾
Consett Fire Brick Works ⎬	23	Sacriston Colliery...................................	16
Consett Iron Works	23¼	Sand Quarry	18½
Consett Tin Works........ ⎭	23¾	Shields Row Colliery	18½
Consett Coal Depot ...... ⎫ *By New Line to Consett Iron Works.*	24	South Moor Colliery...............................	18¼
Consett Iron Works ...... ⎬	23½	South Pelaw Colliery	12½
Consett Tin Works ...... ⎭	24	South Tanfield Coke Ovens....................	17¾
Craghead Colliery...................................	16	South Tanfield Colliery	18
Cresswell Colliery..................................	19	Twizell Colliery	15
Crook Hall Coke Ovens .... ⎫ *By New Line to Consett Iron Works.*	22½	Waldridge Colliery	14½
Crook Hall Fire Brick Works ... ⎬	23	Washington Colliery................................	10
Crook Hall Iron Works .... ⎭	22½	West Derwent Colliery............................	24
Eden Colliery	21	West Stanley Coke Ovens	16¾
Edomsley Colliery...................................	15¾	West Stanley Colliery	16¾
Holmside Colliery	16	West Stanley W. Way Depot	16¼
Leadgate Coal Depot	21¾		

YORK AND NORTH MIDLAND RAILWAY.

STATIONS.	Altofts.	Burton Salmon, L. & Y. Junction.	Driffield Junc.	Hull.	Knaresboro'.	Knottingley.	Leeds Central.	Leeds, Hunslet Lane.	Malton Junction.	Methley Junc.	Normanton.	Starbeck.	York.
Allerton	35¾	32	54	65½	4¼	32¼	44¼	43	34½	35½	36¾	6	12¼
Altofts Junction	...	9½	65¼	47	40¼	9½	11¼	10¼	45¾	2½	¾	42	23½
Arram (Gate Siding)	58¼	54½	8	11	81	54½	66½	65½	57	57¾	59	82¾	64½
Barton Hill	35½	31¾	29¾	65¼	28¾	32	44	43	10	35¼	36½	30¼	12
Bempton	79½	75¾	15	34¼	72¾	76	88	87	33¾	79¼	80½	74¼	56
Beverley	55¼	51½	11	8	78¼	51½	63¾	62½	59¾	54¾	56¼	79¾	61½
Bolton Percy	15¾	12¼	49	45½	24¼	12¼	24¼	23	29¾	15½	16¾	26	7½
Bridlington	78	74	11½	30¾	76¼	74¼	86¼	85¼	37¼	77½	78¾	78	59½
Bromfleet (G. House)	32¾	29	33¾	14¼	55½	29	41	40	61	32¼	33½	57¼	38¾
Brough	36½	32¾	30	10½	59¼	32¾	44¾	43¾	65	36	37¼	61	42¾
Bubwith	22½	18¾	56¼	37	45½	18¾	31	29¾	51	22	23½	47	28¾
Burnby	37½	33¾	60¾	51¾	85¾	33¾	45¾	44¾	41¼	37	38¼	37¼	19
Burton Agnes	72¾	68¾	6¼	25½	81½	69	81	80	42½	72¼	73½	83¼	64¾
Burton Salmon	6¾	3	58½	40¼	33½	3	15	14	39	6¼	7½	35	16¾
Burton Salmon L. & Y. Junction	9½	...	61½	43¼	36½	¼	17¾	16¾	42	9	10¼	38	19¾
Carnaby	75¾	71¾	9¼	28½	78½	72	84	83	39½	75¼	76½	80¼	61¾
Castleford	2¾	6½	62¼	44	37¼	6½	11¼	10¼	42¾	2½	3¾	39	20½
Castle Howard	40	36	25¼	69½	33	36¼	48¼	47¼	5¾	39½	40¾	34¾	16¼
Cattal	33¾	30	52	63½	6¼	30¼	42¼	41¼	32½	33½	34¾	8	10¼
Cayton	66	62¼	28¾	48	59	62¼	74¼	73¼	20	65½	66¾	60¾	42¼
Church Fenton	12¾	9	52½	42½	27½	9	21	20	33	12¼	13½	29	10¾
Cliff	19¼	15¼	47½	27¾	42	15½	27½	26½	47½	18¾	20	43¾	25¼
Cliff Common (Sidg.)	19½	15¾	53¼	33¾	42¼	15¾	27¾	26¾	47¾	19	20¼	44	25½
Copmanthorpe	19¾	15¾	45½	49¼	20½	16	28	27	26	19¼	20½	22	3¾
Cottingham	51	47¼	15½	3¾	74	47¼	59½	58¼	64¼	50½	52	75½	57¼
Crabley (Gate House)	38½	34¾	67¾	8½	61½	34¾	47	45¾	67	38¼	39½	63	44¾

YORK AND NORTH MIDLAND RAILWAY—*Continued.*

STATIONS.	Altofts.	Burton Salmon, L. & Y. Junction.	Driffield Junc.	Hull.	Knaresboro'.	Knottingley.	Leeds Central.	Leeds, Hunslet Lane.	Malton Junction.	Methley Junc.	Normanton.	Starbeck.	York.
Cross Gates	19¾	16	66½	47	42½	16	28	27	48¼	19¼	20¾	44¼	26
Driffield	66½	62¾		19¼	87¾	62¾	74¾	73¾	48¾	66	67¼	89¼	71
Driffield Junction	65¼	61½	...	19¼		61¾		72½		65	66¼		
Drypool	49¾	47¼	23½	6½	73¾	43¼	59½	57¾	67¾	49½	50½	75½	55¾
Duffield (G. House)	20¼	16½	54	34¾	43	16½	28½	27½	48½	19¾	21	44¾	26¼
Eastrington	27¾	24	38½	19	50¾	24	36¼	35¼	56¼	27½	28¾	52¼	34
Fangfoss	36	32¼	54¼	58½	29	32¼	44¼	43¼	34½	35½	36¾	30¾	12¼
Ferriby	39½	35¾	26¾	7¼	62½	35¾	48	47	68	39¼	40½	64	45¾
Filey	69¾	66	24¾	44	62¾	66¼	78	77	24	69¼	70¾	64½	46¼
Flaxton	33½	29½	31¾	63	26½	29¾	41¾	40¾	12¼	33	34¼	28¼	9¾
Foggathorpe (G. House)	25¼	21½	59¼	39¾	47¾	21½	33¾	32½	53¼	24¾	26¼	49½	31
Ganton	58½	54¾	33¼	55¼	51½	55	67	65¾	12¾	58	59½	53¼	35
Garforth	16¾	13	64¾	44	39¾	13	25¼	24	45¼	16¼	17¾	41¼	23
Gate Helmsley	32	28¼	50¼	61¾	25¼	28½	40½	39½	30¾	31¾	33	26¾	8½
Goathland	71	67	45¾	85½	64	67¼	79¼	78¼	25	70½	71¾	65¾	47¼
Goldsboro'	37½	33½	55½	67	2¾	33¾	45¾	44¾	36	37	38¼	4¼	13¾
Gristhorpe	67¾	63¾	27	46¼	60¾	64	76	75	21¾	67¼	68½	62½	44
Grosmont	74	70	48½	88½	67	70¼	82¼	81¼	28	73½	74¾	68¾	50¼
Halton	21¼	17½	69¼	48½	44	17½	29½	28½	49½	20¾	22	45¾	27¼
Hambleton	12	8¼	54¼	35	35	8¼	20½	19¼	40½	11¾	13	36½	18¼
Hammerton	32½	28½	50½	62	7¾	28¾	40¾	39¾	31	32	33¼	9¼	8¾
Harswell (G. House)	30	26¼	64	44½	43	26½	38½	37½	48½	29¾	31	44½	26¼
Haxby	28¼	24½	37	58	21½	24¾	30¾	35¾	17¼	28	29¼	23	4¾
Harrogate	31¼	27¼	61	60¾	45¾	27½	39½	38½	51¼	30¾	32	47½	29
Heslerton	53½	49¾	28¼	60¼	46½	50	61¾	60¾	7¾	53	54½	48¼	30
Hessay	28¾	25	47	58½	11¼	25¼	37¼	36	27½	28¼	29¾	13	5¼

M'Corquodale & Co., Printers.

YORK AND NORTH MIDLAND RAILWAY—*Continued.*

STATIONS.	Altofts.	Burton Salmon, L. & Y. Junction.	Driffield Junc.	Hull.	Knaresboro'.	Knottingley.	Leeds Central.	Leeds, Hunslet Lane.	Malton Junction.	Methley Junc.	Normanton.	Starbeck.	York.
Hessle	42¼	38½	24¼	4¾	65	38½	50½	49½	70½	41¾	43	66¾	48¼
Holme	28¼	24¼	62	42½	45	24½	36½	35½	50½	27¾	29	46½	28¼
Howden	24¾	21	41½	22¼	47¾	21	33¼	32	53	24¼	25¾	49¼	31
Hull (Goods)	46¾	43	21	5¼	69¾	43	55¼	54	69¾	46½	47¾	71¼	53
Hull (Passengers)	47	43¼	19¼	...	70	43¼	55½	54¼	68	46¾	48	71½	53¼
Hunmanby	72½	68¾	23	41¼	65½	69	80¾	79¾	26½	72	73¼	67¼	42¾
Huntington	27	23¼	45¼	56¾	20	23½	35¼	34¼	25½	26½	27¾	21¾	3¼
Hutton	42½	38¾	22¾	71½	35½	39	50¾	49¾	3¼	42	43¼	37¼	18¾
Hutton Cranswick	63¼	59½	3¼	16	86¼	59½	71½	70½	52	62¾	64¼	87¾	69½
Kilnwick Gate (Siding)	61	57¼	5¼	14	84	57¼	69½	68¼	54	60¾	62	85½	67¼
Kirkham	39¼	35¼	26	68¾	32¼	35½	47½	46½	6½	38¾	40	34	15½
Knapton	51¾	47¾	26½	62¼	44¾	48	60	59	5¾	51¼	52½	46¼	28
Knaresboro'	40¼	36½	58½	70	...	36¾	48½	47½	38¾	39¾	41	1½	16½
Knottingley	9½	¼	61¾	43¼	36¾	...	17¾	16¾	42¼	9	10½	38¼	20
Knottingley Branch Junction	6½	2¾	58½	40½	33½	2¾	15	13¾	39	6	7½	35¼	16¾
Leeds Central	11¼	17¾	73½	55½	48½	17¾	...	2	54	8¾	12¼	50¼	31¾
Leeds, Hunslet Lane	10¼	16¾	72½	54¼	47½	16¾	2	...	53	7½	11	49¼	30¾
" Marsh Lane	23¼	19½	71¼	50½	46	19½	31½	30½	51½	22¾	24	47¾	29¼
" Wellington	11¼	17¾	73½	55½	48½	17¾	...	2	54	8¾	12¼	50¼	31¾
Levisham	62¼	58¼	37	76¾	55¼	58½	70½	69½	16¼	61¾	63	57	38½
Lockington	60	56¼	6½	12¾	82¾	56¼	68¼	67¼	55¼	59½	60¾	84½	66
Lowthorpe	70¾	67	4½	23½	83¼	67	79¼	78	44½	70¼	71¾	85	66¾
Malton	45¼	41½	20	68¾	38¼	41¾	53½	52½	½	44¾	46	40	21¼
Malton Junction	45¾	42		68	38¾	42¼	54	53	...	45¼	46¾	40½	22¼
Manston	19	15¼	67	46½	42	15¼	27½	26½	47½	18¾	20	43½	25¼
Marishes Road	52¾	49	27½	67¼	45¾	49¼	61¼	60	7	52¼	53¾	47½	29¼

YORK AND NORTH MIDLAND RAILWAY—*Continued.*

STATIONS.	Altofts.	Burton Salmon, L. & Y. Junction.	Driffield Junc.	Hull.	Knaresboro'.	Knottingley.	Leeds Central.	Leeds, Hunslet Lane.	Malton Junction.	Methley Junc.	Normanton.	Starbeck.	York.
Market Weighton	33½	29¾	64	48	39½	29¾	41¾	40¾	45	33	34¼	41¼	22¾
Marston	29¾	26	47¾	59½	10½	26	38	37	28¾	29¼	30½	12	6
Marton	80¼	76½	13¼	33	73¾	76½	88¾	87½	34¾	79¾	81¼	75½	57
Menthorpe (G. House)	24	17¼	55	35½	44	17½	29½	28½	49½	20¾	22	45¾	27¼
Methley	3½	10	66¾	47½	40¾	10	7¾	6¾	46¼	¾	4¼	42½	24
Methley Junction	2½	9	65	46¾	39¾	9	8¾	7½	45¼	...	3½	41½	23
Micklefield	14¼	10½	62¼	41¾	37¼	10½	22¾	21¾	42¾	14	15¼	38¾	20½
Milford	11¼	7½	59¼	38½	34	7½	19½	18½	39	10¾	12	35¾	17¼
Milford Junction	8¾	4¾	66½	38¼	31½	5	17	16	37	8¼	9½	33¼	14¼
Nafferton	68½	64¾	2	21¼	85½	64¾	77	75¾	46½	68	69½	87¼	68¼
Newton Kyme	19¼	15½	59	49	34	15½	27½	26½	39½	18¾	20¼	35½	17¼
Normanton	¾	10¼	66¼	48	41	10¼	12¼	11	46¾	3½	...	42¾	24½
Old Junction	9¾	6	57¾	37	32¾	6	18¼	17¼	38¼	9½	10¾	34¼	16
Pickering	56¼	52½	31	70¾	49¼	52¾	64½	63½	10¼	55¾	57	51	32½
Pocklington	39¾	36	58¼	54¼	33¼	36¼	48¼	47¼	38¾	39½	40¾	34¾	16½
Poppleton	26½	22¾	44¾	56¼	13½	23	35	33¾	25¼	26¼	27½	15¼	3
Rillington	49¾	45¾	24½	64¼	42¾	46	58	57	8¾	49¼	50½	44½	26
Ruswarp	78¾	75	53½	93¼	71¾	75¼	87¼	86	33	78¼	79¾	73½	55¼
Scarboro'	66¼	62¼	40¾	53½	59¼	62½	74½	73½	20¼	65¾	67	61	42½
Sculcoates	48	45¾	21¾	4¾	72	41½	57¾	56	66	47¾	48¾	73¾	54
Seamer	63¼	59½	38	50½	56¼	59¾	71½	70½	17½	62¾	64¼	58	39¾
Selby	16¼	12½	40	30¾	39	12½	24½	23½	44¾	15¾	17	40¾	22½
Sherburn, Y. & N. M.	10½	6¾	54½	40¼	29½	6¾	19	18	35	10¼	11½	31¼	12¾
Sherburn, Y. and S.	57	53¼	31¾	57	50	53¼	65¼	64¼	11	56½	57¾	51¾	33¼
Shipton	35½	31¾	62¾	50	37½	31¾	43¾	42¾	48¼	35	36¼	39¼	21
Sleights	77¼	73½	52	91¾	70¼	73½	85½	84½	31¼	76¾	78	72	53½

YORK AND NORTH MIDLAND RAILWAY—*Continued.*

STATIONS.	Altofts.	Burton Salmon, L. & Y. Junction.	Driffield Junc.	Hull.	Knaresboro'.	Knottingley.	Leeds Central.	Leeds, Hunslet Lane.	Malton Junction.	Methley Junc.	Normanton.	Starbeck.	York.
Southcoates	49	46¾	22¾	5¾	73	42½	58¾	57	67	48¾	49¾	72¼	55
Speeton	76¾	73	18	37¼	69¾	73	85	84	30¾	76¼	77½	71½	53
Spofforth	26	22¼	65¾	55¾	40¾	22½	34½	33½	46¼	25¾	27	42½	24
Staddlethorpe	30	26¼	36¼	17	53	26¼	38½	37¼	58½	29¾	31	54½	36¼
Stamford Bridge	33¼	29½	51½	61¼	26½	29¾	41¾	40½	32	32¾	34¼	28	9¾
Starbeck	42	38		71½	1½	38¼	50¼	49¼	40½	41½	42¾	...	18¼
Stepney	47½	45¼	21¼	4¼	71¾	41	57¼	55½	65½	47¼	48¼	70¾	53½
Stockton on Forest	30¼	26½	48½	60	23¼	26½	38½	37½	28¾	29¾	31	25	6½
Strensall	30¾	27	34½	60½	23¾	27¼	39	38	15	30¼	31½	25½	7
Stutton	16¼	12½	56½	46	31	12½	24¾	23½	36½	16	17¼	32¾	14¼
Tadcaster	17¼	13½	57	47	32	13½	25¾	24¾	37½	17	18¼	33¾	15¼
Thorp Arch	20¾	17	60½	50½	35½	17	29	28	41	20¼	21½	37	18¾
Thorp Gates (Siding)	14	10	52½	33	36¾	10¼	22¼	21	42¼	13½	15	38½	20
Ulleskelf	14½	10¾	50½	44¼	25½	11	23	22	31	14¼	15½	27¼	8¾
Weldon Siding	4¼	5¼	61¾	44½	35¾	5¼	12¾	11¾	41¼	4	5¼	35½	19
Wetherby	23¼	19½	63	53	37¾	19½	31½	30½	43½	22¾	24	39½	21¼
Whitby	80¼	76½	55	94¾	73¼	76½	88½	87½	34¼	79¾	81	75	56½
Whitwood Junction	1½	8	63¾	45½	38¾	8	9¾	8¾	44¼	1	2¼	40¼	22
Woodlesford	5	11½	67½	49¼	42½	11¾	6	5	48	2½	6	44	25¾
Wressle (G. House)	22¼	18¼	44¼	24¾	45	18½	30½	29½	50½	21¾	23	46¾	28¼
York	23½	19¾	41¾	53¼	16½	20	31¾	30¾	22¼	23	24½	18¼	...
York, Y. N. and B. Junction	25¼	21½		55	15	21½	33½	32½	23¾	24¾	26	16½	1½

IRISH RAILWAYS,

CALCULATED IN ENGLISH MILES.

CORK AND BANDON RAILWAY.

STATIONS.	Cork.										
Ballinhassig and Kinsale Road	10										
Bandon	20										
Cork	...										
Curranure and Innoshan-uan Road	17¾										
Upton and Brinney	15½										
Waterfall	6½										

DUBLIN AND BELFAST JUNCTION RAILWAY.

STATIONS.	Drogheda.	Dundalk.	Portadown.							
Castle Bellingham	15¼	6¾	40							
Drogheda	...	22	55¼							
Dundalk........................	22	...	33¼							
Dunleer	10	12	45¼							
Mount Pleasant..............	25¾	3¾	29¼							
Newfoundwell	¾	21¼	54½							
Newry	38½	16½	16¾							
Portadown......................	55¼	33¼	...							
Poyntz Pass	44¾	22¾	10½							
Tanderagee	50	28	5¼							

DUBLIN AND DROGHEDA RAILWAY.

STATIONS.	Drogheda.	Dublin.	Junc. for Howth.								
Balbriggan	10¼	21¾	17								
Baldoyle	29¼	6¾	2								
Beauparc	12	44	39¼								
Donabate	20¾	11¼	6½								
Drogheda	...	32	27¼								
Dublin	32	...	4¾								
Duleek	4½	36½	31¾								
Gormanstown	8	24	19¼								
Howth	30¾	8¼	3½								
Junction for Howth	27¼	4¾	...								
Kells	27	59	54¼								
Laytown	5	27	22¼								
Malahide	23	9	4¼								
Navan	17¼	49¼	44½								
Port Marnock	25¼	6¾	2								
Raheny	28¼	3¾	1								
Rush and Lusk	18	14	9¼								
Skerries	14¼	17¾	13								

GREAT SOUTHERN AND WESTERN RAILWAY.

STATIONS.	Carlow.	Cork.	Dublin.	Mallow.	Waterford and Limerick Junc.
Athy	11	145	44¾	125¼	87¼
Blarney	151¼	4¾	160	15	53
Buttevant	128¾	27¼	137½	7½	30½
Carlow	...	156	55¾	136¼	98¼
Charleville	120¾	35¼	129½	15½	22½
Clondalkin	51¼	160¼	4½	140½	102½
Cork	156	...	164¾	19¾	57¾
Dublin	55¾	164¾	...	145	107
Dundrum	91	65	99¾	45¼	7¼
Goolds Cross	86½	69½	95¼	49¾	11¾
Hazelhatch	45¾	154¾	10	135	97
Kildare	25¾	134¾	30	115	77
Kilmallock	115¾	40¼	124½	20½	17½
Knocklong	108½	47½	117¼	27¾	10¼
Lucan	48¾	157¾	7	138	100
Mageney	4¾	151¼	51	131½	93½
Mallow	136¼	19¾	145	...	38
Maryboro'	42	114	50¾	94¼	56¼
Monasterevan	27¾	128¼	36½	108½	70½
Mountrath	51	105	59¾	85¼	47¼
Newbridge	30¼	139¼	25½	119½	81½
Portarlington	32¾	123¼	41½	103½	65½
Roscrea	58½	97½	67¼	77¾	39¾
Sallins	37¾	146¾	18	127	89
Straffan	42½	151½	13½	131¾	93¾
Templemore	70¼	85¾	79	66	28

M'Corquodale & Co., Printers.

GREAT SOUTHERN AND WESTERN RAILWAY—*Continued.*

STATIONS.	Carlow.	Cork.	Dublin.	Mallow.	Waterford and Limerick Junc.						
Thurles	78	78	86¾	58¼	20¼						
Waterford and Limerick Junction .... }	98½	57¾	107	38	...						

KILLARNEY JUNCTION RAILWAY.

STATIONS.	Mallow.										
Banteer	11½							.....	....		
Killarney	41							.....	. ...	....	
Mallow	...							.....	...	....	
Mill-street	20							.....	.	....	

IRISH SOUTH EASTERN RAILWAY.

STATIONS.	Carlow.	Kilkenny.										
Bagenalstown..................	10¼	15										
Carlow	...	25¼										
Gowran	18½	6¾										
Kilkenny	25¼	...										
Milford	4¼	21										

MIDLAND GREAT WESTERN RAILWAY.

STATIONS.	Dublin.	Mullingar.							
Athlone	78	28							
Athenry	113½	63½							
Blanchton	4½	45½							
Ballinasloe	91½	41½							
Castletown	58¼	8¼							
Clonsilla	7	43							
Dublin	...	50							
Enfield	26½	23½							
Fernslock	21	29							
Galway	126¼	76¼							
Hill of Down	36	14							
Kilcock	19	31							
Killucan	41½	8½							
Leixlip	11	39							
Lucan	9	41							
Maynooth	15	35							
Moyvalley	30½	19½							
Mullingar	50	...							
Moate	68½	18½							
Oranmore	121	71							
Streamston	61½	11½							
Woodlawn	101½	51½							

WATERFORD AND KILKENNY RAILWAY.

STATIONS.	Kilkenny.	Waterford.
Ballyhale	15¼	15¾
Bennett's Bridge	6	25
Dunkitt	28½	2½
Kilkenny	...	31
Kilmacow	26¼	4¾
Lavistown	2½	28½
Mullinavat	22¾	8¼
Thomastown	11	20
Waterford	31	...

WATERFORD & LIMERICK RAILWAY.

STATIONS.	Great Southern & Western Junc.	Waterford.									
Bansha	7½										
Boher............................	17										
Cahir	16¼										
Carrick	41¼										
Clonmel	27¼										
Dromkeen	11										
Fiddown	45¼										
Great Southern and Western Junction	...										
Killonan	17¾										
Kilsheelan	33¼										
Limerick	22										
Oola	4										
Pallas............................	8										
Tipperary	2¾										
Waterford											

DUNDALK AND ENNISKILLEN RAILWAY.

STATIONS.	Dundalk.										
Castle Blayney	18										
Culloville	12¾										
Dundalk........................	...										
Enniskeen	7¾										

Milton Keynes UK
Ingram Content Group UK Ltd.
UKHW022154180124
436299UK00004B/173